WITH BILLIE

Billie Holiday backstage.
Photograph by George T. Simon (Institute of Jazz Studies, Rutgers University).

WITH
BILLIE

JULIA BLACKBURN

JONATHAN CAPE
LONDON

Published by Jonathan Cape 2005

2 4 6 8 10 9 7 5 3 1

Copyright © Julia Blackburn 2005

Julia Blackburn has asserted her right under the
Copyright, Designs and Patents Act 1988 to
be identified as the author of this work

First published in Great Britain in 2005 by
Jonathan Cape
Random House, 20 Vauxhall Bridge Road,
London SW1V 2SA

Random House Australia (Pty) Limited
20 Alfred Street, Milsons Point, Sydney,
New South Wales 2061, Australia

Random House New Zealand Limited
18 Poland Road, Glenfield,
Auckland 10, New Zealand

Random House South Africa (Pty) Limited
Endulini, 5A Jubilee Road, Parktown 2193, South Africa

The Random House Group Limited Reg. No. 954009
www.randomhouse.co.uk

A CIP catalogue record for this book
is available from the British Library

ISBN 0-224-07589-6

Papers used by Random House are natural,
recyclable products made from wood grown in sustainable forests;
the manufacturing processes conform to the environmental
regulations of the country of origin

Typeset by Palimpsest Book Production Limited,
Polmont, Stirlingshire
Printed and bound in Great Britain by
Clays Ltd, St Ives plc

CONTENTS

. . . and I will sing, that they shall hear
I am not afraid.

William Shakespeare, *A Midsummer Night's Dream*

Grateful acknowledgement is made to Linda Lipnack Kuehl, whose research proved invaluable in the writing of this book, and to Avalon Archives for making this research available.

ONE

The Record Sleeve

———

When I first heard Billie Holiday's voice, I had just turned fourteen. I was at a party and everyone was much older than me and very drunk. Their movements seemed to have been slowed down; even the way they opened and closed their mouths was too slow.

There were two prostitutes at the party. One was a woman called Sally. She had short-cropped hair, but I can no longer find her face in my mind. She lived with a tall thin homosexual called Barry, who had huge front teeth and floppy black hair, and I can see him easily. They used to invite me over to their flat in Mayfair and they liked to show me a cupboard that was full of ropes and masks and whips. On one occasion when the three of us were having tea, a client dropped by, but Sally said she couldn't do anything for him because she had a guest.

She did take me out for an appointment with two American businessmen. We went to the Ritz and ate lobsters, which I had never eaten before, and I was shocked by the sound their claws made when they were cracked open. One of the men asked me how old I was and, when I told him, he panicked and ordered a taxi and sent me away with a book on sexual techniques as a present. Sally and Barry wanted me to sell my virginity. They used to telephone me and tell me about an old gentleman they knew and how easy it would all be and how much he was prepared to pay.

I had never met the other prostitute at the party and I don't know her name. She was plump and blonde. She had taken off all her clothes and she was dancing among the guests. Every so often she would squat down and run her hand between her legs and then lick her fingers with a loud lip-smacking noise. Everyone was laughing, and Barry, who was always competitive, took off all his clothes and did a little shimmying dance with his penis tucked tightly between his thighs. I was very impressed because he suddenly looked almost like a woman.

A man in a dark sweater was staring at me; he kept pursing his mouth into tight kisses and winking one wrinkled eye. I was frightened of him. I was frightened of every person in the room except for Sally, because she had always said she would look after me if there was trouble and I wanted to believe her.

My mother had arranged the party and invited the guests. She was laughing and drinking and having fun. The relationship between us had changed since she had separated from my father. Before, we had been allies of sorts, busy every night with an assessment of the danger and the likelihood of violence; ready to run and hide if things got too bad. But now things were different and we had become two women: one young, the other no longer young. My mother never said she would look after me if there was trouble and it never occurred to me that she might. I was aware of her watching the man who was watching me.

I escaped to a far corner of the room and sat down on the carpet next to the new record player, its wine-red plastic surface stamped incongruously with an imitation of the scales on a snake skin. I looked through the little pile of records that people had brought to the party and stopped at one called *A Billie Holiday Memorial*. There was a black-and-white photograph of a woman on the cover. She was illu-

minated by a stage spotlight and she was wearing a white evening dress that left her shoulders bare. She was standing very
stiff and straight, her head tilted slightly upwards towards the
benediction of the light, her arms bent at the elbows, her
hands clenched into fists. I couldn't see her feet, but I could
tell from her stance that she must have had them planted
firmly on the ground, as though she was on the deck of a ship
and was maintaining her balance in spite of the breathing swell
of the ocean. She was caught in the gaze of lights and cameras
in front of an audience of strangers who were gathered in
the darkness to watch her, and yet she seemed to be completely alone. It was as if the act of singing filled her with
such a wild joy that she was aware of nothing else for as
long as the song lasted.

I lowered the needle onto the spinning black disc. The
music began with the notes of a piano stepping lightly as a
dancer, and then some other instruments whose names I
didn't know joined in. They were like an excited crowd of
people who were all talking, laughing, telling jokes, but
bound together by the sound of a regular beat.

Suddenly and quite unexpectedly, a woman's voice arrived.
She flew in there among them like a bird and I realised that
all the instruments had been waiting to welcome her. To my
surprise she didn't seem to care about the beat which they
wove around her, and she kept pulling at it and stretching
it until I thought she had lost it entirely. But just when it
seemed too late, she was back again.

'I . . .' she sang, her voice as clear and strong as a trumpet,
pulling out that one long vowel of sound. 'I . . . cried for
you, now it's your turn to cry over me.' She sounded so
close and familiar. It was as if she was looking straight at
me.

She was telling me a story about how she had once loved
a man, and he was unkind to her and made her very unhappy.
But then she met another man who was much nicer and
she was happy again. Meanwhile, the man who had made
her sad was beginning to miss her, and so the wheel had
come full circle and it was his turn to cry.

She sounded as brave as a lioness and yet she also sounded as fearful as a child. Listening to her, I didn't have the sense that she was bitter or resentful, or that she was angry with the man who had hurt her and glad to see him suffer. Her message was much simpler: she was telling me that things change, life moves on, laughter is followed by tears, and tears are followed by laughter. After you have been knocked to the floor, you rise up and get on your feet again.

The record went on playing and I listened as more and more stories were told. There was a lot of unrequited love and a lot of longing for a world in which a man and a woman could live happily ever after. But even the saddest songs were full of courage. It was as if just the fact of singing was in itself a triumph and a way of dealing with despair.

The last song on the record was called 'For All We Know'. I had no idea how much time separated the first recordings from this one, but I could hear at once that a number of years had passed. It was clearly the same woman who was singing, but her voice had changed profoundly; it had lost that dancing, light-hearted effervescence and instead it seemed to be pulled forward by a sheer effort of will. But still she was strong and I was made strong by listening to her.

On the morning after the party, I bought myself a copy of the record. I played it over and over until I knew the words of all the songs and they had become my stories as well. It was not that I suddenly believed in eyes of blue and hearts so true, or in cottages by streams where I would just like to dream, but I did believe in Billie Holiday and the way her voice could chase out my fears.

The record has always stayed with me since then, travelling from place to place. I haven't looked after it well; the black vinyl is warped and scratched, and only a few of the songs can struggle to be heard. But I have kept it anyway because of the memory of myself as a young girl at a party and because of the photograph of Billie Holiday on the cover and how she impressed me when I first heard her sing.

TWO

The Cardboard Box

————

I am treading in someone else's footsteps.
  More than thirty years ago a woman called Linda Kuehl
wanted to write a book about Billie Holiday. As a way of
beginning she made tape-recorded interviews with more than
150 people who had known Billie at one time or another
during her short life. It was not just the famous names Linda
Kuehl was after; it was anyone she could find, so long as
they had a story to tell.

  Eventually she had two shoe boxes filled with tapes, each
one carefully named and numbered. Then she began the
slow process of turning all these spoken words into written
words. Turn the tape on, listen to a sentence. Turn the tape
off, type down what is being said. Begin again. Back and
forth, back and forth, until hundreds of pages had accumulated, a great babbling mountain of voices. As well as the
interviews, Linda Kuehl also collected anything else she
could find: newspaper cuttings, legal documents, hospital
records, police files, the transcripts of court cases, royalty
statements, and all the photographs and private letters that
the people to whom she spoke were willing to let her use.
She even obtained a hoard of shopping lists, postcards and

little drunken notes that Alice Vrbsky, Billie's secretary and assistant during the last years, still had in her possession:*

```
75 watt (2)
60 bulb
sugar                2 bars Camy
Bread                2 bars Lux
12 eggs              1 large lestol
4 tolite [sic] paper
1/2 Ham              1 comet
not too small chicken roasting
```

The New York publishers Harper & Row agreed to take on the book and for several years Linda Kuehl was busy with it. But it seems she could never get further than the first few chapters, which she kept on writing and rewriting. It was as if she was looking for the key that would open the door and make everything else follow and fall into place.

On 9 August 1977 Frances McCullough, Linda Kuehl's editor at Harper & Row, explained in a letter that the book wasn't working. She said it had become a 'choppy, patchy mélange, in which you, the reader, very easily lose your bearings'. She said perhaps another publisher could be found who could take it on and 'if that works, believe me, I'll be very happy'. She said, 'God knows, if it's painful to me, it must be awful for you.'

Linda Kuehl moved over to Dial Press and went on with her unfinished manuscript, struggling to find the right form. In January 1979 she had made arrangements to attend a Count Basie concert in Washington, DC, and 'in spite of a fierce snowstorm and major travel snarls to the north-eastern seaboard' she travelled there by train from New York. She arrived a few minutes before the music began, looking 'quite flustered', and then she disappeared and didn't

---

* When she was interviewed by Norman Saks, on 18 February 1985, Alice Vrbsky said rather wistfully that, among many other things, she'd had a letter that Billie sent her from Italy in November 1958, 'which I gave to that woman who was working on the book and I never got it back'.

turn up for the reception after the show. It seems she went back to her hotel room, wrote a suicide note and jumped out of her third-floor window. Passers-by had seen her sitting on the ledge before she jumped.* Her family kept her Billie Holiday papers until the 1990s, when they were sold to a private collector.

He kindly allowed me access to the archive. I was shown bundles of files filled with loose sheets of paper. Everything had been jumbled haphazardly together, either by Linda Kuehl herself or by someone else. Fragments of unfinished chapters, almost obliterated by handwritten revision notes, lay alongside the transcripts of Billie's court appearances and her medical reports. Formal letters from publishers and record companies rubbed shoulders with very informal letters from friends and lovers. There were lists of addresses and several lists of the important dates and events in Billie's life, but each list was uncertain and incomplete and covered with question marks.

If I had been a different sort of person I suppose I might have tried to establish order in this chaos, but order has never been one of my strong points and I wouldn't have known where to begin here. And so I simply raced through the papers as they presented themselves to me and made copies of anything that seemed particularly interesting or relevant, trusting that I would never know what I had missed out. Before I left New York, I also collected a cardboard box filled with typewritten transcripts of the interviews Linda Kuehl had recorded. Even these were in a strange muddle, with pages missing or repeating themselves, and sometimes a whole interview had disappeared completely.

---

* The story of Linda Kuehl's last day was given to me by J. R. Taylor, who knew her in connection with the Jazz Oral History Project, which he supervised while it was based at the Smithsonian Institute in the 1970s. He met her once in 1978 and saw her again briefly on the night of her death. He learnt of her suicide from the drummer Jo Jones, who had been a friend ever since she interviewed him for her Billie Holiday book in 1971. Apart from the problems with getting the book finished, I do not know what other factors were involved in Linda's decision to take her own life.

For about a year I did my best to construct the bones of a biography out of this material. Just like Linda Kuehl before me, I made lists of what seemed to be the main events in Billie's life and I started chapters with titles like 'A Baltimore Childhood' and 'Harlem in the 1930s'. I then arranged the interviews into little groups and tried to force all those voices into the cages I had constructed for them. But in doing so I lost the wildness and the vitality that made them so interesting, and all I achieved in return was a rather bland uniformity in which one voice merged seamlessly with the next. That was when I decided this book must be a documentary in which people are free to tell their own stories about Billie and it doesn't matter if the stories don't fit together, or even if sometimes they seem to be talking about a completely different woman.

So this is Billie Holiday's life, seen through the eyes of some of the people who knew her. I begin with the friends she ran around with when she was a young girl in Baltimore: Freddie Green, Mary 'Pony' Kane, Skinny 'Rim' Davenport, Wee Wee Hill, 'Sleepy' Dean and a woman called Christine Scott, who was an inmate at the reform school where Billie was sent when she was accused of being a 'minor without proper care and guardianship'. I end in the late 1950s, with the lawyer Earle Zaidins, who lived in the same cheap hotel where Billie was staying for a while and who got to know her when they were both out in the street late at night, walking their dogs. And Alice Vrbsky; she of the shopping lists. In between there are all the others.

I lift out a sheaf of papers stapled together at the top left-hand corner and there is an orange stain where the little strip of rusting metal bites into the pages. The interview date, the number of the tape cassette and the name of the person who is speaking are written at the top of the page and there are occasional corrections and notes added in Linda Kuehl's rather bulbous handwriting.

Sometimes an interview includes a brief account of the circumstances of a meeting, 'in a brown Cadillac Eldorado'; or of what the speaker was wearing, 'a shiny red suit and a white cowboy hat'; or of how they looked, 'shaking and sweating profusely from the effects of a cocaine high'. But such descriptions are unusual; mostly the voices are not given faces to recognise or clothes to wear, and so unless the person happens to be a well-known figure in the jazz world, their words float in a haphazard space without any anchors of recognition to hold them steady.

I have listened to a number of the original tapes. The quality of the recordings tends to be very poor and it can be difficult to disentangle what is being said. You might hear the human roar of a late-night bar, juxtaposed with the closer, intimate sound of the clink of glasses on a table top, the cellophane rustle of a cigarette packet, someone coughing directly into the microphone. Or the interview is being held in a car with the activity of the street echoing on all sides, or in a private house where doors bang, dogs bark and children burst in and are shouted to silence. Several of the speakers are quite old and obviously frail and forgetful; others are drunk, or high on something.

It is always strange the way the mind works. We often do not know what we think until we have transformed the amorphous creature of our thoughts into words. We do not know what memories we hold until we have opened the door of recollection. Looking back on a far-away time, the mind often gets stuck on a point of its own forgetfulness and then, like a scratched record, keeps repeating the search for the name it has lost or the event that it cannot quite recapture.

But Linda Kuehl was obviously a very good interviewer and she never seemed to be in a hurry, or to be trying to steer people's thoughts in a particular direction. And so, if sometimes awkwardly at first, the memories soon begin to flood in, the past accumulating on all sides and becoming vivid. And once the talk is flowing easily, then all sorts of unexpected recollections and emotions emerge out of nowhere and float to the surface like strange balloons.

As well as being patient and friendly and not easily shocked, Linda Kuehl was also pretty and flirtatious and people obviously enjoyed talking to her. A lot of the men were very challenging – when asked if he rehearsed before a music session with Billie, the trumpet player Roy Eldridge said, 'Why should I rehearse? Would I need to rehearse before making love to you?' – and several of them, including Billie's pianist and fellow heroin user Carl Drinkard, the bass player (and junkie) John Simmons and the music writer Arthur Herzog, obviously fell in love with her in one way or another.* But over and over again, Linda Kuehl was ready with the relevant questions and a knowledge of dates and circumstances, and people were happy to talk. When I met Billie's pianist Bobby Tucker in 2003, he remembered Linda with great affection. He said she came to see him on three occasions and she took the time to listen.

However, although many of the interviews are rich with information and anecdotes, they are often very complicated and difficult to follow and the stories that are being told emerge in broken fragments. In order to make a coherent sequence out of what is being said, I have had to do a lot of untangling, to separate out the various threads of a narrative before piecing it back together. But although I have reshuffled people's words, I have never put words into their mouths or added any detail that wasn't actually there. I also make it clear when I am quoting directly and when I am paraphrasing.

Take the black narcotics agent, Jimmy Fletcher. He was

---

* Carl Drinkard wrote to Linda Kuehl when he was in jail, asking for help with a legal problem and saying he missed her. John Simmons wrote letters on the First Church of the New World headed paper, calling her 'dearest Tripper'. He said he was 'highly optimistic, waiting for your return when you're ready to resign yourself to the fact as to how I feel towards you. I know we will be good to and for one another.' The songwriter Arthur Herzog had a long correspondence between 1971 and 1976, and when they finally met in 1976, he said he 'had had no ideas of being amorous' and enclosed a limerick about 'a lovely lady named Linda' for whom 'Lowly impulse succeeds when she's highish'.

involved in arresting Billie Holiday on a drugs charge in 1947 and as I read his interview I realised that he had maybe never told this story before and it involved a lot of emotional effort for him to do it. He had met Billie several times, he had talked with her, danced with her, enjoyed her company and had even been in love with her in a way. He knew she had been singled out for a big public arrest and he wished he had not been the one chosen to bring this about. He wished he could have stopped the whole unpleasant business before it unfolded. And as you follow the halting and complicated progression of what he is saying, you slowly begin to realise that he is ashamed of having betrayed her and is struggling to put his shame into words.

On a different note, Carl Drinkard, who worked with Billie in the late 1950s, tells stories that cover more than a hundred typewritten pages, but his stories keep spinning into junkie paranoia and boastfulness and it is hard to tell the real from the imagined. And then there is the pianist Jimmy Rowles, who says he got drunk in anticipation of talking about Billie, and he drinks as he talks and gets more and more excited as the image of Lady Day becomes increasingly vivid and she swims into the room and is there standing in front of him.

In an interview she gave at the Storyville Club in Boston in April 1959, just over two months before her death, Billie said, 'I've got no understudy. Every time I do a show I'm up against everything that's ever been written about me. I have to fight the whole scene to get people to listen to their own ears and believe in me again.'

A huge amount of myth and gossip and savage misrepresentation had already gathered like a thick fog around her during her lifetime and it has gone on growing and proliferating ever since. Of course it is not possible to disentangle an absolute truth about who Billie was or how she lived, but at least we can listen with our own ears to the voices of the people who knew her, and then we can make our own decisions about what to believe and what not to believe.

THREE

The Facts of Childhood

---

7 April 1915: Born in Philadelphia General Hospital. Her mother, Sarah Julia Harris, known as Sadie, is nineteen and her presumed father, the banjo player Clarence Holiday, is sixteen. Sadie gives her occupation as 'housework'. The baby is given the name of Eleanor and is registered as the child of Frank DeViese, a twenty-year-old waiter who then disappears without trace.

The baby is collected from the hospital by Robert Miller, the husband of Sadie's half-sister, Eva Miller. Robert Miller takes the baby to Baltimore and hands her over to his mother, Martha Miller, 'who was always taking in neighbourhood kids who had fallen on hard times or had been abandoned'.*

1918: Sadie returns to Baltimore. For a while she stays with Martha Miller, who is still looking after the child. Clarence Holiday visits occasionally, but in October 1918 he goes as a soldier to France. He is back in Baltimore nine months later.

---

* Evelyn Miller in an interview with Stuart Nicholson (*Billie Holiday*, 1995, p. 19). Evelyn was raised by her grandmother Martha Miller and was ten years old when this new child suddenly arrived in the household.

1919: Sadie starts a relationship with Philip Gough, a twenty-five-year-old driver who lives on Spring Street.

1920: Sadie moves in with Robert and Eva Miller, to a house in Colvin Street, and brings the child with her. Eva Miller looks after the child and Sadie works in a shirt factory. Sadie starts using the surname of Fagan, after her father, Charles Fagan.

October 1922: Sadie marries Philip Gough and moves with him to East Street. The child goes on living with Eva Miller, who has moved to Bond Street in the Fell's Point district, the home of Miss Viola Green and her son Freddie Green. When the child starts school, Eva Miller is registered as her mother.

1923: Sadie separates from Philip Gough and the child returns to Martha Miller in North Barnes Street for a while. 'The child was left with my grandmother . . . Her mother would be off working or with other men. She left her all the time and that was the problem. The child had an attitude, I guess from being neglected.'*

According to Freddie Green, the child moves back to the house of Miss Viola Green on Bond Street and lives with them for 'about a year and a half'. Freddie says that Sadie is mostly absent. 'Miss Sadie used to make trips to New York over the weekend and be back for Monday mornings because she was "working out" as a maid somewhere else in Baltimore.'

1924: Sadie gets a house of her own on Dallas and Caroline Street, near to the docks in the Point district. She moves there with her nine-year-old daughter.

January 1925: The child is brought before the Juvenile Court, for playing truant and being 'without proper care and

---

* Evelyn Miller again. It seems likely that Billie's later stories about the grandmother who loved her were based to a large degree on her memories of Martha Miller.

guardianship'. She is sent to spend a year at the House of Good Shepherd, a reform school in a converted warehouse on Franklin Street and Calverton Road.

3 October 1925: The child is released on parole. She moves to a place on the East Side with Sadie.

26 October 1925: The child stops attending school. She moves with Sadie to Durham Street, the home of Miss Lou Hill. Sadie starts an affair with Miss Lou's son, Wee Wee Hill.

24 December 1926: The eleven-year-old child is raped by a neighbour. She is returned to the reform school as a State Witness.

2 February 1927: The child is released from the reform school after the intervention of a lawyer who uses the grounds of habeas corpus. She goes to stay in Miss Lou Hill's house. Sadie and her lover Wee Wee move to the house next door.

1928: Sadie moves to New York, leaving the child at Miss Lou Hill's.

1929: The child comes to New York to join her mother. Sadie is staying in Harlem, between Lenox Avenue and 7th Avenue in a whorehouse run by Florence Williams.

2 May 1929: The child, along with her mother and several other women, is arrested during a night raid. She is tried and found guilty of vagrancy. She is sent to Welfare Island, first to the hospital and then to the workhouse.

October 1929: The child, who is now fourteen years old, is released from Welfare Island. She joins Sadie in Brooklyn. She sings at the Grey Dawn, a small cabaret bar in Queens.

Spring 1930: She moves with Sadie to a tiny room in Harlem, between 5th and Lenox Avenues. She does waitress work at a club called Mexico's, which is popular with musicians. She sings at tables 'like a gypsy fiddler in a Budapest café'.★ It is around this time that she changes her name to Billie Holiday.

★ The composer and bass player Spike Hughes, quoted in Nicholson, p. 35.

FOUR

Freddie Green

_____

'I'm in your corner, girl!'

On the morning of 27 October 1971, Linda Kuehl had arranged to meet Freddie Green* at the Red Rooster club in the Point district in Baltimore. Billie Holiday's friend Ethel Moore used to have a whorehouse a few blocks from here, down by the docks. Billie always went to see Ethel and other old friends whenever she came back to Baltimore. She'd see Willie Diggs and Hilda and Rosie, the Polish lady who had a bar on Pratt and Bethel Street, and Wee Wee Hill and 'Pony' Kane, and she'd see Freddie too.

In her notes Linda Kuehl said that when she arrived at the club she had to put her face to the peephole and say the word 'Freddie' before she was let in. I imagine her leaving the daylight world behind as she steps into a darkened room, full of murmured talk and cigarette smoke. I imagine her walking carefully between the tables, a tape recorder clutched under her arm. In the one photograph I have seen of her she wears pink lipstick, and she has lines of kohl drawn around her eyes. Her pale face is framed by a waterfall of straight dark hair.

---

* Not Freddie Green the guitarist, 'the quiet guy' who played with Billie in the Count Basie band and with whom Baltimore Freddie said she had 'something going for a while', although he couldn't 'put them together'.

She went to sit next to Freddie at the mirrored bar. She said he was wearing a shiny red suit and a white felt hat with a feather stuck in the brim. She said he was sweating profusely and coming down from what he called 'a wee morning cocaine high'. He called her 'honey' and ordered her a drink. She turned on the tape recorder. Listening to the interview, you can hear the electric buzz of voices on all sides.

Freddie was eager to talk. 'I'm in your corner,' he said. 'You're gonna get it from the horse's mouth. You'll get it together, honey, we'll put that thing together! I can't tell you more than I know, and it's easy to repeat something you know is the truth!'

Freddie said that his mother, Miss Viola Green – known as Miss Vi – rented out three rooms in her house on Bond Street. Billie and her mother had a third-floor bedroom at the front. He remembered that they brought their own bedroom suite with them when they arrived and they had what he called 'some Christian pieces': the figures of Mary and Jesus and a 'little tiny statue of the Saviour on the cross'.

Freddie insisted that he and Billie were the same age and 'we was fourteen', but this must have been in 1922, when Billie was just seven years old. There is a photograph of her from around that time. She wears white socks and a white ruffled dress with long sleeves. Her right elbow rests on the polished surface of a little table and her left hand reaches across to touch the right hand, as if for reassurance. She stands very serious and poised and erect, and a big white ribbon perches like a butterfly on the side of her head, in a curious visual presentiment of the white gardenias that later became her trademark when she appeared on stage.

Freddie said that his mother had two daughters as well as him. There was Goldie, who became a singer and performed at the Diamond Subway in Baltimore for a while, but 'she didn't get nowhere'. And there was Pearl, who was the youngest. Miss Vi did day-work as a maid, but the money was 'so measly' that she needed to take in roomers as well.

Miss Vi had a wind-up Victrola or 'graffaphone', as well as an 'old-time roll piano' in the downstairs room, and Freddie remembered how Billie would 'sing along and could pick up a tune just like that', and on the tape you can hear him snapping his fingers.

You can see that serious child standing transfixed by the miracle of the player-piano, watching as the black-and-white keys come alive and pour out their wild music with no hands touching them. You can see her captivated by the defiant energy in the voice of a great female blues singer like Bessie Smith, who tells the world that she is as blue as blue can be, because her man has a heart like a rock thrown in the sea. Even then, Freddie said, it was the sad songs that Billie liked best.

All the roomers had the use of the one kitchen and on Sunday mornings everybody would gather there and 'It would be tripe fried in batter and eggs and hot biscuits and bacon and a dish of molasses on the side.' But it seems that Miss Sadie was never around for those Sundays. 'She used to make trips to New York over the weekend and she'd be back for Monday mornings, so she must have had a friend there.'

Freddie thought that Billie and her mother kept the room in Bond Street for a year and a half, but 'Sadie wanted her own home' and he remembered her telling his mother that she had found 'this little home on the Point and that she was moving.

'My mother said, "Freddie can help you", and she gave me this money for a harness team. I think I paid two and a half dollars for a horse and a wagon.' The moving was very easy because there was nothing more than the bedroom suite and some chairs and they all fitted in a single load.

The new house was on Dallas and Caroline, right in the heart of the red-light district and very near to Ethel Moore's whorehouse. Freddie described it as a 'two-storey row-house' with three rooms downstairs and two rooms up. 'There was a bathtub in the kitchen and everything was in place . . . Miss Sadie was a very clean lady.'

Freddie would visit Sadie and her daughter once or twice
a week. They lived right at the end of town in a district they
called Bottom of the Point, or just the Bottom, where 'you
could get everything' and 'you had to fight your way to get
down there'. If he came on a Sunday he'd stay for dinner.

He described Sadie as a 'short little lady and a very pretty
lady . . . with a beautiful set of chestnut hair'. Billie was
always dressed 'very plain', in gingham cloth skirts and blouses
that her mother had made up for her. She wore her hair
pulled straight back from her head and cut in a bob.

And then Freddie saw no more of Billie and her mother.
When Linda Kuehl asked him if Billie was working at Alice
Dean's whorehouse, he said he 'got lost with that part of her
life'. The next thing he knew was that she had set out for
Harlem to join her mother there. He thought Harlem must
have been even tougher than the Point in Baltimore, because
it was more of 'a dog eats dog place where you had to
struggle, you had to squeeze more, and people had their
thing and didn't help one another'.

So Freddie's friend disappeared into the big city and for years
he heard nothing more of her. He had been buying records
by a singer called Billie Holiday★ and 'having a ball with
'em', but the name 'threw him off' and he didn't realise this
was 'the same girl he came up with', whom he had always
known as Eleanor Gough or Eleanor Fagan.

And then one day, sometime in the late 1930s, Miss Sadie
came to tell Freddie's mother that Billie was in town over
at the Royale and that they all must go and listen to her. 'It
shocked me,' said Freddie. 'My mother asked, "You know
who Billie is? – Eleanor!"'

So there she was with a three-piece band at the Royale.
She looked very stylish and wore her hair pulled back in a
tight bun with an orchid pinned on the side, just like that

★ Billie's first recording, with 'Riffin' the Scotch' on one side and 'Your Mother's
Son-in-Law' on the other, was issued in 1933. In 1935 she made the first of
a number of recordings for Columbia, with Teddy Wilson and his orchestra.

early photograph. But Freddie was not so impressed by her when she sang, because 'She was more of a stand-still type. She wasn't that exciting type. She just stood still . . . I couldn't see her as a star coming up.'

She sang from about twelve till close-up and then she went on to the Savoy Grill, where they had 'turned it all out for her and they had tablecloths and everything'. There was a chorus girl called Evelyn Randolph, who was a friend of Billie's in New York, and she told Freddie to come and join the party.

As soon as Billie saw him she called out, 'Freddie, hey, Freddie!'

He said, 'Oh, girl, you're fabulous.'

And she said, 'Sit down and shut up!' and he was given a seat right next to her and her mother.

The last time Freddie saw Billie was in 1948. She had come to Baltimore with Count Basie and his band. In the early days she had been smoking grass pretty hard, but now she had got into 'this other bag and . . . she was going for the hard thing', which surprised him because he never thought she would. Freddie was particularly shocked because she was so negligent. 'She'd have grass on her dresser and some powder over there and people could come in and see it.'

He remembered how he called her one evening and she was in bed, but she told him to come on up anyway. When he got to her room he saw this powder and she said, 'D'you want some horse?' and he said, 'Oh, no! I never could do anything but smoke grass.'

But in other ways Billie never changed, 'no matter how much of a star she was. She'd go down in the slums, in the bars, and she'd have her mink, you know, and she'd just throw it on the chair and sit down with a little booze and buy for everyone else. And say "bitch" and "motherfucker" and "what you doin' now?" And she would tell jokes in different voices . . . And there'd be little kids, dirty and all, and she'd grab 'em in her arms and not care, and hold 'em and they'd have molasses on 'em, and she wouldn't care.'

FIVE

Christine Scott

———

'She never bothered with nobody.'

On 5 January 1925, the nine-year-old Billie Holiday was brought before the magistrate at the Juvenile Court in Baltimore. Her mother Sadie was there in court as a witness, along with the probation officer who had reported Billie to the authorities for playing truant. She was described as being 'a minor without proper care and guardianship' and was sentenced to spend a year at the local reform school, the House of Good Shepherd for Colored Girls.

The school was a big, ugly, six-storey warehouse on Franklin Street and Calverton Road in East Baltimore. It was run by a dozen or so nuns who belonged to an order called the Little Sisters of the Poor. They were provided with an annual income of $3,000 by the State of Maryland, but that was not nearly enough for them to feed and clothe themselves, let alone a shifting population of about a hundred girls who were mostly between the ages of fourteen and eighteen.

People who remembered the House of Good Shepherd from that time said it was an awful place, very bleak and grim. When Linda Kuehl asked some of the sisters to tell her what it had been like to live there, they did not want to speak about it; they were simply glad the school had been moved to a new location and that conditions had improved. This was except for one very old and senile sister, who kept saying over and over again that it had been 'Heavenly! Heavenly!'

The sisters supplemented the school's income by taking in washing. The girls helped to run the laundry and also did sewing, crocheting and knitting as well as their household duties. There were lessons in reading and writing for the younger ones and in organ playing for anyone who was interested. The days were regimented by prayers in the chapel.

All the girls had their hair cut short. In the summer they wore blue capes and blue dresses with pleated or gathered sleeves and white cuffs and collars. In the winter they wore the same capes, with black skirts and white blouses. The sisters wore a similar uniform.

Linda Kuehl spoke to two women who had been sent to the House of Good Shepherd. One of them was Billie's childhood friend Mary 'Pony' Kane, who spent a few weeks there in around 1929, just after Billie had left for New York. Pony was then moved on to the training school, 'where they put the real bad girls'. That was followed by a term in the local jail, which was where she learnt to steal and 'do other things'.

Pony Kane said that Sister Margaret, the Mother Superior, was a mean woman who would hit you and make you stand on one foot in the corner if you didn't do what you were told. And every time you used swearwords she'd hit you across the fingers with a ruler. But it was the hierarchy of bullying among the inmates that she hated most, especially since all the sisters seemed to know what was happening, but turned a blind eye.

Pony said, 'Some of the girls were there five to ten years and some of them were tough. Girls used to get together and they used to fuck you, if they seen you and liked you. The older girls would fuck the younger girls, if they liked 'em. They would sneak 'em candy and talk to 'em . . . And if a girl didn't come across with 'em, they would catch 'em in bed and nobody would holler and nobody would tell on nobody . . . Some of the girls would cry . . . a lot of 'em would tell their parents about it and a lot of 'em wouldn't tell nobody.'

Pony Kane mentioned one inmate who had 'been there so long'. She must have been thinking of Christine Scott, whom Linda Kuehl interviewed on 4 November 1971. Christine had been born in the 1890s and sent to the House when she was still very young. I have no idea why; maybe she simply lost all her family and there was nowhere else for her to go. Whatever the reason, she was still an inmate when Billie arrived in 1925 and she stayed on throughout the years that followed until she was eventually moved to an old people's home outside Baltimore, which was also run by the Little Sisters of the Poor.

Linda Kuehl was impressed by Christine. She said she was 'remarkably sharp and her memory was astounding'; she was shown to be correct in all the information that could later be proved. Christine was, however, convinced that Billie was about fourteen years old when she first arrived at the House, and she failed to mention that Billie was there a second time, from 24 December 1926 until 2 February 1927.★

Christine Scott explained that she had never been an affectionate person. She didn't like hugging or kissing; in fact she didn't like to be touched at all. 'Everybody knew it,' she said, 'because I could never let the children take hold of my hand. I was awfully touchy. That's the truth. I am strange. Always was . . . I had nothing to do with nobody. I didn't want to be bothered with people. You get into trouble when you have lots of friends flocking around.'

When she was asked about her first meeting with Billie,

★ In the small hours of the morning of 24 December 1926, Sadie discovered her daughter being raped by a neighbour called Wilbert Rich. Billie was bundled off to the House of Good Shepherd as a State Witness and might have languished there for years had not her uncle Charles Fagan paid for a lawyer to fight for her. She was released on the grounds of habeas corpus. At his trial, Rich was found guilty on the count of 'Carnal Knowledge of 14–16-year-old' (there were six counts against him in total), in spite of the fact that Billie was only eleven at the time and both the court and the House of Good Shepherd held her correct date of birth (Nicholson, pp. 26–7).

she said she remembered how she was sitting on her own in the chapel one Monday morning, when the chaplain beckoned her over. He had a very shy young girl with him, whom he said was called Madge.* Christine had hardly noticed the girl before and had never said more than two words to her, but now she looked at her for the first time. 'She was a very nice-looking brown-skinned girl. She wasn't quite as light as I am, but she was light. And she had a nice suit of hair. And her features were even and light. She was as tall as any fourteen-year-old would be and she was right plump.'

The chaplain explained that he wanted to have Madge baptised because he'd had an 'awful time trying to find out where she came from and where her people came from'. He asked Christine if she would be the girl's godmother.†

Something changed in Billie when she learnt she was going to be baptised; while she was being prepared for the ceremony she was no longer so silent and fearful and she told everyone in the House how excited she was. And when the day came, she was dressed like a bride in a white frock with a white veil and she rushed to show all the sisters how pretty she looked. Christine said, 'She was so happy, poor child, she was grinning from ear to ear – you could almost see her back teeth, and she was just as light as a feather.'

As soon as the baptism and the First Communion that followed were over, the sisters gave Billie a string of rosary beads and her new godmother was told to present her with a prayer book. And Christine said that as long as she stayed

---

* All the girls were given new names when they arrived. In theory this was to protect their identities, although it seems more like a way of making them forget who they were. Billie (whose name at the time was still Eleanor) was called Madge.

† This first baptism was on 19 March 1925 and Billie's place of birth was given as Philadelphia. For some mysterious reason she was given a further 'conditional baptism' on 14 August 1925, when her birthplace had become Baltimore. When she returned to the House of Good Shepherd on 24 December 1926, she was baptised a third time and again her birthplace had become Philadelphia. The ceremony was performed by a different pastor on each occasion, so perhaps people forgot it had been done before and Billie, as always in such situations, kept silent.

in the House, Billie 'had that prayer book in her hand all the time, so she must have appreciated it'.

But once the brief immersion in the limelight had ended, the little girl withdrew back into her shell. She was clearly frightened of the other girls, but she felt safe with Christine and used to follow her everywhere like a lost puppy, padding after her from room to room and then sitting on the floor at her feet, silent and watchful.

'She liked me and she didn't want to be with the girls. She never told me her reason. I didn't ask her a thing about herself or about her parents and she never told me anything . . . She very seldom had anything to do with anybody else and she was always down in the dumps . . . In the classroom she'd go to sit on a chair by herself, and when she went out in the yard she'd go to sit by herself. She never bothered with nobody. She very seldom spoke to anybody . . . She was almost like a stick . . . She sewed a lot: overalls, shirts . . .'

Billie, in the form of a child called Madge, was released back onto the streets of Baltimore on 3 October 1925, three months before she had completed her sentence. This was presumably because her silence and lack of contact with the other inmates were interpreted as good behaviour.★ Christine Scott said she did not know who came to fetch Billie when it was time for her to leave, but she was quite sure it was not her mother Sadie.

Apart from the period between 24 December 1926 and 2 February 1927 that Christine failed to mention, Billie made one final visit to the House, in around 1950. She came because she was planning to go to Europe and needed a copy of her Certificate of Baptism in order to be able to obtain a passport.

She arrived with John Levy, her current boyfriend and

★ In 1994 Stuart Nicholson interviewed one of the sisters from the House of Good Shepherd. He was told that Billie often visited the institution when she came to Baltimore and that Sister Margaret, the Mother Superior mentioned by Pony Kane, 'retained a great affection for "Madge"'. Nicholson concluded that 'in the disciplined environment of the House of Good Shepherd, Eleanor [Billie] found the guidance and security that were missing in her life.'

manager, and in a flurry of excitement showed him around this place that had been one of her many childhood homes. She led him to the chapel where she had been baptised, to the dormitory where she had slept in a narrow bed, to the room where she had kept herself busy sewing shirts and overalls, to the kitchen where she had eaten her solitary meals and to the yard where she had sat in silence, 'almost like a stick'. One of the sisters looked at John Levy's pale skin and smooth black hair and asked him if he was Jewish. 'Half-Negro and half-Jew,' he replied.★

Then Billie agreed to sing a song for the girls. Perhaps one of the sisters was willing to accompany her on the piano, or she had a pianist with her, or she sang without any music at all. The song she chose for the occasion was 'My Man'. The girls squealed with delight, while the sisters were appalled.

> He's not much on looks
> He's no hero out of books
> But I love him.
> Yes, I love him.
> Two or three girls
> Has he
> That he likes as well as me,
> But I love him.
> I don't know why I should,
> He isn't true
> He beats me too.
> What can I do?

Christine Scott missed this performance, but she was told about it later. She thought she must have been out in the yard feeding the chickens at the time, and nobody bothered

★ Almost everyone who knew John Levy hated him with a passion. When Billie heard of his death in December 1956, she said it was the best Christmas present she could have, while her pianist Bobby Tucker's only regret was that he died of a heart attack and 'didn't even have the courtesy to let someone shoot him'. John Levy looked like a white man and people said you could only tell that he was black when you heard him say 'motherfucker'.

to come and tell her that her famous god-daughter had returned. So she never had a chance to see for herself how the frightened child she knew as Madge had been transformed into such a bold woman, full of laughter and talk, her lips painted as red as blood, her mink coat slippery on her shoulders.

Linda Kuehl asked Christine what she thought had happened to Billie and why it had all gone so wrong. Her reply was, 'She got off track. You see things and you know how it is; how a young girl feels.'

SIX

Skinny 'Rim' Davenport

———

'All the old-timers are dead.'

Skinny 'Rim' Davenport was born in 1906. Linda Kuehl interviewed him on 30 October 1971, in the back seat of a brand-new brown Cadillac convertible belonging to Ethel Moore's son, Lenny.* It was parked outside Carter's Club in East Baltimore. When I played the tape, Skinny's voice sounded very old and frail and he spoke in a high-pitched whisper. Linda Kuehl described him as a 'string bean of a man' and said he had lost all his teeth.

Skinny was currently employed as a school janitor, or, as he put it, 'a custodian of the schools system', but in the 1920s and '30s he didn't need to work because he was living the fast life. 'I was pimping, yeah,' he said with a thin little laugh. 'All the fellas was pimping.' That way he was able to make more money in one night than his father could make in a month, working at the steel mill down on Sparrow's Point.†

---

* Ethel Moore was one of Billie's close friends in Baltimore, someone who had 'been like a mother to her'. Skinny described Ethel Moore as 'a fast girl who had a good-time house on North Bond Street'.

† If you didn't have a fixed job, then you might get one month's employment during the tomato or the bean season, or a packing job at the wholesale fish market, but for a black man in Baltimore at that time there wasn't much work

Skinny said it was hard to remember things, because 'all the old-timers are dead and I'm the only one that's living'. But as he spoke, everything started to come back to him. He began with the whorehouses. He knew of four or five main whorehouses in the city, where 'The girls used to trade with the white cats, because the black cats didn't have no money. The black cats had nothing.'

There was Snapper's Big House on Eastern Avenue, but Snapper got killed; she had been shot by one of the big toughs years ago. There was Geneva's, but she's dead too. And there was Alice Dean's house on Dallas Street, but that was not really a house, because Alice had no women who stayed there and so it was more of a 'clip 'em and let 'em go joint'.★ Everyone in this business needed to pay regular protection money to the police, but the police were easier in those days; you might get bail or a short jail sentence if they decided to catch you, but if you had enough money to give them, 'you could always beat it'.

Skinny said that of course he knew Billie. 'The fellas all knew her and liked her and she liked to be with the boys.' He never saw her around the big houses, because she preferred the after-hours places, like Ethel Moore's whisky house on 20 North Bond Street, where there was a little bar upstairs and a jukebox. 'You'd bring your own reefers and drink a little and play records and get high. Reefers was three sticks a quarter, and they was good stuff.' Everyone in those days smoked marijuana, which was still not illegal, or they drank bootleg whisky and sickly home-made concoctions like blackberry wine.† Skinny said, 'They was also usin' a little

---

(cont. from p. 31) to be had. Skinny said it was easier for the women, because they could usually earn a dollar a day scrubbing the white marble stone steps of the houses of the rich or doing domestic work.

★ Linda Kuehl interviewed Alice's son 'Sleepy' Dean, who owned a bar on the Point and lived up to his name by spending each day sleeping in the front seat of his brand-new Cadillac Eldorado, wearing dark glasses and with a hat pulled over his eyes. He didn't have much to say and insisted that his mother rented out rooms, that was all. According to Pony Kane, she and Billie spent as much time as they could at Alice Dean's.

† The use of marijuana was legal until 1937 and then it was classified as a narcotic, every bit as dangerous as heroin.

coke – snortin' now and then. But we didn't make it no habit. It was just somethin' to do. We wasn't usin' no hard stuff.'*

Skinny said you could take a girl to Ethel Moore's place and go to one of her rooms, but her house was just a good-time house and she didn't make any money out of it. Billie was very fond of Ethel. 'She looked up to her as a guardian, you know what I mean. Ethel was older and smarter, and she told Billie right from wrong and tried to steer her right.'

Skinny thought that Billie must have been about sixteen years old when he knew her, although in fact she would have been between the ages of twelve and fourteen. He found her a 'nice, pleasant girl . . . and she wasn't too fast and didn't like to hustle around . . . She liked to sing and she used to sing every night, and every night she'd go to different places and she'd tell people where she'd be and they would follow her.'

She might begin at a club such as George's, which later became a barber's shop; or Carter's on East Fairmount, where Skinny was being interviewed; or the one that got torn down on Pratt and Bethel Street. That would be until about two or three in the morning and then she'd go on to the after-hours joints. 'We'd be partying together, and she would sing a song if we'd ask her.' There was a boy who used to play piano for her, if there was a piano to play. Otherwise they might put on a record that had no words to it and she'd sing to the music, or she'd just sing with no music at all. 'She had singing on her mind,' said Skinny.

By five or six in the morning people would get tired and they'd go home to sleep for a few hours. Skinny had a room at the York Hotel. He had no idea where Billie went; he thought perhaps she stayed with her girlfriends, 'perhaps Tooty or Nitey'.

And then in the early afternoon they'd get up and take a bath and be ready to return to the streets. They'd start in

---

* Skinny said, 'This hard stuff come along for the last fifteen years. The young-sters are on it and that's what makes it so bad. In the '20s and '30s people was more together.'

a bar somewhere and move on to a club. Goldfield, owned by the prizefighter Juan Ganz, was usually the first to open and soon the others would follow and they could again drift from one place to the next. Sometimes Billie was there with Skinny's group, or she might go off with a different lot. She was 'fine and talkin' good' and she was accepted wherever she went.

And then Skinny was gone somewhere and Billie had gone somewhere too, and when he saw her again it was 1937 and she was at the Royale with Count Basie. Skinny went backstage to talk to her a bit and then they went on to Ethel Moore's together. He didn't think she'd changed at all. 'She was high, so it was all the same to me.' Word had got out that she was using hard stuff and that she had a connection on the Avenue, close to Snapper's Big House, but it was only hearsay and Skinny said he saw nothing to prove it was true.

The more he talked, the more nostalgic Skinny became for 'the best days of my life'. He remembered how people were really close then. 'There were nice people in the neighbourhood who knew you. They were good people, working people. It's not like that now.' And on Sunday mornings everybody would be cooking, and 'You didn't have to go out to get nothing to eat. Everybody would say, "Come on over and get some salad, or get some hot chicken and bread!"'

Monday was always the best night of the week. It was called Blue Monday because then even working people went to the clubs and it was also a day off for the girls who were hustling on the streets. Linda Kuehl asked Skinny if his girls went out with him on Blue Monday, drinking and smoking and going to different houses and having a good time, but he got very indignant and said, 'No! no! no! We might pick up a cute chick and take her with us', but his working girls were never included in the party.

Talking about these girls, he explained that 'You had to keep 'em clean, in order to present them in the street. But they didn't need too many clothes, because they didn't go to too many places. I might take them to a nightclub now and then, but very seldom. They never took dope and they only drank a little whisky, but not too much or I beat their ass . . . They didn't have other men, not that I know of, and if I'd a known, I'd a beat 'em to death. You'd have to keep 'em in line. They loved it. They'd be so proud of that black eye. They'd show it to everybody. "Look what mine done to me!" . . . You couldn't be calm with 'em. If you was a chicken, you wouldn't have 'em, 'cos other cats would try to take 'em from you.'*

By now Skinny had forgotten all about Billie and was full of his own memories. He used to have two girls hustling for him on the street and three others whom he took more care of, providing them with a room where they could work and a room where they could stay, always making sure that he kept them in different parts of the city. 'I had a white girl and two others,† and one around the corner . . . I'd see each of the girls each day, because I had to collect that money. I had certain days to go to bed with 'em, once a week. Sure, they knew each other. They had to be friends. But we didn't all go to bed together like some fellas did. I didn't take no chances.'

When Linda Kuehl asked him why the girls gave him all their money and let him use them like this, Skinny laughed his wispy laugh. 'I don't know. Because they loved me. They *said* they loved me. That's what they said. I was a young man and they were satisfied, in the bed.'

He reckoned his girls used to bring in around $300 to $400 dollars a day,‡ but no matter what he collected from them, 'We'd blow it all up in a night. All of it.' He'd go gambling and drinking and partying, but he didn't bother to get himself a car. 'We wasn't so crazy about cars as they

---

* At this point Linda Kuehl tried to bring up Billie's reputation as a 'masochist', saying to Skinny, 'Well, Billie went for men who would beat her up.' But Skinny was not the slightest bit interested in that line of thought. 'I didn't have much dealing with her men. I liked her company,' he replied.

† In *Wishing on the Moon* (1994) Donald Clarke quotes Skinny as saying at this point, 'I had a white girl called Babe. I kept her in a house', but I can't find this in the original interview.

‡ This is a very different sum from the dollar a trick that Pony mentions.

are now. We wanted lots of money so as to spend it. We didn't want to throw it away on no car.'

Clothes were a different matter. 'We'd wear them big hats, ten-gallon hats. I liked white hats. And double-breasted suits, monkey-back or full-back; pin-stripe — you had to have that pin-stripe! I liked purple suits. I had my clothes made by Mike Turk in West Baltimore. A custom-made suit cost me forty to fifty dollars at a time!'

Skinny's way of life came to an end with the Second World War. In 1942 he was drafted into the army and he was gone for three years. He said he never bothered to write to his women because he didn't think he would ever come back, and anyway he knew that somebody was bound to take them from him while he was away.

And when he did finally come back, everything had changed. Two of his women had disappeared and the third had stolen all his clothes and moved to Cleveland. She wrote to Skinny and asked him to join her there, but he said he didn't bother. He just stayed where he was.

SEVEN

Mary 'Pony' Kane

———

'Around where the happenin's was.'

I have been listening to the tape of Pony Kane talking about her childhood. She was interviewed on 27 October 1971 at her home on Bond Street in East Baltimore, which is not far from Durham Street, where she and Billie both lived in the same building for a while.* Pony is sitting in a rocking chair and rocking backwards and forwards so that you can hear the rhythmic creak of the wood as she speaks. A man called Lenny is there with her and other people come and go. She laughs a lot as she talks and her voice is deep and mellow.

The house at 217 Durham Street had been connected to electricity when a white family was there, but in Pony's time there was just the dim blue glow from cobalt lights, combined with the oily yellow illumination from a few kerosene lamps. The house had four main rooms, a 'summer kitchen', a bath in the back and a water tap out in the yard. There was also a tiny attic on the third floor, which was where Billie stayed, except when her mother came to spend a few days with

* Pony said, 'The house is still there, but now there are only white people. It was all coloured then.' Billie arrived in October 1926 when she was first released from the House of Good Shepherd for Colored Girls.

her lover, Wee Wee Hill. Then Billie moved to another bed, somewhere else in the building.

The house was owned by Miss Lucy Hill, whom everyone called Miss Lou. Pony described her as a 'great big fat lady' who was crippled because she had a hole in her leg. Pony thought this was caused by cancer, although Miss Lou's son Wee Wee said it was the result of having slipped and hurt herself on an icy road. But anyway, the hole 'ate and ate and ate' and it gave Miss Lou a lot of pain and made it impossible for her to move about much. Mostly she just stayed in her room on the ground floor, lying on a metal hospital bed, but sometimes she managed to heave herself into a chair next to the stove and then she would sit and stir the cooking pots, while keeping both her legs raised on a wooden box.

Another of Miss Lou's sons had epileptic fits and he lived with her all the time; so did Pony, along with her mother, whose name I have not got. Wee Wee was there with his wife Mary, but she left when he started up with Billie's mother. Pony described Wee Wee as a handsome man, who was always busy with so many different women that no one knew where he was or when he might next turn up. She said there were other boarders in the house as well, and I suppose one of them might have been the man called Wilbert Rich who was discovered raping the eleven-year-old Billie on Christmas Eve in 1926, but Pony made no mention of the rape.

Pony said she never saw much of Miss Sadie; she thought she had an after-hours drinking house on Pratt Street somewhere, but she was usually away in New York on jobs. 'She used to stay there most of the time ... She made nice money in New York.' Miss Sadie would send boxes of clothes to her daughter and, on the occasions when she did come to Durham Street, she would bake cookies and cakes and pies. Pony said that of course Billie was nice when she was around her mother, because 'all girls are nice when they are around their parents', but as soon as Miss Sadie had gone, Billie 'would be gone too'.

Billie was the same age as Pony, but she was a big girl

and 'right plump' and she seemed much older. When she first came out of the House of Good Shepherd, she was 'too rough' for the people in Durham Street. 'She was fighting. She wasn't scared.' But she and Pony quickly became friends and went around together for a while and did things together.

They used to go to a five- and ten-cent store called Broadway and steal clothes, but Billie was not a professional shoplifter; she'd simply see a dress she liked and she'd 'throw it under her coat' and that was all. She once stole a skirt for Pony and told Pony's mother that she had bought it with her own money. In those early days Billie used to wear ordinary pleated dresses and satin blouses with big puff sleeves and shiny belts that looked as though they were made of patent leather.

Billie had been brought up as a Catholic, but, as Pony explained, 'Catholic churches were white',* so she went with the other girls to the little store-front Baptist churches on Dallas Street. Or a group of them might take empty jam jars to the Catholic church of St Michael on Wolf and Lombard, and the priest would come to the door at the back and fill the jars with Holy Water, which he kept in a big barrel. The water brought good luck, especially if you sprinkled it in the corners of a room when you had just moved house. Pony remembered that they were also given old Palm Sunday branches. She said that when Billie came back to Baltimore years later, she never bothered to go to the churches; it was just the bars she'd visit. She'd walk in unannounced 'and we'd be playing her records'.

If the two girls wanted to smoke reefers, they'd go to the shop run by a lady called Miss Lura. She sold 'real skinny ones', which were rolled by a sailor who sat in the shop. They'd 'get 'em and use 'em and go and play records' or they might go to the movies, although they didn't see many films† because they didn't have too much money, and so

---

* Pony said that 'Miss Sadie would sometimes go [to the Catholic church of St Michael] with Miss Butler and they would sit in the back, those two.'
† Linda Kuehl asked if they perhaps saw any films by Billie's namesake, Billie Dove, but Pony didn't think so. 'Westerns were popular . . . *Frankenstein*,' she said.

instead they'd 'hang out on the corner and whisper about the boy we'd like'.

But they spent more and more time at Alice Dean's house on South Dallas Street. Pony said Alice Dean was a very pretty woman, and she was sorry she didn't have a photograph to show just how pretty she was. Alice was quite short and plump and looked as though she had Indian blood in her veins. She had long hair, which she wore parted in the middle. She had diamond rings and nice clothes: flat-topped wide-brimmed hats, trimmed with bird of paradise feathers★ and black and grey Chinese mink, Hudson furs, coats with big collars and big sleeves. She had house dresses and street dresses, but she didn't wear pants because 'they were too much trouble to take off'.

Everyone agreed that Alice Dean ran her house very efficiently. She paid her protection money and never got into any trouble, mostly because 'No one was stationed there, no, no, the girls would just walk in and clip 'em . . . I never seen people getting so much money so quick.' The girls wore red velvet garters and satin slips and panties – 'all colours,' said Pony, 'red, orange, black, lavender, green, you know, all colours . . . yellow', and as she spoke it was as if she could again see those colours flashing kingfisher-bright before her eyes. The pimps would sometimes wear girls' garters on their sleeves, and lots of them had bright silk handkerchiefs emerging like tropical flowers from their waistcoat pockets.

Pony remembered that house as a magical place, full of laughter and beauty and music. She and Billie used to 'do anything to be in there. Just to be there.' They took on any jobs that were offered to them, with maybe a dollar or fifty cents as a day's pay.† Alice Dean's bedroom was painted all white and the furniture was white as well, while the bedroom

---

★ As Farah Jasmine Griffin explains in her book on Billie, *If You Can't Be Free, Be a Mystery* (2001), such hats were the prostitutes' trademark.

† This was more than Pony might make from scrubbing steps. 'I'd go up and down Baltimore Street scrubbing steps and people's houses. Up and down Pratt Street where Jewish people lived. Get ten cents or fifteen cents for doing a group of steps . . . Sometimes I'd make three, four, five dollars a week, a bad week was two dollars.'

next door was all blue. Alice had sewn the lace curtains in the bedrooms herself, and they needed starching and ironing, while the front steps, which welcomed each new stranger through the door, needed scrubbing and Pony would polish the oilcloth on the floors until it 'shone as yellow as the sun . . . so clean you could eat off it!' She laughed as she explained how she would wipe a bedroom door very, *very* slowly, while peeping in through the keyhole to see what the women were doing with the men. 'I tried to see as much as I could. I found out how it went.'

Pony said that the 'rich guys who came around the neighbourhood looking for sport' were white men mostly, simply because 'Very few coloured men ever had the money . . . Shit, there weren't no money in those days. A girl would make a dollar a trick, sometimes a quarter. She'd go to bed all night with a man for two or three dollars.'

A man would go upstairs with a girl, to the blue bedroom or the white, and he would give her the 'few pennies he was going to give her'. But what she wanted was his wallet, especially if she had seen that he had a 'big roll and good bills of money in it'. If he left his trousers folded over the chair by the bed, then it was easy, and Alice Dean or someone else could creep in softly, remove the wallet, empty it and return it to its pocket. But if he kept his trousers on, it was more difficult. Pony was asked in the interview how it was done then, and on the tape you can hear her swivelling her chair round with a noisy squeak as she tells the man called Lenny to stand in front of her so that she can demonstrate the technique.

'OK. So he's going to trade with me. When we lay down I have to put my hands on him, you understand. But my hand is working on his wallet. On the bed. His pants are down.'

Again she laughs her big fat laugh and at that moment you can hear a child calling for her and she tells him to help himself to a biscuit from the biscuit tin.

Pony wasn't going with men then; that came later, after she had been released from prison. But Billie was much quicker. She learnt the trade from working in the house and soon she was 'ready to catch tricks in there too'. But as Pony said, 'She wasn't doing anything unusual. She did just like all the rest of 'em . . . Her friends were all doing that . . . She'd get a pair of stockings, wash 'em out and put 'em on half-dry and go out. She didn't have too much of clothes or nothing . . . She wasn't making money . . . She was getting a meal, missing a meal getting a trick or two . . . She wanted to be around where the happenin's was, round this way, down this corner, out this way.'

Billie already had a lot of men. 'She was a tall girl, shaped pretty nice. She was liked by a whole lot of boys, but she used to call them country boys; they were working fellas and she would get the money and she wouldn't have no time for them . . . Hustling men liked her. They would come around and take her for nights out. She didn't have no time for the others.'

Billie liked men who 'dressed nice': leather nob shoes with wing toes in brown or black or a wine colour; grey pin-striped suits; caps from that shop called Matterburg's. She liked a very 'pretty-skinned' boy called Dee Dee who worked in the packing house, but she found him too much of a country boy and anyway he had another girl. She liked Willie Diggs, who made a lot of money and blowed it, and Charlie Diggs who ran a poolroom, and Douglas Crawly who was young and had women take care of him. As Pony said, 'She wanted who she wanted and they mostly had someone else.'

At first the other women were resentful of Billie, because she was the youngest of them all and tall and light-complex-ioned and well-built, and because she could sing. They used to beat her up, until she learnt to 'get in with them and get rough too'. When Linda Kuehl thought this was the moment to ask if Billie 'went for women', Pony replied, 'There used to be some women around there like that, but she wasn't with them . . . Most girls I know in their youth do that. The average woman would go to bed with another woman – that's just for kicks. Billie always dug them guys.'*

* Again Donald Clarke in *Wishing on the Moon* quotes this very differently, and has Pony saying that she thought that 'Billie went with women . . .' (p. 27).

All the men were keen to hear Billie sing. 'She used to sing in nightclubs and maybe make two or three dollars a night. She'd be singing "Stormy Weather" and "Stardust" and all those popular tunes. She sang fast and slow numbers. There used to be an after-hours place called Pitts on Caroline Street, where a man would play piano and everybody would pile in there at nights and she would be the big attraction . . . Everybody would get her on Blue Monday for the singing and they'd be drinking whisky and balling, and she would sing and booze and dance.' Pony added, 'She'd sing like it hurt her, like it did her good to sing.'

Billie was drinking bootleg whisky during that time, usually a corn whisky called White Lightning. 'She'd be feeling good and high and drunk and she'd go up to a man and say, "Kiss my ass, motherfucker!", right in his face, in front of all his friends.' Pony explained that it was 'a natural thing for a woman to cuss, you'd pick it up right off the street . . . but they didn't mostly say it to their men because if they said it to their men they knew they was going to get their behinds beat.* Billie'd say it to anybody, she didn't have no special ones.' Some of the men would ignore her and let it slide, but others would get angry and they'd chase her down the street while she ran ahead, still taunting them. '"Come on cocksucker, suck my ass! Suck my ass!" She'd be about half a block from them and then they would beat her up. She'd holler. She wouldn't say it when they were beating her.'

Pony remembered how Billie often came back to Miss Lou's house in the early morning with bruises all over her face, 'looking like she'd been put through the mill'. But the house was dark and she'd be all made-up and so you wouldn't

---

* Linda Kuehl asked if Billie 'liked being beaten up', but Pony was quite evasive. 'She'd get slapped around a lot. She must have liked it, though she wouldn't say much about it. She liked the guys.' Charlie Ray, who was also interviewed in Baltimore in October 1971, said that when Billie went around with a 'hustler type' called Calvin Atkins, 'She used to like to wear his shoes, just to come down and go to the store. He was always saying, "Don't wear my shoes!" but she'd wear them anyway. And one day he caught her coming from the store with a pair of his shoes on, so he smacked her on the side of the head and said, "Goddamn it! Didn't I tell you not to wear my goddamn shoes!" And she haul-assed back inside and took off them shoes.'

notice much, and 'She wouldn't tell; no, she wouldn't tell.'

But then Miss Lou got sicker and could no longer cope with this girl who was only thirteen years old, but who looked like a grown woman and was getting around so fast. Miss Lou didn't know what Billie was doing, but people began telling stories about how she was drinking bootleg whisky and fighting and causing trouble. And so she sent for Miss Sadie in New York and told her she must take her daughter away.

Miss Sadie turned up and stayed for a while at Durham Street and, when she left, she had arranged for Billie to come and join her in Harlem. I wonder if she explained that she was living and working in a whorehouse run by Miss Florence Williams at 151 West 140th Street; a place where a wild and good-looking young girl could earn plenty of money. Or at least more than she was earning in Baltimore.

Pony saw Billie on the day of her departure. She said she had chosen to wear a white voile dress, something like her Communion dress perhaps, but with a shiny red belt pulled tight around her waist. You see her there, waiting for the train that would carry her to a strange new city, where she could find other beds in which to sleep, and other bars and whorehouses and after-hours joints where she could be invited to sing and drink and smoke and have a party. You see her there, a young girl dressed all in white with a little gold cross hanging round her neck, and perhaps she has the rosary beads and the prayer book which the Sisters of the Poor gave her, tucked neatly into her suitcase, among the silk slips and panties.

EIGHT

Wee Wee Hill

———————

'I was her stepfather.'

Linda Kuehl went to interview Wee Wee Hill at his home in Baltimore, a 'renovated, pretty, brick row-house, on a wide southern boulevard on the Point'. She obviously liked him and described him as being 'still youthful, handsome and charming'. His wife Viola, 'a small chunky woman', was there throughout the interview, but she kept silent apart from occasionally muttering, 'I don't know nothing about no Billie Holiday!'

Wee Wee was twenty-three years old when he first 'went with' Billie's mother Sadie. She was thirty-four at the time, although to him she didn't seem like an older woman. He described her as a 'nice-looking, brown-skinned person . . . with beautiful pitch-black hair', and said it was obvious she took after her father, Charles Fagan, who was 'part Indian and real light'.

According to Wee Wee, Charles Fagan loved both his daughter Sadie and his granddaughter Billie; in fact he was 'crazy about them' and would often come down from North-West Baltimore to visit them when they were living in Durham Street.★

★ Footnote on page 46.

Wee Wee thought he must have started going with Sadie in around 1924, or it could have been later — 1927 perhaps, or even 1928. He said they were together for about four years. He first met her when she was living on Spring Street and then she moved in with him to the house at 217 Durham Street. His mother, Miss Lou Hill, was living next door in number 219.

Looking back through the tunnel of the years, Wee Wee admitted that in those days he was often a very bad man who couldn't be satisfied with one woman. He gambled and ran around. Of course he knew that Sadie had a lot of trouble with her daughter; but what he remembered, or at least what he wanted to remember, was a time when everyone was good and kind and loving and they were all part of one big happy family. Billie and her mother were 'real close' and Sadie would 'do anything in the world' for Billie. He said nothing about Billie being sent to the House of Good Shepherd, or of the occasion when he and Sadie came home in the early hours of Christmas Eve and discovered her being raped by a neighbour.

Wee Wee talked about the house at 217 Durham Street as if he and Billie and Sadie had lived there together. He said Billie was going to school, and then she'd come home and help to keep the house clean. He said even then she had a nice voice and he used to hear her singing around the house. Maybe she'd be upstairs doing the cleaning, or in the bathroom, and he'd hear her.

Sadie didn't have a bad temper, but she'd get angry with him because of the way he was running around. He said that one time she caught him in a good-time house on Bond

---

* Billie's first cousin John Fagan gave a very different account of these family relationships, saying that Sadie was treated 'kind of cool, because of Billie'. It wasn't the fact of her illegitimacy (he calls it bastardy), but it was because Clarence Holiday, 'he ain't from the Point, from the East Side, I don't know exactly where he's from. So they gave Sadie a hard time . . . Billie was disgusted by this . . . One night we went to the Astoria — me and my father and my sister, and after she finished a set . . . she came over and she made a remark that, "So far as I'm concerned, all the Fagans are dead!" What she meant was that she carried that feeling over till after she was successful, because her mother had gotten this hard time from her family when she was small.'

Street. She couldn't go into the building because 'the people there was white', but she rapped on the door and he looked out of the window and saw her. He was afraid to go down because Sadie was carrying a gun, which surprised him because he 'didn't know she cared that much'. When he finally got home that night, Sadie was waiting for him. She hit him with a wooden cigarette stand and cut his wrist and arms. She was cursing him, but still he wouldn't fight her, because he knew he was in the wrong. He remembered that Billie was there as well, trying to talk to her mother and calm her down.

Sadie wanted Wee Wee to marry her. She was divorced from Philip Gough by then, so nothing stood in their way. He told her he'd think about it, although the truth was he 'didn't have the mind' to get married.* That was why she packed up and went to New York. She asked Billie to go with her, but Billie said she wanted to stay in Baltimore because she wanted to be with her grandfather. Wee Wee said that even though Billie couldn't visit her grandfather, she knew he wouldn't let her down, not if she ever needed anything.

Wee Wee used to write to Sadie in New York and in the end he did go and join her for a while. At that time she was living in Long Island and working as a maid-cook for a Jewish family named Levy. They managed to get Wee Wee a job as a porter in a cotton store down on Broadway and Times Square, but then he heard that his mother was sick because of the trouble with her leg, so he came back to Baltimore. He never went back to New York because he met Viola and set up house with her and even married her, after his mother had died.

Anyway, there was the twelve-year-old Billie on her own in Baltimore, fending for herself. Wee Wee said she never needed to work scrubbing steps because he provided her with enough funds to pay for a furnished room on Pratt

---

* This is contradicted by Pony Kane, who said that Wee Wee was married to a woman called Mary who moved out of Durham Street when he started with Sadie.

Street. He 'used to give her money now and then, when she used to ask me for a couple of dollars'. Her grandfather would also give her money 'when she went up there to get her dollars from him, or when he came down to see her on weekends'. And on top of that, her father Clarence was 'good to her' as well.

Linda Kuehl was obviously not convinced. She asked Wee Wee, 'Well, how did she make money?'

'Well, like I said, her grandfather was pretty good to her,' he replied.

'And she was hustling?' said Linda Kuehl.

'Yeah, probably so,' came the answer. 'Yeah, definitely so. When she hung around with Alice Dean and them girls, that's what they did. So she had to be doing the same thing . . .* She was on her own for maybe two years. People knew. That's what gave her a bad name. My mother loved her, and Billie would come and spend a night at Durham Street and eat, and my mother tried to talk to her, about being a good girl. She'd come up to the house, get a meal, listen, but she never give a damn.'

Wee Wee said that Billie stayed with him and his mother at the house on Durham Street on the night before she set off to join Sadie in New York. Wee Wee took her to the station the following morning. He didn't mention that she was wearing a white voile dress with a shiny red belt around her waist.

He heard nothing more about her until the summer of 1932 or 1933, when Sadie contacted him to let him know that Billie was coming to Sparrow's Beach and was singing with Count Basie's band, and could Wee Wee 'spread it around and build her up'.

---

* When John Fagan was asked the same question, he said, 'Of course Billie turned tricks. What else are you going to do in those times. You had to make ends meet. You had to survive.' He also insisted that she was 'not like a slut. No, no, no, no! She was not staggering from one bar to another. She just lived fast. The difference is this. Some people are good-time people, but they have their principles about themselves. They are out after hours and . . . they go in and wash their faces and clean up and sleep half the day and go out all night and sleep again. Billie had that pride and respect for herself.'

'A lot of her friends were excited and a lot didn't believe it,' he said. 'They didn't think it could be her. All of East Baltimore went to Sparrow's Beach that Sunday to see if she could sing. They said she did good. She was all right. She could sing. She made good . . . Practically all the guys I knew went that Sunday.'

After this meeting Billie always tried to see Wee Wee whenever she came back to Baltimore. As he said, 'I was her stepfather. She knew I wasn't her father, but she didn't have no father.'

The last time they met was when Billie was appearing at the Royale. She had heard that Wee Wee's wife Viola was sick in bed and so she went to visit her at the house. When she learnt that Wee Wee was in the barber's shop downstairs she followed him there and sat with him while he got a shave and a haircut. The people in the shop wanted her to sing and Billie said she couldn't because of her contract with the Royale. She bought drinks for everybody instead.

NINE

The Pursuit of Happiness

———

In 1776 the Declaration of Independence stated that all men were created equal and every American was promised 'certain unalienable Rights'. These included the right to 'the pursuit of happiness', as if happiness were a wild animal lurking in the woods and bushes of life, and you and everyone else must go out and follow its trail, dogs on the scent, guns at the ready.

You search and search, trying to flush out this elusive, fleeting creature, and there is always the possibility that as the years move on you might fail to catch a glimpse of it, or even fail to recognise it as it races past you. But what happens if you do manage to find happiness and you have it in your grasp? Must you allow it to escape, just so that you can continue with the joy of the hunt? Or is it something you can keep hold of for ever, in spite of the vicissitudes of time and circumstance?

And if you have the right to pursue the promise of happiness, do you also have a similar right to eradicate any evidence of unhappiness that gets in your way? To remove all the perceived threats that surround you, in order to provide more space, where the happy things you long for can increase and multiply?

Alcohol is a case in point. During the years after the Civil War the American press was flooded with articles and editorials that blamed alcohol as the chief cause of poverty, crime, disease and insanity. In the isolated rural communities of the South, huge crowds would flock into the Baptist and Methodist churches to listen to their preachers describing the abominations caused by the demon drink. It was said that in order to clear the path for paradise on Earth, it was first necessary to stamp out this sin, and whole congregations were united in a mood of wild hysteria. It was suggested that fatal poisons should be added secretly to hard liquor and, if thousands died as a result, the price would still not be too high. It was said that drinkers should be deported, excluded from the churches, forbidden to marry, branded, tattooed, sterilised, tortured, whipped and even executed along with their children, as far as the fourth generation.★

For white southerners, the dangers of alcohol took on an extra dimension. As Congressman Richmond Pearson Hobson from Alabama explained to the House of Representatives in 1914, 'Liquor will actually make a brute out of the Negro, causing him to commit unnatural crimes . . . The effect is the same on the white man, though the white man being further evolved, it takes longer to reduce him to the same level.' At this same debate, Congressman Edward W. Pou of North Carolina reminded the House that the South had been 'forced' to take away the ballot from the Negro, 'as an adult takes a pistol from the hand of a child', and now it was time to remove the bottle as well.

The Eighteenth Amendment, bringing in Prohibition, was finally passed on 16 June 1920, in the aftermath of the First World War and at a time when America saw itself as a last refuge of peace and virtue in a degenerate world. As the leader of the Anti-Saloon League explained in 1919, 'It is the business of the Church of God to make a democracy that is safe for the world, by making it safe and sober everywhere.'

★ Much of the material for this chapter is taken from Andrew Sinclair, *Prohibition: The Era of Excess*, 1962.

As a result of these new laws, no more intoxicating liquors were to be manufactured, sold or transported within the United States. The legal loophole about *drinking* the stuff was immediately apparent; all that needed to be organised were the logistics of illegal production and distribution.

Prohibition was not responsible for creating the criminal gangs, syndicates and protection rackets, but it did provide a means for criminals of all sorts to make an easy and steady income. And money was soon made on such a vast scale that the underworld was able to 'buy' judges, state attorneys and whole police forces. In some instances they had the power to take over local and even State government.*

Prohibition was brought to an end on 5 December 1933, but by then a new demon was all ready and waiting to be attacked. Drugs, rather than alcohol, were seen as the cause of 'crime, disease, poverty and insanity'.

There were laws against the use of cocaine and opium, but during the years of Prohibition it was marijuana that had become increasingly popular, especially among those on the fringes of society. It was cheap and legal and easy to obtain and was considered to be no more harmful than tobacco.

In 1930 the Federal Bureau of Narcotics was created and H. J. Anslinger was appointed its first director. He was of Swiss extraction and had been raised in a small town in Pennsylvania. He was short and thickset with a pock-marked neck and a fondness for dressing like a gangster in irides-cent suits and big ties decorated with Chinese pagodas.

During the early 1930s, the Bureau did not do very well. Its budget was cut by almost half during the three worst years of the Depression and it was in danger of being closed down altogether. In 1935 Anslinger was hospitalised with nervous strain, but when he returned he had a new fighting spirit and a new zeal. For the sake of increasing and main-taining the power of his Bureau, this man waged an almost single-handed fight to bring in federal legislation against

* Sinclair, pp. 221–4.

marijuana. His campaign was conducted with all the fiery rhetoric of a Baptist minister and he used his natural flair for publicity and vivid scaremongering to get his point across.

Anslinger confidently assured the House of Representatives that, under the influence of marijuana, 'some people will fly into a delirious rage and may commit violent crimes'. He gave talks on the radio and addressed public meetings in which he blamed many of society's ills on this one drug, asking his audiences if they had any idea 'how many murders, suicides, robberies, criminal assaults, hold-ups, burglaries and deeds of maniacal insanity' were precipitated by the use of marijuana.

On 14 June 1937, the Marijuana Tax Bill was brought before the House of Representatives and successfully passed. It was now illegal to grow, transport, use or sell marijuana. The new Act came into force in October, and a week later a fifty-eight-year-old man was arrested, charged with possession and sentenced to four years' imprisonment and a hefty fine. The presiding judge declared enthusiastically, 'I consider marijuana the worst of all narcotics – far worse than the use of morphine or cocaine . . . Marijuana destroys life itself.'

Suddenly there was no distinction to be made between cocaine, opium, heroin and marijuana. In spite of the prevailing scientific evidence, Anslinger insisted that marijuana had all the characteristics of a narcotic and, as far as he was concerned, it was the most dangerous of all the forbidden drugs. Of course this meant that he and his agents now had access to a huge number of potential criminals; enough to keep the Bureau well funded and in business for years.* It also meant that people like Billie and her friends

---

* Research by New York hospital physicians published in 1942 showed that 'the use of marijuana does not lead to physical, mental or moral degeneration and that no permanent deleterious effects from its continuous use were observed'. Another report put together by psychiatrists, physicians, chemists, sociologists and officials and published in 1945 also challenged Anslinger's claims about the dangers of marijuana, calling it 'essentially a harmless drug'. Anslinger disregarded the study.

in the jazz world, who were fond of smoking reefers, were suddenly in serious contravention of the law and liable to be arrested and punished whenever the police decided it was time to teach them a lesson.

TEN

Billie Comes to Harlem

A fter Emancipation, those who had once been slaves were now in theory the equal of everyone else, but in practice they were never allowed the freedom of movement that was part of the definition of the freedom of the individual. Other men and women could move from one state to another and could vanish into the swelling hubbub of the cities, forgetting their past and inventing a new future for themselves at will. But for black Americans it was different, because when they abandoned the southern states in their thousands in search of a better life in the North, they were denied their democratic rights wherever they went.*

---

* Many of the poor white immigrants who arrived in the USA welcomed the chance of feeling superior, claiming, as a delegate to a conference in Alabama said, 'No black man in the world is equal to the least, the poorest, lowest-down white.' During the First World War the headquarters of the American Expeditionary Force issued an explanatory document that called on the French 'not to treat [Negro soldiers] with familiarity and indulgence which are matters of grievous concern to Americans and an affront to their national policy . . . [and] not to commend too highly the black American troops in the presence of white Americans'. In spite of such warnings, the first two American soldiers to receive the Croix de Guerre were both blacks from the Fifteenth Regiment of New York's National Guard, and that entire regiment, nicknamed the Harlem Hellfighters, was also awarded the same honour for bravery. Much of my information comes from Nat Brandt, *Harlem at War: The Black Experience in World War II*, 1996.

Duke Ellington, in a talk he gave in Los Angeles just before the outbreak of the Second World War, gave an unexpected interpretation of one of the effects of this broken promise, saying, 'I contend that the Negro is the creative voice of America, *is* creative America, and it was a happy day in America when the first unhappy slave was landed on its shores. We stirred in our shackles, and our unrest awakened justice in the hearts of a courageous few, and we re-created in America the desire for true democracy, freedom for all, the brotherhood of man, principles on which the country had been founded . . . [We've kept] America and its forgotten principles alive in the fat and corrupt years intervening between our divine conception and our near tragic present.'★

Although the majority of black Americans lived and worked in the South, they also had a long connection with New York. Already by 1771 they made up about one-sixth of the city's total population. But this number began to decrease once New York became the destination of hundreds of thousands of immigrants escaping from hunger and persecution in Europe. Each newly arrived group fought for its share of territory and power in the city, and throughout the nineteenth century the black population was driven out of areas where they had established themselves. They were pressed further and further to the north. They had to escape from the violence and intimidation that was brought to bear on them in Soho and in Greenwich Village, in the Five Points district (which became Chinatown) and in Little Africa (which was transformed into Little Italy).† All this was in spite of the fact that, as Jacob Riis explained in 1890, ‡ 'There

---

★ Quoted in Geoffrey C. Ward and Ken Burns, *Jazz: A History of America's Music*, p. 311.

† There were several particularly bloody battles with the Irish Catholics who arrived in the late 1840s, escaping from the horrors of the potato famine. They were at once thrown into conflict with the resident black population, competing for the lowest-paid jobs and the cheapest housing. In 1854 there were open street fights between the two groups, and in 1863 there was a riot when Irish youths went on the rampage. In 1900 another Irish-led riot left hundreds dead and wounded. By then the police were mostly Irish and did little to control the violence, and even participated in it.

‡ *How the Other Half Lives*, 1891, p. 156.

is no more clean and orderly community in New York than the new settlement of coloured people that is growing up on the East Side . . . In this respect the Negro is immensely superior to the lowest of the whites, the Italians and the Polish Jews, below whom he has been classed in the tenant scale.'

By 1905 the first of the more well-to-do black families had moved into Harlem, occupying the elegant red stone houses that had been left empty after a slump. They were prepared to pay higher rents in exchange for the space and dignity that could be found here, and at first the neighbourhood was 'stable and unified', with blacks and whites living in close proximity to each other. However, most of the properties in Harlem were owned by white landlords, who could charge rents as much as 58 per cent more than the average in the rest of the city. Of the 12,000 retail stores operating in Harlem in 1930, only 391 were owned by blacks and 172 of them were groceries.

With the internal migrations from the countryside to the city and from the South to the North, Harlem's population increased by 600 per cent between 1910 and 1935. The grand houses in their wide boulevards were transformed into 'filthy, vermin-ridden buildings' as more and more people were crowded into the one area of the city where they were able to live. By the late 1920s there were around 200,000 people crammed into three and a half square miles.* The overcrowded houses had become tenement blocks; schools, sanitation and all the basic amenities of life were neglected by the civic authorities, and the death rate was twice as high as in the rest of the city. There was just one hospital, the Harlem General, which was known locally as the Butcher Shop or the Morgue. In 1931 it was providing 273 beds for the entire community.†

---

* By 1940 that number had increased to 500,000, still contained within the same area.
† According to Gunnar Myrdal, *An American Dilemma*, 1944, in 1928 in the United States as a whole there was one bed for every 139 white persons and one bed for every 1,941 coloureds (p. 172).

As well as employment, housing and health problems, there were also the persistent humiliations and social discriminations. In Blumstein's or Koch's, the big Harlem department stores on 125th Street, a black woman was not permitted to try a dress on in the store. The people of Harlem were forbidden to use the toilet facilities in shops or restaurants. Black movie-goers could only sit in the balcony at Loew's Victoria on 125th Street. A black person could not be served at a bar with a white friend.

The tensions in Harlem reached a crisis during the First World War, when many black Americans wondered 'why we fight for democracy abroad when we don't have democracy at home'. A similar crisis came with the onset of the Second World War. James Baldwin, in his essay *The Harlem Ghetto*, spoke of the 'furious bewildered rage' that was taking root throughout these years, as 'all over Harlem, Negro boys and girls are growing into a stunted maturity, trying desperately to find a place to stand; and the wonder is not that so many are ruined, but that so many survive'.

But people made the best of what they had, and Harlem in the first decades of the 1900s was full of clubs, ballrooms, speakeasies, hole-in-the-wall joints, whorehouses and reefer pads; all sorts of enclosed paradise worlds where you could forget your troubles for a while, with the help of music and dancing, and sex and liquor, and whatever drugs were available at the time.

For wealthy white New Yorkers, the word Harlem was a 'national synonym for naughtiness', and the 'pleasure-loving' would go 'slumming' in search of excitement and entertainment. Some places, like the Cotton Club, maintained strict rules of segregation,★ while others – and in particular the famous Savoy Ballroom that opened in 1926 – had a mixed clientele.

The Savoy occupied an entire block on Lenox Avenue.

★ The strange madness of segregation was strictly maintained at the Cotton Club, where the 'high-yeller dancing girls, who in white company could pass for Caucasian', were not allowed to mix with the all-white audience who had come to be entertained.

You came in via a marble pillared staircase lit by cut-glass chandeliers and stepped out into an orange-and-blue dance hall, which had a revolving stage for a band at either end so that the music never had to stop. Louis Armstrong, Ella Fitzgerald and Cab Calloway were regular performers. Wednesday-night shows were reserved for fraternal organisations, and Thursdays for kitchen maids, who had one free night in the week. Everything was kept very dignified and orderly and, even when Prohibition had been repealed, the Savoy served only ginger beer. One in five of the guests was white and mixed dancing was commonplace.

But the excitement of the 1920s gave way to the Great Depression and, by 1934, half of the black working population in all of the United States was without employment, as opposed to less than a quarter of the white population. Almost half of all families in Harlem were receiving benefit, and because the provision was eight cents a meal for food, and nothing at all if a man of working age was part of the household, it was not uncommon to see whole families foraging in garbage cans in search of scraps to eat.

When Billie first arrived in Harlem in 1929, she stayed with her mother in a brothel belonging to a woman called Florence Williams on 151 West 140th Street, between Lenox and 7th Avenues. A few weeks later, on 2 May, the Police Department of the 19th District organised a big round-up of prostitutes in that area and Billie, along with her mother and Florence Williams and two other women from the same address, were brought in for questioning. Billie gave her age as twenty-one and called herself by her grandfather's surname of Fagan. Her mother gave her age as thirty-four and used her middle name of Julia and her maiden name of Harris. Neither of the two women let it be known that they were related.

Sadie and the three other women were discharged, but Billie was taken into custody. She had the misfortune of being tried by a woman magistrate called Jean Hortense Norris, who was notorious for giving harsh sentences in an effort to rid the streets of New York of what she called 'wayward minors'. Billie was found guilty of being a 'vagrant and dissipated adult' and was sent to Welfare Island, now known as Roosevelt Island, on the East River.★

Billie was released in October 1929. For a while she and Sadie lived in Brooklyn and then in 1930 they returned to Harlem, to a small room off Lenox Avenue. A report on Negro housing was presented to President Hoover around that time. It stated that 'one notable difference appears between the immigrant and the Negro populations. In the case of the former, there is the possibility of escape, with improvement in economic status in the second generation', whereas for African-Americans there was hardly any opportunity to make a decent living and to climb onto the ladder of success, because 'the more things changed, the more they worsened'.†

So this is the sort of world that Billie came to know and to see as home. No doubt in the early days she sometimes turned to prostitution in order to make a few dollars, but she also had her voice to sell. Her first singing job in New York was in 1930 or 1931 with the Hat Hunter Band, playing at the Grey Dawn cabaret bar on Jamaica Avenue. She earnt whatever money was thrown down on the floor for her.

When she and her mother moved to a tiny room on West 127th Street, Sadie had a job working at Mexico's restaurant, while Billie waited at the tables and sang for tips. This was followed by Ed Small's Paradise, the Alhambra and then Pod and Jerry's, where she was accompanied by the pianist Bobby Henderson and was able to earn a steady two dollars a night as well as the tips.

She spent all the spare time she had with musicians; smoking marijuana with them, drinking with them and luxuriating in their company. Everyone said how shy she

---

★ Welfare Island housed a hospital and a workhouse. Most of the women who were sent there were charged with prostitution and, according to Harry Anslinger at the Federal Bureau of Narcotics, 'practically all the prostitutes committed were drug addicts' (*The Traffic in Narcotics*, 1953, p. 94).
† Quoted in David Lewis, *When Harlem Was in Vogue*, 1981, p. 306.

was, 'with a shyness so vast that she spoke in practically a whisper'. And everyone was impressed by her character. 'She was an uncompromising, devastatingly honest kind of girl . . . very attractive, very cool, very gentle . . . an extremely quiet person who liked to laugh . . . She had a gingham gown on her and she was vivacious and young and nice. Oh, she was so vivacious, she was like sunshine!'*

It was during this period that she decided to change her name. She took the first name of Billie, after the white actress Billie Dove, who was billed as the 'American Beauty' of silent films and who was often cast as a damsel in distress, awaiting rescue at the last minute by a handsome hero.† And she chose the strangely evocative surname of her young father, the banjo player Clarence Holiday, who was only sixteen years older than she was.

---

* John Chilton, *Billie's Blues*, 1975, p. 22.
† Dove was born Lillian Bohny in New York in 1900. She joined the Ziegfeld Follies in 1917, made her first film in 1921 and hit the big time in 1923, playing opposite Douglas Fairbanks in *The Black Pirate*. After twelve years she retired from show business, and in her private life she was a pilot, a painter and a poet.

ELEVEN

Elmer Snowden

'She'd call me her daddy.'

Elmer Snowden* was seventy-one years old when he was interviewed by Linda Kuehl in October 1971. He said nobody could believe he was so old, and anyway he didn't care because he could still 'get almost as much at seventy' with the young girls who hung around the bandstand as he did when he was a young man.

He first met Clarence Holiday in Baltimore around 1910 when they were just 'kids in short pants'. They went to school together at the Tin Factory on Calvin and Gold, and then Clarence moved to somewhere in the east of the city, but Elmer couldn't remember the name of the street. He thought Clarence was about two years older than him and had been born in Baltimore, but he wasn't sure.†

They were both learning to play banjo. Elmer started with the Northwest Baltimore Group and Clarence was with the East Baltimore Group; and then Elmer was in Eubie Blake's

---

* Elmer Snowden, guitar, banjo, saxophones, band leader and very successful businessman. He was born in 1900 and died in 1973.

† Elmer kept changing the date of their first meeting and later in the interview he said it was in 1914 or 1915, when 'I was about seventeen and he was a littler older'.

band, but Clarence was not taken on there because he couldn't read music. They'd see each other when they played a dance. 'We weren't that close because we were from different sections of town. But he was a fine guy to hang out with and when we got together we were good friends; he was a musician and I was a musician, and musicians have a language of their own.'

While they were still young they played Murray's Casino on Preston Street and St Mary's Hall and the Pitheon Castle, and Elmer remembered going to big rough places like Galilee Fishner's Dance Hall in East Baltimore. They'd change into long pants when they went out on a job. The girls were always there, 'hanging around when we was playing. You never had to worry.' As soon as the performance was over the musicians set down their instruments while they went to get paid, and that was the sign for the girls to move in. The one who managed to grab your instrument was the one you'd be with for the night and 'you were her man'.★

The bands used to have 'battles' to see who got the most applause on a particular instrument, and Clarence and Elmer competed on the banjo. Elmer said he was the best at that time and 'It got so they wouldn't let me play and made me a judge.' The prize for winning was five dollars.

Everyone who spoke of Clarence Holiday remembered him as a 'happy-go-lucky guy' who was full of fun. The trombone player Sandy Williams was in Fletcher Henderson's Orchestra with Clarence in the early 1930s. He tried to explain more about this happy-go-luckiness. He said, 'All sorts of things would seem funny to him. If he saw a guy walk across the street and break his neck, he'd be laughing. He was that type. He and Billie were not the same. He was more of a clown, but I've never seen Billie being a clown.'

Clarence laughed when he was sober, but he laughed even more when he was drunk. According to Sandy Williams,

---

★ According to Wee Wee Hill, Billie's mother Sadie met Clarence at a carnival and he 'romanced her' on that first night. Maybe he was playing banjo and she was the one who picked it up. Elmer Snowden never saw her together with Clarence in Baltimore, although he met her later.

'He was a liquor-head, just like his daughter . . . he loved his booze. He'd drink anything you put into a glass.' He remembered how he and Clarence were once in Atlantic City together with the orchestra, and every morning they'd get up early and go down to the beach with bottles of whisky – or was it gin? – and they'd bury a bottle in the wet sand to keep it cool. On one occasion the tide came right up, leaving the bottle buried far out to sea. Clarence didn't want to wait for the tide to turn and so he waded out into the water. He went as deep as his armpits, fully dressed, and never mind that he couldn't even swim! That was the kind of man he was.

Everyone who spoke of him agreed that Clarence was not ambitious. He never wanted to set up his own band and he was never a soloist. People remembered him for his steady rhythm. He was also said to be a good singer, 'a shouter not a crooner', but he never recorded, so it's not possible to compare his voice with his daughter's. He earnt himself the nickname LibLab, because he knew how to chat up the girls, but even when he was drunk he was never violent to women.

Elmer remembered the first time he heard of Billie's existence. This was in October or November 1917. Clarence said to him quite casually, '"You know I'm a daddy now!" I said, "You're a what?" I never even heard of a wife or nothing, but in those days it was one of those things. A wife? What's that? Because there were kids here, there and everywhere.'

And then Elmer was introduced to Billie – he thought it was in 1918 or 1919. Anyway, he was with Eubie Blake's band at the time and a piano player called Joe Rochester invited them all to go over to the house where Clarence was living on Jefferson Street in East Baltimore. And there in the house Elmer saw a three-year-old child whom he described as 'an ugly little thing, a homely-looking baby'. Clarence explained that this was his daughter and asked Elmer to be the girl's godfather. 'I was too young to know what godfather meant, so I asked the piano player, who was a man, and he told me it meant I had to take care of her. But I thought, I can't even take care of *myself* with the money I'm making . . . so I never said if I would or wouldn't be her godfather.'★

The next time Elmer met Billie was in New York in 1927, or it might have been 1929. By then he was running five different bands and doing very well. She was singing in a little back room at a club called the GoGrabbers, and he told her that he liked her sound and that she shouldn't be performing in such a dump. He tried to persuade her to go to the Hot Feet Club. She said she'd see about the Hot Feet, but went to Pod and Jerry's instead. He felt it was not such a bad choice because 'you could make good money there too'. He remembered how the gangsters used to come in at Pod and Jerry's and they'd say, 'Close the door! Put the floor show on!' And there was one gangster who liked to produce a 500-dollar bill and put a match to it and let it burn. Sometimes the musicians would try to grab the bill from him before the serial number was destroyed, because then it could still be redeemed at a bank.

After a while Elmer got talking with Billie, but he didn't 'put her together with Clarence'. And the name Holiday 'didn't ring a bell'. Then she told him she was from Baltimore and said, 'My father's a musician too', and it all fell into place. Elmer didn't want to confess that he was more or less her godfather, because he had not done much in the way of taking care of her, but when he finally got round to it, Billie told him not to worry, she knew the story already.

Elmer found her a lovely, beautiful person. He'd often come to see her with his girlfriend when he'd finished playing at Small's Paradise and she was always friendly and lively. They'd sit and talk, and then they'd go through a side door to a bar at the back where they could buy 'needle beer, which had something in it − usually ether − to make you high', or they'd have 'bath-tub gin' − another Prohibition speciality. After that they might go to a basement place west

---

★ Elmer said he was making fifty-six cents a night, fifty cents for overtime and seventy-five cents for an 'out-of-town engagement'.

of 7th Avenue where Art Tatum was playing piano, and they often ended up at Elmer's reefer pad, because he had 'the biggest reefer pad in New York. If they had raided my place, not a show in New York would have gone on. A girl from Chicago used to come with a shoe box of the stuff . . . She was selling the reefers and I was selling the reefers, and between the two of us we made good. And we paid off the elevator man who kept the cops off us. I had all the white bands, all the coloured shows . . . Glenn Miller's band . . . and Tommy Dorsey and his group, and Jimmy Dorsey and his . . . They'd call in for their orders and I'd have it all wrapped up for 'em, every night. And Louis [Armstrong] — every night when he got off from work, I'd put forty reefers in a kitchen matchbox for him.'

Sometimes Elmer was with Billie when she met up with her father. They didn't see too much of each other because Clarence was often away on tour with Fletcher Henderson,★ but when they were both in town, they'd 'hang out and have a ball'. They'd meet at the Rhythm Club or the Band Box, or at a place called Big John's. Big John was an Italian who was 'father to all the musicians, and he'd have a pot of soul food — lima beans and pigs' feet — always on the stove in the back of his gin mill,† so you always had something to eat and a place to sleep if you needed it.

Billie wanted everybody to know that Clarence was her father, even though Clarence preferred to keep this fact a secret because he felt it made him seem old. Elmer said that the two of them had 'very different dispositions' but 'They were just like this. Like brother and sister. Very close.'

★ Billie was keen to work alongside Clarence in the Fletcher Henderson Orchestra and for a while she did until Clarence's wife Fanny became jealous and Billie was made to leave. John Hammond gave a very different account of Billie's relationship with her father. 'I said, "Clarence, you didn't tell me you had a daughter. She's the greatest thing I ever heard!" He said, "For Christ sake, John, don't talk about Billie in front of all the guys. They'll think I'm old. She was something I stole when I was fourteen." . . . I never heard a parent referring to a child with so much contempt and horror. So I knew there was no relationship between the two.'

† 'Any cheap saloon, bar or night-club', but, during Prohibition times, 'a speakeasy, selling bootleg whisky without a licence' (*Dictionary of American Slang*).

Clarence had a 'very warm feeling towards his daughter', and whenever he was on his own with Elmer he'd always say, 'Now don't you forget. I want you to take care of her.'*

On 23 February 1937, Clarence died as a result of influenzal pneumonia. He claimed he had always had weak lungs, ever since he had been gassed in the trenches in France during the last year of the First World War,† and because of that even the slightest cold could lead to life-threatening complications. He was on a tour of the South, and he first got sick when they were in Fletcher Henderson's home town of Cuthbert in Georgia. He stayed in hospital there for a couple of days and then went on with the band to Texas. It was there that the sickness got much worse, but nowhere would take him in until they reached Dallas, where he was admitted to a servicemen's hospital. Billie was told of his death on 1 March.

Elmer said Billie never wanted to talk about her father's death. 'It hit her harder than her mother's death, because she loved her father so.' And after Clarence died she made a point of always trying to come and see Elmer anywhere he was playing, and he would try to go and see her too. 'And when I went to where she was working she would jump off the bandstand and hug and kiss me and call me her daddy. Because her daddy had gone.'

---

* Elmer was sorry that he couldn't take care of her and was upset when he saw Billie without work and in difficulties. 'I remember Billie in 1941, 1942. She wouldn't have a job. She'd just be sitting in a corner like this. And she'd see me coming in and I'd put my arms around her and I could feel the warmth coming from her, and I'd say, "How are you doing?" And she'd say, "So-so."'

† According to Nicholson, Clarence's ship set out for France on 20 October 1918, twenty-two days before Armistice Day, and so he had little time to see action.

TWELVE

Fanny Holiday and Clara Winston

'She was a fat thing with big titties.'

People described Clarence's wife, Fanny Holiday, as a short, dumpy woman, who was quiet and nice and friendly. But that was not the way she saw herself. She said she certainly wasn't as short as Billie's mother Sadie and on top of that, she was from Virginia and 'we're the meanest women in the world'.

Fanny first met Clarence one night in 1920 when she went to a dance at the Waltz Dream Ballroom in Philadelphia; but he wasn't in a band playing the guitar or banjo, he was just running the elevator. They started to live together in 1924, when he was 'working to be a musician' and had got himself a room in New York. They were married in 1927.★

Talking about him more than thirty years after his death, Fanny still had fond memories of Clarence. She said he was a good-looking boy who loved to romance her, and he'd sing songs to her in the house. Of course he was a 'liquor-head' just like his daughter, but he was also the boss and Fanny looked up to him and listened to him.

★ Clarence had already married an eighteen-year-old Baltimore woman called Helen Boudin, on 16 October 1922 when he was twenty-three, but they only stayed together for a few months. He never obtained a divorce.

Clarence wasn't considered to be a lady's man★ and his friends insisted he was no pimp, either. For her part, Fanny accepted that her husband went out catting sometimes† and she knew all about his relationship with a big white woman called Atlanta Shepherd, who worked as a dime-a-dance dancer at Remie's Dance Hall on 66th and 67th Streets. Atlanta had borne Clarence a daughter called Mary,‡ on his birthday in 1932, but even that didn't seem to bother Fanny; she always referred to Atlanta as 'wife-in-law' and the two of them were on friendly terms. But she hated Billie's mother Sadie with a vengeance. She saw her as a serious rival who was always hanging around her husband and 'dibbin and dabbin' and following him wherever he went.

Fanny remembered an occasion when she and Clarence were at a club on Lenox Avenue, along with a whole party. He was minding his own business, but then Sadie came in and started to talk to him. Fanny was sure 'she was trying to agitate me. My temper went up. I took up my fists and beat her. A guy picked me up and took me out of the club and wouldn't let me come back.' Another time she had a hunch that Clarence and Sadie were together somewhere and so she took a ride around 125th Street until she found them. And that was when she said she did her best to try to kill Sadie.

When Billie first came to New York, she wanted to stay with her father and her stepmother, but Fanny wouldn't hear

---

★ This is according to his friend, the musician Walter Johnson. Ken Burns in *Jazz* gives a very different impression of Clarence, whose 'flashy example helped lure her into the music business [and] whose hustling ways were mirrored in many of the predatory men she would later call "Daddy"' (p. 206).

† 'Catting' comes from the word 'tomcat' and means 'to seek women for sexual reasons'. It can also mean to gossip or to loaf about (*Dictionary of American Slang*).

‡ She was so light-skinned she could pass as white. She turned up towards the end of Billie's life and for a while tried to contest the will. In March 1987, the Attorney at Law, L. Mifflin Hayes, who was representing the estate of Billie's last husband Louis McKay, wrote a very stern letter regarding a Grammy award that had been claimed on Billie's behalf by a woman called Nicole Holiday, who said she was Billie's half-sister: 'It should be noted that the name Billie Holiday was a stage name, not her real name. Secondly . . . to the best of my knowledge, she had no sisters or other close blood relatives.'

of it. She and Clarence had recently moved to an apartment on St Nicholas Avenue★ and they had three bedrooms as well as a sitting-room, so there was lots of space. Clarence was often away on tour with Fletcher Henderson's Orchestra while Fanny made herself a bit of money by running an 'after-hours in-the-home place' where you could go and 'have a little taste' and take your girlfriends up. But it was just for friends who knew the family well; she had to know who you were, and you had to be invited.

As far as Fanny was concerned, Billie was no better than her mother, what with calling Clarence *Daddy*, 'just to be insulting to me', and trying to win his sympathy in one way or another. She said that Billie was nothing but a 'fat thing with big titties', and she didn't approve of the kind of life she was living and certainly didn't want her to be 'doing it in my home . . . She was growed up then. I couldn't teach her nothing. Couldn't do nothing with her. She didn't look no thirteen. She looked like a growed woman.'

One night Billie turned up and complained that a boyfriend of Sadie's had approached her; she pleaded to be allowed to stay in St Nicholas Avenue because she was scared. But Fanny was sure this was just a cunning way of trying to get Clarence's sympathy and wouldn't change her mind.

For a while, however, Billie did sometimes sing with Fletcher Henderson's Orchestra, and Clarence was pleased to have her around. But Fanny saw this as a threat and persuaded Fletcher to throw Billie out, saying that if he kept her it was going to cause the break-up of her marriage and there would be 'a lot of hair pulling and a whole lot of things'.

Clara Winston had also known Fanny and Clarence at this time. Linda Kuehl described Clara as a 'plump, bleached-blonde woman who had been one of the biggest madams

---

★ Fanny was in the same apartment when she was interviewed by Linda Kuehl in December 1971.

in Harlem'. When they met for the interview she was wearing a blue shortie negligee and at one point during the conversation she lifted it up to show off a naked buttock.

Clara explained that, as a woman, she'd 'been through hell' and nowadays she was a bit of a lush and liked to drink beer or maybe some Henessy brandy, because she figured it stimulated her a bit. She said in that way she was different to most of her friends because they didn't 'go for the wet stuff any more. They go for the dry stuff. They go for cocaine. Everybody is each for his own. They can have it.'

Clara used to have two apartments at 135 West 142nd Street. She kept one for business purposes while the other was for living. She was nostalgic about the old days when 'people used to come into my house, from the best to the worst; even Tallulah [Bankhead] used to come to my house. They were beautiful times. You could walk up and down Lenox Avenue and go in and go out and there was no sticking up. Everything was peaceful, and people could have beautiful evenings and mornings and look beautiful and not be afraid, and they were all nationalities . . . And there was a shop on 8th Avenue had the most beautiful flowers you ever heard of, honey, and even the President didn't have no more beautiful flowers.'

It was Clarence who arranged for Billie and Sadie to rent a room from Clara for a while. Clara said she wanted to make it clear that she wasn't 'cloaking' Clarence at the time, and she only met him once or twice when he came to the apartment to visit his daughter. She said you could tell straight away that the two of them were related because Billie 'looked just like her daddy, only she was taller and he was a little shorter. But they had the same freaky-looking eyes, sort of slanty eyes . . . In fact, Clarence looked something like a foreigner.' She remembered how Billie 'always did what she wanted' and how Sadie would run after her, calling, 'Billee, Billee, Billee.' 'She just loved her, just like a little baby, and used to worry herself to death about her.'

After a few months Sadie got a place on 142nd Street, near 7th Avenue. Clara said Sadie had a little business there, where she used to serve food. 'There were no real tables, but people could sit around and drink and go with girls and everything. White fellas and girls would go on up.' The trumpet player Harry 'Sweets' Edison confirmed that Sadie was a 'groovy person . . . who ran a little whorehouse, and a lot of musicians used to go up there and buy some pussy'. Clara said she didn't know about Billie 'doing any prostitution' at the time, but in her view it was always 'better to sell it than give it away!'

Clara said that Billie was 'beautiful people', having a good time and living her life. She had lots of friends and 'she did everything everybody else did . . . There's nothing bad I can say about her . . . She was a spodie-odie good time. She'd come into some place and she'd say "OK, come on! Rack 'em up and run 'em around!"' At one point during the interview Clara announced that Billie 'could have been real famous, with that voice'.

Clara remembered Clarence's funeral. She said the Reverend Monroe was the preacher and he had 'some Baptist church' down on 115th and St Nicholas Avenue and 'he'd preach for anybody'. Clara used to call him Motha because he was 'a gay baby and he loved those nice-looking boys'.

Fanny also spoke about the Reverend Monroe. She said he was often called in for the funerals of musicians who didn't have church connections. She described him as a light-brown-skinned man with a deep 'religious voice'. He could really preach a funeral; he could preach anyone into heaven with fire and brimstone and his hands waving. Clarence's body was brought to Duncan's Funeral Parlour and the Reverend Monroe did his preaching there because 'he had no church'. Then Clarence was taken to Forest Hills cemetery in Queens, and Billie accompanied Fanny and Atlanta Shepherd in the limousine. There was no question of Sadie coming with them, so she went on her own in a separate car and somehow got lost on the way and arrived too late to see the coffin lowered into the ground.

THIRTEEN

Pop Foster

———

'It was only show people.'

Clarence 'Pop' Foster was a vaudeville comic who performed with various partners on the black theatre circuit in America and in theatres throughout Europe. Linda Kuehl first interviewed him in January 1972 while he was doing the Wednesday Night Amateur competitions at the Apollo Theater in Harlem. She said that when he came on stage, 'He stood before the curtain with a frayed tweed overcoat over his shoulders as though it were a luxurious cape. His voice was thick with alcohol, but elegant and almost-British just the same.' She interviewed him a second time in the nearby Paradise Bar in May 1972. Here he is talking:

I met Billie when she was sixteen years old, but she was big. She was a big fat slob and she'd wear the same dress every night; a common dress, not an evening gown. She used to put on anything and I'd call her a big fat slob.

In those days she did a little prostitution up here in Harlem. Along 136th Street was kind of the main drag and 132nd Street by the Lafayette Theater. I used to see her every night and every day. I knew she was doing it because I was in that life myself. You dig? So I knew everything that was going on. But you wouldn't say she was one of those common prostitutes that you see hanging out on the streets; she was a girl that was a very lovable person and she had her own way about things. She was an all-around girl.

She was young and she didn't know what was going on until she won this amateur contest and that's when she went on to stardom. That's when she found out she could sing. Then she began to know where she was really at.

She was singing in nightclubs and getting whatever they would pay her, and some nights she didn't get nothing. She just wanted to sing, you dig, she wanted to sing but she needed money and at that time she wasn't making money. We were working to be working. We'd work for whatever they threw on the floor. When she was working for me we got paid off at Jerry's Log Cabin in chicken and waffles. We'd get money and we'd split up maybe ten or twenty dollars between us.

About 1928 or 1927 she was singing at the Hot Cha and this was really when people began to notice her, and from then on it was *Billie Holiday*! From then on. All the show people were nuts for her! We used to jam in every night at the Hot Cha, just to hear her sing. And then some actor gave her the name of Lady Day and then we started to call her Lady Day. Billie had a lot of white friends and a lot of *ofay*★ men used to go for her, because she could sing.

We used to smoke pot a lot together. In the hotels there in Harlem, in the Braddock, in the Theresa. Or we'd bump into each other at parties. She wasn't a loud girl; she was kind of a shy girl, quiet in a way, unless somebody flustered her, and then she was a bitch and she'd raise hell. She had a very good sense of humour and a big smile. When we got high, everyone would

★ 'A white person . . . common Negro use since *c.* 1925' (*Dictionary of American Slang*).

be telling stories because it was really good in those days and everybody used to laugh, and she had just a belly laugh when she really laughed. There was a big black boy with great big white teeth and a great big broad smile. We called him High Jivin' Smiley and he used to make everyone laugh because he was so *unfunny*, and Billie used to pass out when he started, she used to die laughing.

In the tea pads they'd say, 'Lady Day's in the house!' and they would play all her records and she used to sing along. This is where they sold marijuana. There'd be fifteen or twenty of us, passing the pot around with the door wide open, and the cops didn't bother us. There were four or five tea pads uptown. One was called Kaiser's, and then there was Reefer Mae's on the corner of 143rd Street and 7th Avenue. Mostly show people were there and they'd say 'We're crazy and we're happy' and we used to have a ball.

You could get anything at that time: booze, cocaine, and some used to drink 'top and bottom', gin and wine mixed together, but no one would really get drunk because we had marijuana. We got it from Texas and Mexico. We found out we was getting happy on this marijuana. Oh yeah, we were getting happy! Oh my God! You could see the black gum of the marijuana coming out of the end of the cigarette.

Lester Young used to come into the tea pads and he carried a brown leather zipper bag, this big, full of marijuana. But Billie and Louis Armstrong made marijuana popular. They were the idols of the marijuana people. You could say they were King and Queen. But once they got really big they kind of waned away from public smoking, because they could get all the dope they wanted and only once in a while they came uptown.

When Billie wanted to blaze it, to get drunk and have a ball, she would check into a hotel with Dexter Gordon. After Dexter Gordon she fell in love with Lester Young. She used to change boyfriends like you change your pants, but Lester Young was the boy she *really* loved, and after he died I don't think she lived more than five months.★

There was a place called the Daisy Chain† on 141st Street, between Lenox and 7th Avenue, and we all used to go there. It was just a cat house, owned by a very, very pretty girl called Hazel Valentine, an ex-chorus girl who died five or six years ago. You'd go up to this big railroad flat house and you had to pay five dollars a piece and everybody would get buck-naked. I used to go up there quite often. I was quite young. Everyone was doing everything, but you don't care, you just have a ball. Billie used to frequent it, just to look and see what was happening.

There were these rooms over here and rooms over there and a long hall, and you'd be going from room to room and you'd see people on the floor getting their thing. Fantastic! Women going with women. Men going with men. They had a girl called Sewing Machine Bertha and she went down on all the girls. All the lesbians used to go up there, but I couldn't quote names because some of them was real big-time stars, so it was husha-husha. Entertainers went up there and it was half-coloured and half-white. Hell, yeah! *Real* integrated! Nobody paid it any mind. The public didn't know anything about it. It was only show people. Everybody was gay and having a lot of fun, twenty-four hours a day.

★ 'When she died they wanted to have her funeral at St Patrick, but Cardinal Spellman wouldn't allow it. This is the truth. I know it. So I never did like Cardinal Spellman after that. Billie was a real Catholic and she gave the Catholic Church a lot of money, and Cardinal Spellman knew her.'
† 'The act or an instance of several persons having sexual intercourse with each other at the same time' (*Dictionary of American Slang*).

FOURTEEN

Bobby Henderson

'The way she handled a fork.'

M ae Barnes first got to know Billie in 1928, when they were both 'doing the tables' at a club called the Nest.★ Billie stood out from the other girls because she refused to sing dirty songs and only took tips with her hands. 'She felt if she couldn't make a dollar standing on her own two feet, she didn't want it. And if a guy offered her ten dollars to go with him to a house, she'd say, "Shit! I can make that standing up!" Even for a hundred bucks, she'd refuse.'

Mae Barnes met Bobby Henderson around 1930 when he and Billie were sweethearts for a couple of years. She saw how different he was from the other men Billie went with later, the 'hustlers, pimps and all kinds of smooth-talking cats,

★ Mae Barnes was a dancer and singer who started in show business when she was twelve years old, touring Europe with Ethel Whiteside, a 'big fat blonde' who had a group called Ethel Whiteside and her Ten Pickaninnies. In the late 1930s she performed by special invitation for the Duke and Duchess of Windsor in their Waldorf Towers residence. Her most famous song was a very slow version of 'Sunny Side of the Street', with Lester Young. The Nest later changed its name to Monroe's Uptown House when Clarke Monroe was running it. Mae Barnes said that when Billie was singing there, 'She was doing everything that Louis Armstrong was doing, doing every song that Louis ever did. She'd slide and do the Louis run as he'd do it on the trumpet, but she'd do it with her voice.'

rough-talking cats, who could protect her'. She said that Bobby Henderson was the only man Billie ever loved. He was someone who 'showed her a lot of affection and he was a good man and a beautiful pianist . . . He had his own style.'

People spoke of Bobby Henderson as the warmest, kindest, gentlest person they knew.★ He was quiet in the company of strangers and he could be aloof in his way, but when he was working in a club he was very lively and would 'juice a lot' along with the best of them. He always got on well with everyone: with the girls who were singing or dancing, with the club owner and with the guests; he was even on friendly terms with difficult men such as the gangster Dutch Schultz and the pimp Dickie Wells.†

Away from the night-life of work, Bobby Henderson lived quietly with his mother on 109th Street, just across from Mayor La Guardia. He spent a lot of time alone, walking the streets of New York with a bottle of wine in his pocket to keep him company. He said that was the only way he could think about what he called the 'process' of his life and could listen to the stream of music playing inside his head. 'I had a habit of walking . . . I know every path in Central Park; I know every path in every park in New York City. I'm one of the few people that walked from the Battery to the Bronx, from the Hudson River to the East River – you hear what I say? Through Chinatown. I don't think there's a street in New York I haven't walked on. It's a big city, but since I was a kid I knew it. And thank God I could always hear some music when I was walking, whether a jukebox

★ Bobby Henderson (Robert Bolden Henderson) was born in New York City in 1910 and died in 1969. He was interviewed in December 1967 by Millard Lampell and John Hammond, in preparation for the Third World Cinema film *The Billie Holiday Story*, which never got made.

† Not to be confused with the trombone player, singer, arranger and composer of the same name. Mae Barnes said of Dickie Wells the pimp, 'He was a light, beautiful boy. He was smooth and he had line and jive and he was a bitch. Classy. He was a big pimp. Dickie and Billie were friends, but Dickie never had a coloured woman. Rich white women were taking care of him. When he died, his mother had his clothes changed every day while he was in that coffin, right down to his shoes and socks. He was in Salem church and you couldn't get near that church. A girl I know said, as she looked at him in his coffin, "I don't know. He's dead, but he's sharp."'

was playing or not, I was hearing sounds. And when I came to the piano at night, the girls used to say, "Where you been today? What you been doin'? You sound mighty fresh on those keys!"'

Bobby's mother was unmarried and already middle-aged when he was born in Harlem in 1910. He was her only child. She worked as a janitress and brought him up on her own, but she was visited regularly by a much younger man who 'acted like a little chippy girl' and ran a musicians' club on 134th Street and 7th Avenue. Bobby had always known this man as Uncle Fred, but when he was seventeen a friend told him that Uncle Fred was his father. He kept this knowledge to himself for another ten years. He remembered the one occasion when Uncle Fred 'showed me that he loved me'. He clapped Bobby on the shoulders and said enigmatically, 'This is *my* boy.'*

Bobby said his mother was full of love and never judged him, but she was also very strict and very religious. She was keen for her son to go to college to study bookkeeping so that he might have a better life than the one she had known. But then, when he was twenty-two years old, he was sitting one day in the classroom with the music of Duke Ellington's 'Sophisticated Lady' going round in his head and suddenly he asked himself, 'Who is going to keep whose books in *this* administration?'

His teacher was calling to him, 'Mr Henderson! Mr Henderson! Where are you, Mr Henderson?'

And right then he *knew* what he had to do and he said, 'I can't tell you, Mr Marquet, but give my books to the Principal with my best regards, because I'm leaving school right now!' And all the class turned round and laughed at him, but he walked out and never returned, even though he later admitted that it took 'a lot of guts' to do it.

---

* Bobby Henderson explained the situation by saying, 'He loved my mother, but he had a family that was supposed to be on the other side of the railway tracks, and they thought my mother was not good enough for him. This was the only thing I didn't respect about him, because I would have fought them and lived on the other side of the tracks with her. But I could understand, I guess.'

He remembered how he hopped on the back of one of those open streetcars and rode right up to Harlem. He told his mother what he had done and 'The tears came down and I grabbed her and hugged her and explained to her, "Mama, I'm playing music now!"' He had already been earning seven dollars a night by playing at parties and he was sure he could earn even more.

Not long afterwards a man called Jack Sneed★ took him one morning to Pod and Jerry's. It was an integrated club where the 'sporting element', Negroes with plenty of money, mixed with white people from downtown who also had plenty of money. Bobby Henderson said that in those days the area was 'completely integrated and people could walk on the side-streets anywhere and nobody was knocked on the head'. And in spite of Prohibition, at Pod and Jerry's there was always a jug of corn liquor in the corner, made by people from the South who knew how to make real corn liquor. It gave you 'an appetite like a horse'. The musicians would come and 'hit the jug' and send out for another milk bottle full, which cost a quarter for a quart.

So there was Bobby Henderson at Pod and Jerry's and the boss, Jerry, came over and said, 'Hello, son, can you play the piano? That's Willie "The Lion" Smith† you see there. He's one of the greatest piano players playing. Well, Willie's made plenty of money, and Willie's going to move downtown to another spot . . . So, play a tune, kid.'

Bobby Henderson was very scared, but he said to himself, 'Play what you can play and that's all you can do.' He started with 'I Got Rhythm' and after a while he relaxed and went on for about twenty choruses.

★ 'A cat who played the four-string guitar and who was one of the most mischievous cats in the whole world, on the whole block, and the most hippest too,' said Bobby Henderson.

† Duke Ellington said, 'The Lion has been the greatest influence on most of the great piano players who have been exposed to his fire, his harmonic lavishness, his stride . . . I can't think of anything good enough to say about him.' A vital figure in the Harlem stride school, he was born in New York in 1897 and died in 1973.

Somebody said, 'Who is this kid?'

Somebody else said, 'You're all right, kid!'

And the boss said, 'Don't stop there, kid. Play a little blues. I like you. What you drinking? You want the job?'

So Bobby turned up again at eleven o'clock that night. There was a mirror fixed over the piano so that he could watch the girls dancing and picking up the money between their legs. 'I'm looking around and my eyes are poppin'.' But the girls who were singing loved him at once for the way he could transpose to any key they wanted, even to the difficult F sharp. 'Nobody played for us like you play for us,' they said.

There was a waiter who had the job of gathering up all the money and putting it into an 'entertainers' fund' that could be shared out at the end of the night. This waiter had to make sure that the girls didn't secretly stuff dollar bills down their fronts, or hide them 'you know where', and as the night moved on the waiter was putting more and more money into Bobby's pockets. By the time the club was closing in the early morning he had earned himself $150.

Bobby Henderson went home and, before falling into bed, he emptied the money from his pockets onto the kitchen dresser. His mother woke up and looked at 'all those twisted-up twenty-dollar bills, ten-dollar bills, five-dollar bills, two-dollar bills, one-dollar bills and she let out a yell. "What's the matter, Mom? House on fire?"' he said, and explained that he had not stolen the money and she could go right out and get herself some new dresses.

Later that same day he took ten of his own dollars and bought a bottle of dry white wine. Then he walked to the boating lake in Central Park and hired a boat and rowed out as far as he could go. He sat there quietly for a long time, thinking about this sudden change in his fortunes and the new direction his life was taking.

It was not long after this that he met Billie Holiday. He thought it was at Dickie Wells' Clam House, but it might have been at Brownie's next door. In those days the clubs were 'so close together and you only needed twenty-five

cents to open a new one'. He remembered that Gladys
Bentley* was singing and she was dressed as a man.

Anyway, Billie was there as well and she and Bobby were
briefly introduced. Her pianist, a tall girl called Dot Hill,
said, 'Why don't *you* play a tune, Bobby? What are you going
to play?'

Bobby Henderson hesitated and then he played 'Sweet
Sue'. He said he did something so simple 'in there' that he
thought the other musicians might laugh at him, and in the
second chorus he added 'some tiny things'.

Billie was standing and watching and she said, 'Hey, do
that again. Just what you did.'

He turned around to look at her and that was the first
time he really saw her, 'because she was interested in what
I was doing'. And what he saw was 'this well-built girl over
there. You could say she was statuesque. She was well-
groomed, man, and she was a woman, a woman you would
admire.'

So he played the song again and Billie listened and said,
'That's it! That's what it is!'

Later they all went up the street and stopped off at a
couple of places, and Bobby played and she sang and they
ended up at Pod and Jerry's. When Billie sang a song there,
Jerry liked her and said, 'Why don't you come on up here
and work?' And so she was hired.

Bobby Henderson loved to play for Billie because 'you
could go anywhere and she'd be there, man. Perfect time
and perfect diction . . . I used to play full chords for her. I
had a knack, I guess . . . and I could stay just behind her,
so you don't pay no attention to the piano and you just
listen to the singer.'

And that was the start of their love affair.† Bobby said,
'We had a liking for each other, me and Billie. I never met
anybody like her. She was more of a hip woman than I was

---

* Gladys Bentley was a lesbian singer who was very open about her sexuality
  and wore men's clothes. She was born in 1907 and died in 1960.
† According to the guitar player Jack Sneed, who was selling meat pies outside
  the Musicians' Union in Los Angeles when he wrote to Linda Kuehl in May
  1976, 'Bobby fell like a tree when he met Billie.'

a hip young man. I was just a square. She was *a woman*, and it surprised me when I knew she was sixteen years old.'

He introduced Billie to his mother, because he wanted his mother to know whom he liked and to know that this was the greatest woman he had ever met in his life. His mother was 'as gracious to her as she would be to anybody'. She fixed Billie coffee and breakfast and they all talked together.

In return, Billie sometimes invited Bobby to the apartment where she was living with her mother. Bobby thought Sadie was a 'wonderful woman, a very simple woman, kind-hearted', but as soon as the two of them were together, all sorts of old wounds began to open up and Sadie 'made Billie so mad you'd think she was going through the roof . . . Billie was burning at her mother, and her mother was burning at her.' They quarrelled over small things, like where had Billie been and why didn't she come home and where was she working? Sadie would sometimes try to tell Bobby why she felt her daughter was in the wrong, but he refused to take sides. 'I made up my mind to keep my mouth shut because you don't know what they are really arguing about. I just said I didn't like to hear them hollering and arguing, and so I'd rather leave. I always had that respect for people. I'd want to get away from there because it's private and it don't have nothing to do with me.'

Bobby said he learnt how to avoid arousing Billie's temper. 'She had a temper,' but she had the 'right kind of patience too'. This was one of the reasons why musicians and entertainers liked her, and as they got to know her they 'got to know that she had a way of her own and mind of her own'. For his part, Bobby felt 'She respected me because I respected her mind. I might have asked her questions in my mind, but I never questioned her actions or decisions. I just said, "Well, she's got to have a reason for it", and I tried to be understanding. In her way she had to fight a lot of things that a lot of us didn't have to. She had to fight her way and she wasn't going to let nobody stop her.'

He never saw Billie 'come to blows' with anyone, but he

remembered the time when he went with her to an after-hours spot in Washington. It was a crummy old nightclub at the top of some stairs that creaked so loudly it was like a scene from a horror movie. When you got there, the bar was nothing but a plank propped up at either end. But right in the centre of the room there was a full-size Steinway grand, all wrapped up in blankets.

The owner of the joint was called Louis and he was waiting for Fats Waller to arrive.★ When he did eventually arrive, somebody 'took the wrappers off the piano and it lit up the whole crummy joint. You could just see it shine . . . And Fats had his Derby hat on and he sat down at this Steinway and, brother, you never heard no record like this cat played!' And then Bobby and Fats sat together, and Bobby played the treble and Fats played the bass, 'And this was an honour, man, to play anything when Fats was playing. And I'm hitting the right notes and the right chords.'

All the while Billie was standing up at the bar. Suddenly Bobby caught sight of her throwing a glass full of liquor at a man's head and missing him by a fraction and just missing the piano players as well. He realised that the man had insulted her by saying 'something derogatory' and so she had fought back. He understood that.

Bobby spoke of the love he felt for Billie. He said there were times when she 'let her guard down and she was like a little girl. It was as if nothing had ever happened in her life.' He talked of how she laughed 'from the bottom of the soles of her feet to the top of her head, plus some'. He loved to watch her eat. 'She was very dainty and Billie was − what could you say? − a full-bodied woman, but she was very graceful in anything she did. She was very clean, very neat . . . the way she handled a fork. We'd be in a restaurant and we'd be eating. Somebody would say, "Hey Bobby, what's the matter

---

★ Bobby had long been an admirer of Fats Waller and had just met him a few days previously. 'We went out on the town and we stayed two days and I found I couldn't drink with Fats, I couldn't eat with Fats, I couldn't do nothing with Fats, 'cos anything you did, Fats done better and much more.' When Fats Waller died in 1943, Bobby Henderson was considered his successor and was acknowledged as 'one of the other immortals of the piano'.

with you?" I'd say, "Nothing." But deep in my mind I'm looking at her and saying, "You do things in a beautiful way."'

They used to sit up till all hours talking to people and Bobby said it was obvious that Billie had problems, because she was always drawn to other people with problems. 'She was attracted to people that way and that's where her patience came in.'

Bobby knew that Billie was one of the greatest people he ever met in his life, 'God rest her.' He said, 'If we were both born in a different set of circumstances it would have been a lot different. We had a beautiful thing there.' But at the same time he realised he could not have done more than he did, 'Because I couldn't have fought the people that abused her. I wasn't cut out for that. I would have wound up getting hurt or washed away.'

Billie never told him much about her childhood, but he could sense what a difficult time she had experienced and how isolated she had been. He felt that 'Had I been a woman in her boots, I would probably have fought in the same way . . . She saw a lot of things that a lot of us didn't have to see. She had to fight and she wasn't going to let anyone stop her . . . When I came here I was lonely, but maybe I had some protection Billie didn't have. I didn't have to go through the things that she had to go through. And she was a girl and that made it tougher for her.'

The last place where they worked together was the Bar Harbor in Utica, New York, towards the end of 1932. In the interview Bobby did not explain what happened next, but the newspapers were full of reports about the break-up between Billie and her 'fiancé'. It was around that same time that Bobby failed to turn up for an important recording session arranged by the record producer John Hammond. He then went into self-imposed exile★ and pretty well disappeared from the jazz scene until he was rediscovered

★ Footnote on page 90.

and recorded by John Hammond in 1956. He appeared at the Newport Jazz Festival in 1957.

Bobby Henderson died in December 1969. According to an obituary that appeared in the *Albany Times Union*, 'There is only one good thing to say about his death. He knew. He really knew, that a whole lot of people loved him.'

★ He changed his name to Jody Bolden, in honour of his namesake, the famous New Orleans cornet player 'King' Buddy Bolden (1877–1931), who was arrested for dementia in 1906 and was committed to a mental institution in 1907, where he remained until his death.

FIFTEEN

Aaron and Claire Lievenson and Irene Kitchings

'*Afternoon of a Faun*'

On 8 December 1971, the pharmacist Aaron Lievenson and his wife Claire sat side by side at their home at 736 Riverside Drive, New York City, and were both busy with very different memories of the past.

Aaron was the first to speak. Before saying anything else he felt it was important to explain that 'Billie Holiday was someone who was only happy when she had a drink or a fix. This I know. She was a customer of mine.'

His wife Claire suddenly interrupted him to announce, 'At that time in her dressing room she used to wear a lot of Tweed perfume. And I'd say, "Goddamn, Billie! All this Tweed!"'

Then Aaron was talking again. He met Billie in 1939 when the war was just beginning. He had a pharmacy and she used to come in to buy things.* That would be about

---

* According to Claire, Billie bought everything from the pharmacy: deep-red Cutex nail varnish, Maybelline eye pencils, Stein's brown powder, cold cream. But even when she was appearing on stage, 'She wasn't vain, didn't have too much shit on the table. She took a little pain in putting her lipstick on, she'd put it on her top lip, then bite down on her lower lip and put a circle on the lower lip again. She took her time with everything . . . but she wouldn't take too much pain with her appearance, she could be looking at herself but just staring, not seeing herself.'

midday, and if the weather was nice she often appeared
wearing a housecoat and slippers, which he said was not
something you would expect. Presumably she'd gone home
after a long night and then, just before going to bed, she
remembered she needed something, headache pills perhaps,
or bicarbonate of soda. She called Aaron 'Doc', and she was
always very civil to him. He said she didn't really stand out
from anybody else in the neighbourhood, except that she
was attractive.

Aaron's pharmacy was on the most densely populated block
in Harlem, on the corner of 142nd Street and 8th Avenue.
He was there from 1933 up to 1959, when all the slum
dwellings were knocked down, leaving only the Church of
St Charles standing. In those early years a few white families lived quite close by on 135th Street, but then they sold
their businesses and moved on. White doctors continued to
practise, but they were mostly refugees who had recently
arrived in the city and needed somewhere to begin. And
there were Jews too, running laundries, candy stores, that
sort of thing. A Jewish dentist lived on 141st Street.

Aaron said he loved being in Harlem. The atmosphere
was very friendly and most people were not hustlers; they
were simply off every day doing menial jobs because that
was all that was available for them. There wasn't really any
crime, although there might be a 'knifing now and then, but
nothing special'. He said that anyway the black people in
the city were being raped and mugged long before the white
people ever were, it was just that the news only made it to
the papers if the victims were white.

Of course you had to be rough to live in Harlem, just to
get along. Everybody was rough, and as a pharmacist Aaron
was up against the 'usual things', such as pilfering and the
drink problem. You could smell the alcohol in the streets
and the police would pick up the drunks in their squad cars
and take them away. The police used to stop off at the nearby
candy store to collect their weekly share of money from the
gambling rackets. They all took bribes; it was part of their
job.

Aaron had known Billie's mother Sadie ever since he arrived in Harlem. He found her a marvellous woman, short and stout and very jolly, with a strong southern accent. She worked in service and used to come to the shop almost every day, because she'd go to the stamp machine to mail letters and then she'd buy a few household items as well. She never mentioned that she had a daughter.

Then Billie turned up. She and her mother had moved to 142nd Street. The house was on the right-hand side, either number 232 or 242. Aaron thought Billie always seemed high, although he had no idea what she was taking.

At this point Aaron wanted to make it clear that although he wasn't interested in gossip, he knew Billie was hustling, selling her favours to a number of men. He had the story from Willie Jones, who never told a lie. Willie Jones used to work in the grocery store right next to the pharmacy, and one time he delivered groceries to Billie and she propositioned him, and he had sex with her then and on several other occasions, in her mother's house. Then there was the famous white band leader, Blue Barron, who played at the Strand and the Paramount; he went upstairs, too. And there were others, lots of them. There were goings-on all the time. Aaron found it odd that he never heard the neighbours talking about what was happening; only Lorraine who worked for him in the pharmacy luncheonette, she talked.

Now it was Claire Lievenson's turn. She said she met Billie in 1934 in the Hot Cha on 134th Street. She was an actress and a 'bachelor girl' at the time and her maiden name was Leybra. Along with the singer Carmen McRae,★ she became a close friend of Billie's. Billie was a few years older and they 'adored her'. As Claire said, 'She was so elegant. I don't give a damn if she was high, it was a gas to watch this bitch walk up to the microphone. She had a very feminine walk, short steps, feminine, and she just melted into the

★ Carmen McRae was born in New York in 1920. She sang and played the piano and was later an actress. When she was eighteen she wrote 'Dream of Life', which was recorded by Billie. She died in 1994.

microphone. BOOM. And most times the eyes would be closed and when she opened them, she was such a magnetic thing to look at and to hear, you were spellbound by her. Even when she was *high*, she can still give it to you, baby. I don't know where it came from . . . I felt she knew she was doing her thing for you, giving it to you, to you, giving it to you; this is me, my other me, sharing it with you . . . And when she finished her last tune she smiled that beautiful smile of hers. She didn't bend down in no low bends or that shit, no: a beautiful smile, a lovely smile, a big open smile, and her head would go down just a little bit . . .

'She didn't have much of an education, but that didn't matter . . . She was very good-hearted. She was kind. Anything you wanted and she had it, you could have it. She gave me a ring I admired. That was in her dressing room on 52nd Street, and Carmen was mad because she didn't get one . . .

'We used to go back into her dressing room and she really laughed when she was really herself . . . All we ever did would be to sit there and look at her, but she didn't care. When she was herself she'd tell a lot of jokes about her boyfriends. I'd talk about being an actress and Carmen would talk about her singing.'

Sometimes Billie was moody and she'd say, 'I don't feel good.' She would stay in her mother's house and not open the door for anybody. But when she did feel good she was ready for anything; singing through the night and drinking through much of the day. She used to collect Claire from her place on 142nd Street, ringing three times on the doorbell and waiting for her to come down. Claire lived on the fourth floor and Billie said, 'I ain't making *no* steps. Now, you bitch, when I ring three times, you come on down. Be cool.'

Claire said Billie always spoke like that, using a lot of profanity – 'Hey, bitch, I ain't see you! Where the fuck you hang out at?' – but because of the *way* she said things, it all sounded like words of endearment. She used to call Lester Young 'the greatest motherfucker I ever met' and that told you how much she loved him. When they saw each other they wouldn't kiss, but their faces would just light up. 'Goddamn son-of-a-bitch, how you *doin'*, Daddy?' she'd say.

After Billie had finished singing at around seven in the morning she and Carmen and Claire would go out drinking together. They went from block to block, to the Silver Dollar, the Brown Bomber, the Poucepateck. Their favourite place was Jimmy's Chicken Shack, where whisky was served in a teacup.

They'd also go to the beach at Rockaway, meeting up with other friends and going by train or taking a car. Billie never entered the water; she didn't even own a bathing suit. She'd just come and sit and watch the others. Claire said she wasn't marked with needle scars, so that wasn't the reason; maybe she was just afraid of water.

Billie met Jimmy Monroe at Rockaway and that's where he started going with her. Claire said before that Billie had been with Bobby Henderson and the guitar player Freddie Green, and Sonny White the pianist, who gave her an engagement ring, and everybody hoped she would stay with him because 'He was a nice boy and didn't like her for what she had, like most of them did.' But it was Jimmy Monroe who got her. Claire said he was a 'suave sort of cat' who used to go round with the gangster Dutch Schultz. Jimmy was also an 'out-and-out hustler' with an opium habit he'd brought back from his time in Paris.

In those days 'everyone' went to Irene Kitchings'★ house. They went there when she was still married to the pianist Teddy Wilson, and they went there when she and Teddy had separated and she was living on her own. Claire remembered how Billie and her friends would turn up in the morning and Irene would cook a whole lot of New Orleans food, and her dog Gypsy would run around and people would be talking and laughing and drinking.

And then, if Billie felt like singing, she'd sing. She'd only do it if she wanted to and there was no point in asking her for a certain song because that never worked. But she'd start

★ Pianist and composer. After she and Teddy Wilson parted she wrote 'Some Other Spring', one of Billie's favourite songs.

humming and Irene would go right up there to the piano and start playing. Claire said it was different from when Billie was performing in clubs. She'd just be sitting there with a drink and a cigarette, and the singing was like talking to herself. 'It was as if she was having a love affair with herself.' She wasn't bothered if the lights were on and the dog was making trouble, for she was in her own world. She'd do torchy songs mostly. Claire loved to hear her sing 'Yesterdays'.★

Irene Kitchings also spoke about those visits to her house in an interview she gave to Linda Kuehl on 27 November 1971. Her second husband Eldon was sitting beside her, but he mostly remained silent, although he did say that Billie 'respected people who were strong . . . She got along so well with my wife because my wife has such a strong will and she respected her for that. Billie thought that if a person was permissive with her, they didn't care about her.'

Irene was still married to Teddy Wilson when she met Billie at the Hot Cha in around 1934. She remembered her as being 'robust and carefree and just like a big kid'. And then Billie and Teddy started rehearsing for the Columbia recordings, and one time she came up to the house on her own, 'And we became friends right there. She told me, "Renie, I've met a lot of wives, Duke's wife and other wives, but you're the first wife I've met that seems *real*. You're just a top chick. I can dig you because you're a real person."'

Irene used to go to listen in on those early recording sessions, and once Billie asked her how to pronounce a word in one of the songs. As Irene said, 'She had to feel close and comfortable with me, to ask something like that.'

The two women went out together in search of good music. They went to an Irish bar where Billie sang Irish songs. They went to a place where they'd heard a good trio

★ Callye Arter remembered a surprise birthday party for Teddy Wilson in 1934, arranged by Earl Hines' wife. People were singing and Billie was 'sitting there and nobody was saying one word to her. She was nothing but a kid. And then she gets up and says, "Teddy, will you play 'These Foolish Things' for me?" And Teddy played it and Billie broke the party up and people started talking about her then.'

was playing, but 'It was nothing but a whorehouse. I had never seen anything like it.' Billie, who knew all about whorehouses, told Irene, 'Now, if you have to go to the restroom, you just let me know, because you can't go in there by yourself because those chicks are too rough, uh! uh!'

When Irene's marriage to Teddy Wilson fell apart, she went to live with Billie and her mother for a while. By this time Billie was going with Jimmy Monroe, and Irene remembered her coming home in the morning and putting something in her coffee that Jimmy had given her, while Sadie fussed over her and accused her of 'acting strange'.

I told Lady, 'What you put in that coffee?'

And she said, 'Aw, Renie, this is just something. Don't pay Mom no mind!'

So I said, 'No, what is it?'

She said, 'Aw, it's not going to hurt me.'

Next thing I know, Lady's in the bathroom, as sick as a dog. Next thing I know Monroe had her smoking hop.* And next thing I knew, he had her using coke.

But it was still the music that mattered. Billie had a collection of records, including *Rhapsody in Blue* and *Porgy and Bess*, and she'd sing along with them. Irene said, 'She had a remarkable ear and didn't know one note of music, not one note. She had opera and stuff like that on her machine. *Afternoon of a Faun.*† She loved *Afternoon of a Faun.*'

Irene saw Billie over the years, but she never judged her harshly as some others did. She said, 'Once she got big, it didn't matter to her. All she wanted was to have some decent music to accompany her, and the people to be quiet and listen to her sing . . . Singing was all she knew how to do. That's all that made her real happy.'

---

* Opium.
† Claude Debussy's *Prélude à l'après-midi d'un faune*.

SIXTEEN

Ruby Helena

———

'She didn't have the right, being who she was.'

Ruby Helena was a dancer and entertainer. She got to know Billie and her mother Sadie when she stayed with them in an apartment on 99th Street in Harlem. According to John Hammond, it was 'a beat-up flat, an awful, after-hours place'. Ruby Helena thought that must have been in 1939, or it could have been 1940; it was difficult to be sure because it was such a long time ago. Anyway she was with them for about six months and Billie used to refer to her as 'my half-sister', while Sadie spoke of her as 'my other daughter'.

Ruby Helena had been told that when Billie first arrived in Harlem she lived with her mother at Florence Williams' whorehouse at 151 West 140th Street. Neither Billie nor Sadie ever mentioned that they had been arrested while they were there, although Ruby Helena did know that Billie had spent almost a year in prison while she was still a young teenager. She thought it was because Billie had refused to have sex with a man called Big Blue Ranier and he'd got his own back by telling the police that she had tried to rob him.

Ruby Helena said that when Billie was released from jail,

Sadie had found her a room in a reefer pad just off 7th Avenue. She was only there for a short time before 'something came up' and she had to leave in a hurry. She moved to another place, but the man who owned it kicked her out because she 'thought she was cute' and refused to do the things that all the other girls were doing. And then she was in the house next door and Ruby Helena suddenly wondered if *this* was where she was raped by Big Blue. She explained to Linda Kuehl that she hadn't known Billie or Sadie at that stage in their lives and was simply trying to piece together the fragmented stories they had told her later.

Ruby Helena was asked to describe a reefer pad. She said 'some of the cats' took her to one in the 1920s when she was still a very young girl. No one bothered her, but it was the first time she saw the things that happened there. She said a reefer pad was just a room lined with couches and with 'dull lights – red; sometimes a blue light or a green one. You could hardly see the person sitting next to you.' There were low tables and music playing on a gramophone, or perhaps someone was busy on the keys of an old piano. Bootleg whisky was sold by the tumbler and cost between two and five dollars, depending on how wealthy the client appeared to be.* Ready-made reefers were sold by the stick at two dollars or more.

There were always girls there, ready to dance and entertain. They usually danced in short costumes, but some of them were a 'little bashful' and preferred long dresses with a slit up the front. The 'rich white people' who had come here 'to see some spice' were 'millionaire businessmen, newspaper men, celebrities – all the people who were getting all the money'. They would be sitting at the tables, listening to the music, smoking, drinking, watching what was going on. And then a man, or it might be his female companion, would place some money on the table and the trick was for one of the girls to pick it up with her vagina. 'They would put

---

* Ruby Helena explained, 'They knew you; they knew what kind of money you had, where you were working . . . and if you were a person who was making big money, you'd pay five dollars for it.'

a fifty-dollar bill on the table and these girls would take their vaginas and pick up the money. They would even pick up silver money. They picked up quarters the same way and the more the girls would pick up, the more they made . . . They were *so* skilled, how they could pick up that money! . . . Some of the girls left out of there very wealthy. One fella put down a hundred-dollar bill.'

Listening to Ruby Helena's voice, it is easy to imagine a scene from an old movie full of gangsters and romance. You can see the whisky in shining glasses and the smoke from the reefers illuminated in ghostly spirals by the shaded lights. You can see the pale faces of wealthy smiling men in well-cut suits; the glint of a woman's jewellery. And you can see the faces of the people who lived in Harlem, and their smiles and clothes and jewellery.

But then there is the sound of laughter. All the people who have money to spare are laughing uproariously as they place a tightly folded banknote or a little metal coin on the corner of a low table. And the intensity of their laughter gathers momentum as they watch a dancing woman dipping down onto the prize like some strange creature gathering food. And if she cannot get enough of a grip, then the coin is dropped, or the piece of linen paper, certified by the United States Treasury and carrying the proud face of one president or another, flutters listlessly to the floor. So then the whole process must be made to begin again. People laughing to see how even the smallest amount of currency is worth such an effort.

People said that Billie was called 'too cute' because she refused to do dancing work in the reefer pad where she was staying. And Ruby Helena said that when she wouldn't go to such places to sing, people complained about her being high and mighty because 'She thought she was better than anyone, but she didn't have the right, being who she was, because they knew where she was living. She didn't have the right to that "air".' According to Ruby Helena's version of things, this was why Billie was given the name of Lady Day and why the name stuck, because she was determined to 'make it' in the entertainment world and she already felt herself to be such a grand lady. But then, thinking it over, Ruby Helena added that it might have been more than just putting on airs. 'She was a person with a lot of pride . . . It could have been something inside of her – some decency.'

Ruby Helena remembered meeting Billie for the first time at Ginnie Lee's restaurant, behind the Apollo Theater on 125th Street. It was around two o'clock in the morning and Billie was there with a group of friends. She suddenly turned to this new stranger and announced, 'I don't want *them* to take me home, I want *you* to take me home.' And so that was decided and they turned up together at the apartment Billie was sharing with her mother.★

So there they were and Billie was making coffee when Sadie called out, 'Billie, is that you?'

'Yes, Mom, it's me . . . Meet my friend Helen.'†

Ruby Helena stayed for what was left of the night and the next day she drove Billie to a recording studio and then went home. They didn't see each other again until they met by chance when Ruby Helena was working at a club somewhere out of town with a troupe of entertainers and Billie happened to turn up and agreed to be 'the special artist for the night'.

When Ruby Helena got back to New York she discovered she had been thrown out of her rented room and that the suitcase in which she kept all her money had been stolen. She contacted Billie and told her what had happened and Billie said, 'Well, that's just wonderful. You can come on down and stay with us.'

Ruby Helena was immediately swept into this family of two women, who behaved towards each other as if they were sisters rather than mother and daughter. She planned to be there with them for a week, but it turned out to be six months.

★ When Linda Kuehl asked Ruby Helena to describe the apartment, she replied, 'It was small . . . It was a slum area. It was a ghetto during that time. It was moderately pleasant.'

† Ruby Helena said, 'Of course my name was Ruby Helena, but Billie always called me Helen.'

Ruby Helena said that at this time Billie was just starting
to change her appearance, although really she was still nothing
more than 'a great big old bundle – just like her mother,
only taller. She was a great big out-of-shape person in tacky
dresses.'★ Sadie didn't know anything about glamour, but
there was a woman called Lucille who gave Billie advice on
what to wear and how to 'look the part'; she'd also borrow
jewellery from Ruby Helena.

At this time Billie was fiercely protective of her mother,
promising that she would never ever leave her and would
always be there to look after her. Although she went out a
lot, she never failed to tell Sadie exactly who she had been
with, at what time she had dinner and all the things that
happened next. It was as if she was giving her mother the
chance to live her life vicariously, through her daughter's
adventures and romances.

But it seems that Sadie was not at all happy with how
things were going and soon turned to her 'other daughter'
as a confidante with whom she could share her worries. In
spite of the fact that she had done so little to care for her
daughter and protect her from the dangers of the world,
Sadie now felt that Billie was neglecting her and failing in
her duties. She asked Ruby Helena to keep an eye on her,
to go with her to the clubs where she was singing and to
make sure that she got home at night.

For her part, Billie got on well with her new 'sister' and
talked openly about her troubles and her difficulties with
Sadie. Her father Clarence had died only recently and she
often spoke of her daddy and how much she had loved him.
'She swore she'd never get over it, because she thought they
let her father die.'†

Sadie was also very busy with thoughts of Clarence
Holiday. She told Ruby Helena that he was the only man

★ Regardless of her looks, Ruby Helena conceded that Billie already had 'something in her voice that struck the public like lightning'.
† Ruby Helena seemed to think that Billie had had no contact with Clarence
Holiday. 'The reason she felt that way about her father was that she knew
how much her mother loved him. She didn't know anything about her father
[but it] made her closer to her mother.'

she had ever loved. They had been married for a while, but then he had walked out on her and had left her on her own with a young child to raise. He was like all men, she said; he only wanted to break a woman's heart. 'Look what your father did to me!' she would say to Billie, weeping piteously, as if it was her daughter's fault that Clarence had abandoned them both all those years ago.

According to Ruby Helena, Sadie never wanted Billie to be close to a man and did everything she could to stop her daughter from becoming attached to any of the men she spent time with. Billie was forbidden to invite a man to stay the night, although Sadie apparently encouraged her to bring women back to the apartment. As Ruby Helena said, 'She didn't mind if she slept with girls, she just didn't want her to sleep with men.' And so Billie would often come home with different girls, white girls mostly, 'society girls', and in the morning they would all get up and have breakfast together. Some of these women were regular visitors.*

But there were men in Billie's life as well, lots of them. For a while there was Clark Monroe, who had a club called the Uptown House. Then she set her heart on his brother Jimmy, even though she said she couldn't stand him when they first met. Ruby Helena described him as a 'very fair-complexioned, nice-looking, frail type' who was just back from spending a few years in Paris and was full of the cosmopolitan sophistication of Europe. He was also 'a person who didn't talk much. A quiet type of person. You would wonder what he was thinking about, or if he *was* thinking. He seemed to be in some kind of other world; in a daze.'

When Billie met Jimmy Monroe he was married to an actress called Nina McKinney, but he was also 'running' two or three other women as well. He was known to be a pimp, but, as Ruby Helena explained, 'He wasn't always busy being a pimp. He was just running a few girls. His mother and

---

* It was at this time that Billie earnt the name of Mister Holiday and took to introducing herself as William or Bill, especially when she was meeting a new woman. Later she told her pianist Carl Drinkard that she went with women, 'But I was always *the man!*'

his brother Clarence had a reefer pad in Harlem and he would go there and pick up girls from the club, for his own purposes.'

Sadie hated Jimmy Monroe. There was a simple reason for that. 'Billie was always devoted to her mother, very devoted, and all of a sudden she started directing her affection towards Jimmy. Sadie thought Billie was giving him too much attention and neglecting her attention to her mother.'

Sadie became obsessed with the idea that Jimmy had 'pulled Billie with drugs'. She did everything she could to stop the two of them from seeing each other. Finally, Sadie confronted Jimmy and said, 'I don't want you coming around here. If Billie's going to hang out with you, then she'll have to go someplace else to stay!'

Ruby Helena was in the apartment on the morning Billie came back, having been out all night without phoning her mother to tell her where she was or what she was doing. When Sadie began to scream at her, Billie produced a sheet of paper that she flung down on the table. It was a marriage certificate. 'We're married,' she said. 'So can he come in *now?*'★

Shortly after this confrontation, Billie moved out with her new husband, leaving her mother abandoned and weeping. The newly-weds began their life together by taking a room on 110th Street, until Billie discovered that Jimmy's ex-wife Nina was living much too close by. They 'jumped up' and moved on. For a while they were somewhere in Maryland, then they rented a room upstairs from the prestigious Symphony Chord Club, which was run by a childhood friend of Jimmy's. The club was in a basement and next to it was a soundproof music room shaped like a baby grand piano, where all the entertainers used to go to rehearse. Anyway, that didn't last long.

Ruby Helena said something changed in Billie's character around 1942. She was no longer friendly or nice to be with

---

★ Linda Kuehl asked, 'Do you think she was rebelling against her mother?' Ruby Helena replied, 'Of course. *You will*, when you are on drugs . . . You feel everyone else is your enemy.'

and she'd swear a lot and act strangely with the people she knew. She never saw Billie taking anything, but she was sure she must have started to use hard drugs. 'Even when she wasn't on drugs, she still wasn't herself. She'd be nervous, edgy.'*

By now Sadie was convinced her daughter was 'doing something wrong' and suspected that Jimmy Monroe was turning her on to drugs in order to have financial control over her. After all, Billie was making a lot of money, singing at the Famous Door and at other places on 52nd Street, and yet she was always broke. Sadie wrote a letter to Ruby Helena in which she said, 'I'm writing this with tears in my eyes. Billie is gone. She is always drugged. I know this is going to take me to my grave.'

Less than a year after the marriage, Jimmy Monroe went to California and (according to Ruby Helena) took most of Billie's money with him. He set himself up with a stable of women there.† She said that Billie was heartbroken once he had gone, not because she missed him, but because she suddenly realised how she had abandoned her mother and had failed to look after her properly.

---

* Ruby Helena and Billie got into big fights, but this seems to have been because Billie resented the way Ruby Helena was keeping a watch on her. One night when they were leaving the Famous Door in a taxi Billie told the driver, 'You take me home and take this bitch uptown.' 'I couldn't believe it,' said Ruby Helena. 'That's when I left the family.'

† In May 1942 Jimmy Monroe was arrested for drug smuggling. He was given a twelve-month prison sentence for marijuana possession. Billie raised the money for his defence, but broke up with him after he was released from prison.

SEVENTEEN

'Strange Fruit'

———

Southern trees bear a strange fruit,
Blood on the leaves and blood at the root,
Black bodies swinging in the southern breeze,
Strange fruit hanging from the poplar trees.

Pastoral scene of the gallant South,
The bulging eyes and the twisted mouth,
Scent of magnolias sweet and fresh,
Then the sudden smell of burning flesh.

Here is a fruit for the crows to pluck,
For the rain to gather, for the wind to suck,
For the sun to rot, for the tree to drop,
Here is a strange and bitter crop.

I have been looking at a photograph that was taken in Omaha, Nebraska, in 1919. The upper part of the picture shows a group of about forty individuals gathered together on a dark night to watch the final stage of a lynching.* I can see three women and a young boy who can't be more than twelve years old, but the rest are grown men. They are

---

* Much of the information for this chapter is taken from *Long Memory* by Mary Frances Berry and John W. Blassingame, 1982. Between 1882 and 1951 there were 4,720 recorded cases of lynching in the US, but the figures are very vague and the number of unrecorded cases is almost impossible to assess.

all wearing hats of one sort or another, some are smoking cigarettes, and one is holding a walking stick in his leather-gloved hand. A number of them look straight into the camera with a triumphant and smiling gaze, while others seem more distracted.

It was between 1900 and 1920 that lynching was at its most virulent. As the contemporary Baltimore journalist and sardonic humorist H. L. Mencken explained it, life in the South could be lacking in entertainment and 'lynching often takes the place of the merry-go-round, the theatre, the symphony orchestra and other diversions common to larger communities'. Thousands of people would turn up for the well-publicised spectacle★ and Baptist and Methodist minis-ters often worked hand-in-hand with the Ku Klux Klan by delivering sermons that incited further racial hatred and violence. Although the myth of protecting white women from black men was maintained, a lynching was often provoked by any signs of what was known as 'uppitiness', such as a black man seeking employment above his station, offensive language or boastful remarks. Even evidence of material success, such as the acquisition of a new car or a soldier returning home with a medal for valour, could be interpreted as uppitiness.

Racial discrimination eased a bit during the 1930s and cases of public lynching had almost entirely ceased by 1940, although as one more cynical commentator pointed out, 'public opinion is beginning to turn away from this sort of mob activity . . . but the work of the mob goes on . . . Countless Negroes are lynched yearly, but their disappear-

---

★ There would be extensive coverage of such events, with photographs and 'light-hearted' articles. Postcards with photographs of the victims were sold in large numbers, including one that showed five men hanging from a tree, along with a little poem about the lesson to be learnt from the Dogwood Tree. People who wanted a tangible keepsake from such an event could take home a fragment of human bone, a scrap of cloth or some charred rope. There was a terrifying obsession with the male sexual organ, and many lynch victims were castrated or otherwise defiled. See *Trouble in Mind* by Leon Litwack, 1988.

ance is shrouded in mystery for they are dispatched quietly and without general knowledge.'*

Billie Holiday had never personally witnessed a lynching, but of course she could imagine what it would be like and she must have spoken to many people with first-hand experience. Her friend Lester Young managed to help his cousin 'Sports' Young escape from a lynch mob when they were both still in their early teens, and the singer Lena Horne must have told Billie how she witnessed a lynching in a small town in Florida when she was a child with her mother's touring theatre troupe.†

In 1938 Billie joined Artie Shaw's all-white band and went on tour with them. It meant she was often refused entry to the hotels where the other musicians were staying, couldn't eat with them in restaurants or drink with them in bars; and in the South she was turned into a fugitive, not even able to use public toilets and always ready to hide from danger. It was during this tour that she had one of many violent and potentially dangerous confrontations when a man in the audience asked the 'nigger wench' to sing another song. Artie Shaw later described the whole southern experience as a nightmare from beginning to end.

When the band came back to New York City they played at the Lincoln Hotel and even there, in an establishment named after the President who had proclaimed the equality of all Americans, Billie was treated like a second-class citizen. She said later, 'I was never allowed to visit the bar, or the dining room. I was made to enter and leave by the kitchen and I had to remain alone in my little room all evening until I was called to do my numbers.'‡ The band was also making a series of radio programmes, but the tobacco company promoting them insisted that Billie's voice could not be

---

* Myrdal, pp. 566, 1350. There was also the sinister suggestion that the police and the judiciary took over some of the tasks that had previously been managed by the mob.
† Speaking about this experience, Lena Horne said, 'I knew about the fear it aroused in people and in my mother. It's something I wanted to forget, but it stayed with me.'
‡ Interview in *Ebony*, July 1949, pp. 26–32.

allowed on the air waves and so she was replaced by the white singer Helen Forrest.

Billie gave up in disgust and went to work at a newly opened club called Café Society. It was run by Barney Josephson, a Jewish ex-shoe-salesman who wanted a place where a black and white audience could mix together with dignity and mutual respect.★ Billie liked the atmosphere and stayed there for nine months. Barney Josephson described her as someone who was sensitive and proud and who did what she liked. 'She could tell a good joke. She knew all the words to use if you rubbed her the wrong way. When she told you off, you damn well were told – white, black, rich, poor!'

In April 1939, a young Jewish schoolteacher called Abel Meeropol was invited to Café Society. He had written a song called 'Strange Fruit', which was his response to a photograph he had seen of a lynching.† Josephson wanted Billie to sing it and so Meeropol sat down at the piano with her and they went through the song together.

According to Josephson, who always liked this kind of joke, Billie didn't at first know 'what the hell the song meant', and only later did its meaning percolate through. But Meeropol gave a different account of her response. He said that at first he thought 'She didn't feel very comfortable with it because it was so different from the songs she was accustomed to. This is quite understandable.' She asked him what the word 'pastoral' meant and he did his school-

---

★ The club was 'a milestone along the long road to racial integration in America' (Nicholson, p. 110). Barney Josephson said he wanted to establish such a club because 'I always had strong feelings of social consciousness. I guess I just had a democratic upbringing.' He was later accused of being a Communist during the McCarthy era and was hounded out of business for a while.

† Abel Meeropol later changed his name to Lewis Allan. In a letter to Linda Kuehl, dated 8 July 1971, he said, 'Way back in the Thirties I saw a photograph of a lynching . . . It was a shocking photograph and it haunted me for days. As a result I wrote "Strange Fruit" as a poem . . . I set it to music and my wife Anne sang it around at small gatherings.' In a letter to the *New York Times Book Review*, on 15 July 1956, in which he objected to the way his part in the genesis of the song was described in Billie's ghosted autobiography *Lady Sings the Blues*, he said, 'I wrote "Strange Fruit" because I hate lynching and I hate injustice and I hate the people who perpetuate it.'

masterly best to explain that it referred to shepherds and shepherdesses and green fields, and here it was used ironically, as a way of shocking the listener.

Meeropol said that the next time he saw Billie was a few days later, and 'She gave a startling, most dramatic and effective interpretation of the song which could jolt the audience out of its complacency anywhere. This was exactly what I wanted the song to do and why I wrote it. Billie Holiday's styling fulfilled the bitterness and the shocking quality I had hoped the song would have. The audience gave a tremendous ovation.'[*]

People started to come to Café Society, just to hear that one song. And for the rest of her life Billie sang it all round America and in Europe. She even had a clause put into some of her contracts allowing her to sing it in those clubs where they would have preferred her to stick to happy and unhappy love songs. She always claimed that 'Strange Fruit' was one of the reasons why she was hounded so fiercely by the Federal Bureau of Narcotics and the FBI. She said it was no coincidence that she defied an order not to sing it at the Earle Theater in Philadelphia and the next day was arrested on charges that eventually led to her imprisonment.[†]

Lena Horne said that, in singing 'Strange Fruit', Billie 'was putting into words what so many people had seen and lived through. She seemed to be performing in melody and words the same things I was feeling in my heart.'[‡] Leonard Feather called it 'the first significant protest in words and music, the

---

[*] Lewis Allan (Meeropol) in a letter to Linda Kuehl, dated 28 July 1971. Although Columbia Records had a contract with Billie at that time, they would not agree to do a recording of 'Strange Fruit', although they did give her permission to record it on the Commodore label with 'Fine and Mellow', on the other side. The record was produced by Milt Gabler in April 1939. It quickly rose to number sixteen in the charts and eventually sold more than a million copies.

[†] In a 1947 interview for *Downbeat* magazine she said, 'I've made a lot of enemies. Singing that song hasn't helped any. I was doing it at the Earle Theater 'til they made me stop.' According to William Dufty, the ghostwriter for *Lady Sings the Blues*, 'Billie has been kicked around and harassed for years by the authorities. One of the reasons is that this song "Strange Fruit" made her well-known and politically controversial.'

[‡] David Margolick, *Strange Fruit: The Biography of a Song*, 2001, p. 41.

first unmuted cry against racism', and for the record producer Ahmet Ertegun it was 'a declaration of war . . . the beginning of the civil rights movement'. The drummer Max Roach believed it was 'more than revolutionary. She made a statement that we all felt as black folks. No one was speaking out. She became one of the fighters, this beautiful lady who could sing and make you feel things.'

In the same year that the record was released, copies of it were sent to all the members of the US Senate, as a form of protest against lynching. The civil rights campaigner Walter White sent a letter to Billie congratulating her for what she had done. There was even talk of awarding her the Spingarn Medal, given annually to a black person of special achievement, but that came to nothing because church leaders disapproved of entertainers.

Billie often said the song reminded her of how her father had been 'killed by the Jim Crow laws of the South', and it was thinking about him that brought tears to her eyes as she sang. Her pianist Mal Waldron said she often chose to sing it to give herself courage when she felt under threat. 'Whenever things were not going right she would sing that tune. If her dressing room wasn't too beautiful, or maybe the police were waiting outside or had stopped her or something like that.'★

There is a film sequence of Billie singing 'Strange Fruit' at the Chelsea Palace Studios in London in February 1959. By then she has become painfully thin and the dress she wears is stretched over the angular scaffolding of her bones. Her hair is pulled back from her face and tied in a long pony tail. She looks austere and beautiful and her face has taken on the abstract iconography of a mask. Even though she is performing in front of an audience, you have the impression that she is lost in her own thoughts and oblivious of her surroundings. She sings very slowly, giving full weight

★ Mal Waldron worked with her from 1956 to 1959.

to the power of each word, allowing the images to grow in their terrible intensity.

But now I have one more photograph in mind. It shows the scene of Billie's funeral, which took place in New York at St Paul the Apostle Roman Catholic Church on 21 July 1959, just five months after that film was made. A crowd of some 3,000 men and women has gathered to watch as her open coffin is carried towards the steps of the church. Some have obviously come to pay their last respects with dignity and sadness, but others, who don't seem to belong to the jazz world at all, have a strange look of eagerness about them. It is as if they have come to enjoy a spectacle.

EIGHTEEN

Harlem at War

When Poland was invaded in 1939, the United States was faced with the possibility that it might be drawn into the conflict. The key issue for the black community was whether they were prepared to support America's involvement overseas, while still being denied their democratic rights at home. At first many blacks looked upon world events with a certain optimism because they felt that there might be a chance of work for everyone, as well as the opportunity to serve their country and prove their patriotism. But by the winter of 1940, in spite of 'the war plants begging for men and women workers, those with black skins were daily told contemptuously that they were not wanted.'[*] An estimated 75 per cent of all jobs in the newly booming defence industry were closed to them.

By the spring of 1943, more than half a million blacks were in the army. But only 79,000 were overseas, and repeating the traumatic experience of their fathers in the First World War. Walter White, the leader of the National Association for the Advancement of Colored People, spoke

---

[*] Walter White, quoted in Brandt, p. 189.

of 'the gratuitous insults and beatings and humiliations suffered by men who had fought in the Pacific and had been returned home to train other fighters ... the countless stories of lynchings and mistreatments of Negro soldiers'.

The tensions in Harlem were building up during the spring of 1943 and they were exacerbated when the authorities decided to close down the Savoy Ballroom on 21 April 1943. The police charged that the ballroom was a 'base for vice' and a major cause of the spread of venereal disease among white soldiers. It was alleged that 164 servicemen had contracted venereal disease in the past nine months as a result of meeting women there. To prove their point the police picked up three prostitutes and a pimp outside the Ballroom.

Ninety employees lost their jobs, and the people of Harlem were indignant. Walter White argued that prostitution was a fact of life at other public places, including the Waldorf Astoria Hotel, but everyone knew that it was really the mixed dancing the police were angry about. As Roy Wilkins observed, 'Chiefs of police, commissioners, captains, lieutenants and plain rookie cops get purple in the face at the very thought of Negroes and whites enjoying themselves socially together.'*

James Baldwin remembered that before the summer of 1943, he had never been aware of so many policemen on the streets of Harlem, 'on foot, on horseback, on corners, everywhere, always two by two'. And then on 1 August a riot finally broke out, triggered by a scene at the Braddock Hotel in which a black soldier in uniform tried to intervene in a quarrel between a white policeman and a woman called Margie Polite. There was a scuffle and a shot was fired. The crowd that gathered in front of the hotel was convinced the soldier had been fatally wounded.

The rage and despair burst its banks and soon thousands of men and women were sweeping through Harlem, looting and burning and breaking street-lamps so that whole areas were plunged into darkness. The writer Claude Brown was

---

* Quoted in Brandt, p. 171.

six years old at the time and remembered how 'the crashing sound of falling plate-glass windows kept me awake for hours. While I listened to the noise I imagined bombs falling and people running through the streets screaming.'★

Five thousand police were rushed to Harlem from throughout the city, but they were under a restraint order, which meant that the fatalities were not as high as they might otherwise have been. Nevertheless six people were killed, nearly 700 were seriously wounded and there were 600 arrests.

The following morning the main streets looked as if they had been swept by a hurricane or an invading army, and Walter White, who had lived in Harlem for twenty-five years, said he had never seen 'such concentrated despair' as he witnessed that morning. Arthur Garfield Hayes, writing in the *New York Times* five days after the riot, blamed it on 'conditions in Harlem: the wretched housing, unduly high rents, lack of recreation grounds, discrimination in industry against coloured people, are largely responsible for an emotional situation which might at any time cause a flare-up. But in addition to this is a lack of proper treatment of the people by the police.'†

Until the outbreak of the Second World War, Harlem had not been an all-black community. The transformation had a lot to do with relations between the black and white soldiers. These relations were so strained and volatile that, however equal the soldiers might be deemed to be, it was thought best to keep them separate when off base. Harlem was effectively off-limits for white soldiers. Nevertheless white soldiers did come there in search of amusement of one sort or another, and all through the winter and spring of 1943 scenes of racial provocation turned into clashes on the city streets.

Billie was singing at the Onyx Club and staying in an apartment above the Braddock Hotel at the time of the riot.

★ Ibid., p. 187.
† Ibid., p. 208.

Even if she missed the worst of it, she must have seen the chaos the following morning and of course she knew all about the heightened racial tensions that the war had released.

By now she was the acclaimed Queen of 52nd Street⋆ and night after night she played to standing-room-only crowds.† Her songs of love and longing exactly reflected the feelings of the entire nation, as soldiers said goodbye to their sweethearts and set out to face their destiny in unknown lands. But throughout the war years there was a deepening gulf between her popular success and the realities of her life in Harlem. This was the mood in the air when she smashed the top off a beer bottle and brandished her weapon at a naval officer who had come up to her in a bar and called her a 'nigger'. And it was the mood in the air when she single-handedly attacked three white soldiers who were burning her mink coat with the lighted ends of their cigarettes.

It was at some point towards the end of 1943 that Billie became involved with the bass player John Simmons. Simmons had been a junkie for years. Perhaps it was under his influence that she started injecting heroin, protecting herself from the knowledge that nothing really changed, no matter how successful she became.

In an interview with Linda Kuehl, Simmons described the way Billie was eager to please her public. 'She would go over and have drinks with them, sit down and laugh and talk . . . and people would ask her about her life and when she started singing, and what does she think about when she was singing, and things like that; and that would wear her down and she would run upstairs to her dressing room to fix, and get this nervous condition away from her, because it's like they'd inflicted real pain on her just from holding a conversation.'

⋆ When *Esquire* magazine conducted a poll among jazz critics at the end of 1943, Billie was the clear winner of the vocal section. In October 1943 a photograph of Billie at a studio jam session dominated the centre spread of *Life* magazine.

† As Stuart Nicholson said, 'The Street provided her with an ideal forum; it allowed her talent to blossom.' Frank Sinatra, among many others, went to see her. 'I used to watch Billie in New York night after night, as much as I could,' he said. 'She was a great contributor to my career in the sense of articulating a song.'

John Simmons also described how, in this new world of fame, total strangers would say, 'Hello, Billie!' and she'd say, 'Kiss my ass! I don't know you!' Then she would turn to Simmons in a panic and ask if he thought she was crazy. And talking about it later he said, 'No, she wasn't crazy, but she wanted to be . . . She got to the point where she thought everyone was trying to use her and so she said "Fuck the world!"'

Now that she had money, Billie gave it away as fast as she earnt it. The singer Babs Gonzales remembered, 'She fed everybody in New York for about four years with no sweat. Any musician could go there and eat and get money for the subway or to go to the movies. Every day they could do that. And if she was out of town she would leave money with her mother.' The trombonist Trummy Young said, 'She couldn't do enough for the men she loved, or even her friends. She spent a large portion of the money she earnt on heroin, but she also spent a lot on down-and-out friends . . . Billie was, with all her weaknesses, an honest person.'*

Billie often referred to herself as a 'race woman'. The blues folk singer Josh White, who became friends with her during the early 1940s, was one of the few people to assert that 'She had more thought for humanity and was more race-conscious than people thought.'† In October 1943 she appeared at the Golden Gate Ballroom in Harlem for an All Star Victory Show in tribute to Lieutenant Benjamin O. Davis Jr, who, along with his father, made up the only two black officers serving in the army.‡ In May 1944 she appeared at the Golden Gate Auditorium in New York at a Celebration and Rally to end Jim Crow (segregation) laws in New York

---

* Chilton, p. 97.
† Chilton, p. 104. In her book *If You Can't Be Free, Be a Mystery*, Farah Jasmine Griffin says, 'At times she was militantly pro-black, often referring to herself as a "race woman" . . . but eventually the stories of her arrests and drug addiction joined with her stage persona of the torch singer to create a new image, that of the tragic, ever-suffering black woman singer who simply stands centre-stage and naturally sings of her woes . . . [a woman who] feels but does not think' (p. 31).
‡ The army continued to insist that only whites could command black outfits. Moreover, no black could be ranked higher than the lowest-ranking white. As a result, few black lieutenants were ever promoted and, apart from Benjamin O. Davis Sr, none achieved the rank of general or, in the navy, flag rank.

City, attended by the Reverend Adam Clayton Powell and Benjamin O. Davis Jr, as well as Count Basie, Teddy Wilson and others. In June she took part in the Negro Salute to the Fighting Jews of Europe at Town Hall in New York.

She was not a political activist or speaker, but she fought back physically whenever she was insulted because of her race. And she went on singing 'Strange Fruit', even when club owners tried to stop her and the song jeopardised her career. According to John Hammond, she was 'pretty well gone by 1940 . . . She was still marvellously musical, but she had gotten self-conscious. I felt that the beginning of the end was "Strange Fruit" when she became the darling of the left-wing intellectuals. I think she began taking herself very seriously and thinking of herself as very important.'★

Others, especially the new breed of tabloid journalists and various police departments, had a different opinion of what was happening. They said that Billie was going downhill because she was leading a selfish and dissolute life and she deserved to be punished for her sins.

★ For her part, Billie resented John Hammond's condescension, saying, 'John's a square, John's just rich, John wants to run my life, tries to tell me and everybody else what to do.' Quoted in Margolick, p. 59.

NINETEEN

Lester Young

———

Billie first met him in 1936, when he had just arrived in New York. He moved in with her and her mother after a rat jumped out at him from the cupboard in the hotel room where he was staying. Talking about that time years later, he said, 'She was teaching me about the city, you know, which way to go . . . because I didn't know my way around. She taught me a lot of things, you know, and got me little record dates, you know, playing behind her, little solos and things like that.'*

Lester Young had green eyes with dark rings of permanent tiredness around them. He had red-tinged hair and it fell in soft curls when he let it grow long at the back. He thought of tying it up with ribbons, until his friends stopped him. He had pale skin that looked grey in the daylight, but he avoided the daylight as much as possible. He was a night person – always had been.

---

* This is from the longest and the last interview made with Lester Young by the French jazz critic François Postif in the Hotel Louisiana in Paris in February 1959. A photographer came along as well, but took no pictures because 'Lester was lying quite nude on his bed, unshaved and ill-looking. He was drinking port wine . . . and was not quite in his normal attitude' (*A Lester Young Reader*, ed. Lewis Porter, 1991, p. 174).

He was very shy and often silent and preoccupied. He tended to look for signs to tell him how things were going; if a butterfly landed on his hand, that was a sign that somebody loved him. When he did speak he used his own coded language so that only the people who knew him well were able to understand what he was saying. For those who did understand, he was a gentle philosopher who spoke in riddles. He had a high, whispery voice.

'How's it going, Lester?'

'Ding dong, I feel a draught. Bob Crosby and another grey just walked in.'

'How's it going, Lester?'

'No eyes, no eyes. Things are bad. All the popes are dying.'

'How's it going, Lester?'

'Seeing is believing, and hearing is a bitch . . . It's fight for your life, that's all.'*

Lester gave nicknames to the musicians he worked with: 'Sweets' for the trumpeter Harry Edison, 'socks' for the pianist Bobby Scott; 'Lady Tate' for his fellow saxophone player Buddy Tate, because 'You're so refined and you're so nice, I got to give you a Lady name, because I don't see you mad at anybody or anything.'† And Lady Day for Billie Holiday because he found her so nice, and she found him nice too and called him 'Pres', short for President.

Billie and Lester made numerous recordings in which you can hear their closeness in the way that the voice and the saxophone work together with such an easy intimacy. They were never lovers, but were more like a brother and sister who shared many character traits. They had the same sort

---

* 'Ding dong' was a form of greeting. Bing and Bob Crosby were the police, and so was Alice Blue Gown. 'Feeling a draught' meant a racist was somewhere close by. Whites were 'greys' and blacks were 'Oxford greys'. Lester had eyes for the things he liked and no eyes for the things he didn't like. Women were different sorts of hats, according to the way they fitted a man sexually. In music, the bass player was the deep-sea diver and a pianist's hands were the little people on the left and the little people on the right.

† Many of his favourite musicians became Lady this or that, and a band could be 'all you ladies'. People he was less sure of became Miss, as with his agent, Miss Carpenter.

of fears and lack of confidence, and the need to keep the
world at bay with drink and drugs; they also had the same
easy generosity and hopeless business sense. But beyond that
there was their shared ability to give power and poignancy
to the most sentimental lyrics.* They both favoured torch
songs about lost or unrequited love, and Lester used to know
all the words to all the verses of a song, thinking along with
them as he played.

Towards the end of his life, Lester explained his 'philosophy of the spiritual' to his friend Willie Jones. He said, 'A
musician is a philosopher and a scientist and he uses the
science of music to project the particular philosophy he
subscribes to.'† He believed that jazz expressed the principles of democracy and equality and said, 'We have made
a major contribution to this country and we are Americans
. . . Our music must be melodious and melodic and the
songs universal and that's about equality.' Towards the end
of his life, Lester was flying across the United States with
the pianist Bobby Scott, the one he called Socks. He looked
down at the vastness of his homeland stretched out beneath
him and said, 'Sure as hell is enough room for everybody,
ain't there, Socks!'‡

But now here is Lester Young stepping out onto the stage.
The audience roars a welcome and the spotlight follows him
and holds him at its centre, but he seems to be hardly aware
of his surroundings. The pianist and composer Gil Evans
said he moved like a parakeet on its perch, while Bobby
Scott described his walk as 'more of a shuffle than an honest
walk. It had something Asiatic about it, a reticence to barge
in. He sidled. It was in keeping with the side-door quality
of his nature.'§

He stands there in a pool of isolation, clutching the saxophone, one leg placed in front of the other to give him

---

* Lester believed that, as a musician, you must 'Go down the audience, see what
  the plumber is thinking, what the carpenter is thinking, so that when you are
  on stage you can help tell their story.'
† Quoted in Frank Büchmann–Møller, *You Just Fight for Your Life,* 1990, p. 193.
‡ *A Lester Young Reader,* p. 103.
§ Ibid., p. 112.

better balance, and his heavy-lidded eyes almost closed. If the music goes well he might suddenly break into a private tiptoeing dance – he was a wonderful dancer, with such a quality of looseness in his movements that he seemed to float just above the surface of the floor. But if things are not going well, then he might turn his back to the audience to hide his tears.*

Lester was always meticulously dressed. He had a long black coat with a high fur collar, which he liked to keep on even when he was indoors. He wore sunglasses when the sun was not shining and crêpe-soled shoes that made a soft scrinch-scrunch sound as he walked. He was fond of well-tailored suits with padded shoulders, wide lapels and high-waisted trousers that were full in the leg and narrow at the ankle. Sometime in the early 1930s his attention was caught by a picture of a group of Victorian ladies in their riding habits wearing broad-brimmed, flat-topped black hats. He had the design copied and the resulting porkpie/matador-style hat became his trademark.†

Lester was almost six feet tall and during the last years of his life he became painfully thin. He ate very little and could rarely be persuaded to touch any food at all before three o'clock in the morning; then he might start with a tin of sardines and follow that with some ice cream. Drink provided him with his nourishment. He drank port wine or sherry mixed with gin, whisky or Courvoisier mixed with beer, along with all those other mezzo-mezzo, up-and-down, top-and-bottom combinations that Billie also favoured. As a young man Lester said he never wanted to lose that 'nice feeling' he had at the beginning when he moved from orange sodas to the harder stuff, but towards the end of his life, as he explained to Bobby Scott, 'I have to drink. When I drink,

---

* At a concert in Paris in 1953, 'he showed more fear and trembling than usual, turned his back to the audience and walked towards the wings, hesitant and sombre', quoting Büchmann-Møller, p. 165, Maurice Cullaz, *Mon Ami Lester.*
† The original copy cost him twenty dollars. There is a famous photograph taken in New York's Alvin Hotel, where Lester spent the last months of his life. It shows the hat hanging from a hook on the wall and the saxophone leaning against a chair on the floor – nothing else.

the pain goes.'* The drinking had begun in earnest in the 1920s while he was with Count Basie and doing a lot of one-nighters: playing for eight hours, followed by a jam session for five or six hours more, and then bundling into a rackety bus for the long ride to the next booking in the next town.

By the time Lester was in his mid-thirties, he was drinking almost two pints a day of 100 proof spirits; sometimes he bought six bottles of spirits at once, just to be safe. It was important for him to feel safe whenever possible. In the days when it was still legal, he used to carry a little leather suit-case filled with marijuana. When Prohibition had ended and marijuana took its turn to be the illegal substance, he would carry a bottle of spirits in a little red plaid bag, which he kept on his lap. His tenor saxophone was always somewhere close by, even in later years when he was not so often in the mood to play. 'Hold it carefully,' he said to the photographer who wanted to move the saxophone in order to get the composition of a picture just right. 'Hold it carefully, you dig. That's my life!'

Along with many of the other musicians he worked with, Lester took Benzedrine tablets to keep him going and barbiturates to help him sleep, and he smoked marijuana every day. People said there was never a moment when he was not high on what he called his New Orleans cigarettes, except for the period between 1944 and 1945 when he was in the army.

So there was the drink and the dope and the pills, but never anything else; no cocaine and no 'needle dancing' as he called it. If someone was using heroin, Lester would ask them to leave the room when they needed to give themselves a shot. He didn't like what heroin did to people, but he also had a terrible fear of needles and injections, as well as a fear of hospitals and medical men and women in white coats. That was why he refused to go to the dentist even

* Bobby Scott, 'The House in the Heart', *A Lester Young Reader*, pp. 99–118.

when his teeth were falling out and why he avoided doctors, no matter how ill he felt.*

He was a man of many fears. He was afraid of the dark and needed to have a light on while he slept. He was afraid of silence, and when he was alone he had the radio babbling to itself and keeping him company, or he put a record onto repeat and let it play through his wakefulness and into his dreams. He liked to listen to Billie singing the old songs they had recorded together and he admired Frank Sinatra, someone who also knew how to turn a simple lyric into something meaningful.

Lester was afraid of death. He said he didn't want to meet Johnny Deathbed when he was in the wrong place, because he felt it was important to die quietly, and preferably in one's own 'crib' at home. He was also afraid of violence. As a child he had run away whenever his father wanted to take the family band on a trip down South, and as an adult on tour he always checked into a black hotel to avoid any unpleasantness, even if the other members of the band were staying in a much smarter establishment that accepted clients from all races. If he felt the presence of a racist somewhere close by, he would always leave at once to avoid a confrontation. In that way he was very different from Billie, who would attack anybody who abused her verbally.

In September 1944 Lester was thirty-five years old and was doing very well in his personal life and in his career. He was married to an Italian nurse called Mary† and they had bought a big house together in Los Angeles. He had

---

* Billie had a similar fear, especially of dentists. Lester's third wife, Mary, did persuade him to go to hospital for an alcohol cure in 1957, and he got on well with a psychiatrist who bore the wonderful name of Dr Luther Cloud. Cloud came to visit him at the Alvin Hotel in 1958 and gave him high doses of vitamin pills, as well as talking to him about some of his fears.

† Lester's first wife, Bess Cooper, was Jewish. They married in 1930, but she died the following year, not long after giving birth to their daughter Beverly. The marriage to Mary lasted from 1937 until 1945. In 1946 he married another Mary, who bore him two children, Lester Junior and Yvette. All his women remained deeply attached to him and he would sometimes visit old girlfriends when he was on tour – he called them 'way-backs'. They were all of a similar physical type, small and fragile, which is perhaps another reason why he and Billie were never lovers.

just taken part in a documentary film called *Jammin' the Blues* and he was in the final week of a very successful nine-month tour with Count Basie's band, playing at the Plantation Club in San Francisco.

And then one night a young man wearing a zoot suit, with a long golden chain dangling around his neck, came to listen to the music. When the performance was over he invited Lester and Harry 'Sweets' Edison and the drummer Jo Jones to come and join him at his table. He said he was a fan and the drinks were on him because he wanted to repay the performers for the pleasure they had given him.

So the four of them talked and drank and laughed until the early hours of the morning. Then the stranger suddenly produced his FBI badge and said that if Lester and Jo Jones did not report to the military draft board by nine o'clock that morning, they would be liable to a five-year prison sentence.

Lester had been sent his call-up papers several times already, but he had ignored them. Now he had no choice but to face the authorities. His friends presumed that his obvious alcoholism, his strange manner, his age and his look of physical exhaustion would exempt him completely. Or, if the worst came to the worst, then he would be made to join a military band along with many other contemporary musicians.

But something went badly wrong. Perhaps the people who interviewed him thought that this pale-faced man with his whispered babbling language needed to be taught a lesson. In the military report he was described as an 'English-speaking Negro', with brown eyes, black hair, a dark complexion, good eyesight and hearing and 'no psychiatric or physical abnormalities'. His profession was given as 'bandsman . . . specialising in tenor saxaphone [*sic*] . . . did solo work'. He was declared to be a suitable candidate for ordinary military service and there was no suggestion that he might join a band.★

★ This is about someone who is considered to be one of the most influential jazz musicians of the twentieth century. When Malcolm Little, the future Malcolm X, was brought before the same sort of military board he managed to persuade them that he was not good army material by telling them, 'I want to get sent down to the South; organise them nigger soldiers, you dig. Steal us some guns and kill us crackers!' (Brandt, p. 110).

After a couple of months' training on the West Coast, Lester Young was sent to the Infantry Replacement Training Center in Alabama and enrolled as a mess orderly in E Company under the command of Captain William Stevenson, a white officer from Louisiana. On New Year's Day 1945, he was badly injured while trying to do an obstacle course exercise, and as a result spent three weeks in the military hospital. The neuropsychologist who examined Lester there described him as being in a 'constitutionally Psychopathic State, manifested by drug addiction (marijuana, barbiturates), chronic alcoholism and "nomadism"'. (The term must have referred to the fact that Lester had been on tour with Count Basie.) In spite of this diagnosis it was felt that he had a purely 'disciplinary problem' and should be dealt with accordingly.★

On coming out of hospital on 24 January, Lester was immediately forced to take up his full exercise duties, even though he was in considerable pain. On 30 January he was seen to be acting strangely and, when he was asked what was wrong, he explained that he was high. His locker was searched and was found to contain one and a half marijuana cigarettes, three barbiturate capsules and eleven barbiturate tablets, as well as an alcoholic mixture that he had apparently concocted himself. His locker also contained a photograph of his Italian wife, and some people believed that this was the real problem as far as the authorities were concerned.

Lester Young was arrested and brought before the military court on 16 February 1945. When Captain Stevenson was asked during the trial what first made him suspect drug abuse, he replied, 'Well, his colour, sir, and the fact that his eyes seemed bloodshot and he didn't react to training as he should.'† He was punished with a dishonourable discharge, total forfeiture of pay, and confinement to a hard-labour

★ Quoted in Büchmann-Møller, p. 121. Jo Jones, who had far less traumatic experiences during his military training in the South, said he went by the prison gates to wave to Lester while he was in the exercise yard. He said, 'The way they treated Lester in the army . . . They had dogs in there they didn't treat like that and I would cry at night thinking about what they did to him.'
† Ibid., p. 122.

camp for the period of one year. He was sent to the Detention Barracks in the State of Georgia. He never spoke about the time he spent there, except to say it was 'a nightmare, man, one mad nightmare'.

When he came out of the army, Lester's playing changed. He had always used silences, but now 'the silences grew longer, the whisper-to-shout shifts were more startling and the sound was darker and more anguished'.* When asked about this development in his style, he said, 'I play different. I live different. This is later. That was then. We change. Move on.'† But he was also more nervous; he felt his audiences were not interested in this change in his playing and were quick to judge and condemn him. He began to call himself 'Old Pres', to distinguish himself from the numerous saxophone players who imitated his early style. He found it disconcerting and even frightening to hear a piece of music in which he could not be sure if he was playing, or someone else was playing just like him.

By the 1950s it was very hard for Lester to get good work‡ and there was relentless gossip about how he had lost his touch and was nothing but a burnt-out drunk or, as one newspaperman put it, 'a living drama of personal weakness, a victim, it seems, of drugs'. Lester said he knew the record companies were eager to celebrate his achievements and produce memorial volumes of his recordings just as soon as he was dead.§

In the spring of 1958, Lester took a room on the fourth floor of the Alvin Hotel, on the corner of Broadway and

---

* Ward and Burns, p. 323.
† *A Lester Young Reader*, p. 73.
‡ According to Willie Jones, 'Some young musicians thought [Lester] was old and dated, that he was losing it. I don't think so. He was just depressed because he couldn't get good work … He was hurt, because he had said certain things to certain promoters that he didn't like, so they didn't like him, and they wanted to punish him' (Büchmann-Møller, p. 197). Billie was also dogged by similar talk of her unreliability and the decline of her talent. There was also a lot of talk about how she and Lester had quarrelled, but this seems to have been just journalists looking for copy.
§ He was quite right. The market was flooded with Lester Young 'classics' once he was no longer around. The same happened with Billie Holiday.

52nd Street. A young woman called Elaine Swain moved in with him and did her best to look after him. The psychiatrist Dr Luther Cloud came to talk to him, and visiting friends tried to persuade Lester to eat. His porkpie hat hung from the wall, and a dozen bottles of Gordon's gin stood in a careful line in front of a mirror on the dresser. Lester spent hours at a time sitting in an armchair with the saxophone on his lap, staring out of the window and down at the Birdland club and the 'street that never slept', watching people come and go through the long days and the hectic nights.

He gave a number of performances during his final months, some of them desultory, others triumphant. In June 1958, his friends arranged for him to take part in a celebration at Birdland called 'Thirty Years in Show Business' and the evening was such a success that he was given a three-week booking. He started with a painfully slow and halting version of 'Pennies from Heaven', a song that Billie had also transformed into something much deeper than the lyrics implied.

> Every time it rains, it rains pennies from heaven.
> Don't you know each cloud contains pennies from heaven.
> You'll find your fortune falling all over town,
> Be sure that your umbrella is upside down.
> Trade them for a package of sunshine and flowers,
> If you want the things you love you must have showers,
> So when you hear it thunder, don't run under a tree,
> There'll be pennies from heaven, for you and me.

In January 1959 Lester agreed to perform for eight weeks at the Blue Note in Paris.* When he arrived, he told people that he had been very ill and would die soon. Night after

---

* Norman Granz said how different European audiences were from their American counterparts. 'They listen to you, applaud and stamp their feet, indicating they'd like more, but there is no shouting or whistling during the solo, nor any of the outcries that mar a pretty tune.' Oscar Peterson echoed this same observation: 'Europeans regard jazz as part of American culture, as an art form . . . Over here it's regarded as just entertainment, a background for drinking and conversation' (Ward and Burns, p. 160).

night he played with all the energy he had in him, struggling to produce enough breath. Between the breaks he would slump against the grand piano, leaning his forehead on the open lid. He would get back to the Hôtel de la Louisiana at four or five in the morning and then could be seen like his own ghost, wearing pyjamas and his faithful hat, pacing silently up and down the corridors, the saxophone in his hands and a look of blank despair on his face.

Lester left Paris a week earlier than planned because his strength was giving out. Elaine Swain collected him from the airport in New York and took him back to the Alvin Hotel. He sat in the armchair by the window for half a day and half the night and drank a bottle of vodka and most of a bottle of bourbon. Then he went to bed and died at around 3 a.m. on 15 March 1959.* Billie wanted to sing at his funeral, but she was prevented from doing so. Lester's eldest daughter Beverly said in an interview, 'The law wouldn't allow Billie to sing', but according to other accounts it was Lester's wife who stopped her, saying that she might make a fuss and cause trouble.

---

* A doctor was called shortly before his death. The police arrived just after he had died. They confiscated his saxophone, a ring, a wallet and $500 in traveller's cheques, as surety for the $76 he owed to the hotel. The property was returned to his wife. The saxophone is now at Rutgers Jazz Institute in New Jersey.

TWENTY

Tallulah Bankhead

———

There was a time when everyone knew about Tallulah Bankhead. She was a highly successful actress and her 1939 role in Lillian Hellman's play *The Little Foxes* was described as 'one of the great performances of the American theatre'. She was also acclaimed as a classic American beauty, with a small and sexy body, an alabaster complexion, aquiline features and long, wavy, auburn tresses.

Tallulah was born in 1902 and was a true child of the Deep South. Her grandfather John Hollis Bankhead came from slave-owning stock and ran a lucrative cotton mill in Jasper, Alabama. He had been elected to Congress in 1887 and became a Senator in 1905, keeping that prestigious position until his death in 1920. He was one of a group of powerful southerners who successfully opposed any attempt to put a ban on lynching.

Tallulah's mother died shortly after her birth and she and her elder sister were brought up by their paternal grandparents in the wealth and opulence of the family mansion.*

---

* Tallulah's father, Will Bankhead, also moved back to his childhood home. It was said that he never recovered from the loss of his wife. He was an alcoholic who often entertained thoughts of suicide. Tallulah doted on him and always referred to him as 'Daddy Dearest'.

Tallulah used to tell the story of how her grandmother would ride out every Thursday to the Negro section of Jasper, bringing the dirty laundry that needed washing and baskets of food to be distributed to the poor. And on Saturdays certain Negroes were allowed to come onto her land so that she could present them with cornmeal for their families. She had a little black book in which she kept a record of who had died and who had been born, and in that way she knew exactly how much cornmeal was required and there was no chance of anyone cheating her and 'getting a bit extra for their chickens'.

According to one biographer,★ Tallulah inherited this ability to be 'touchingly loyal and tender to individual black people, but if they transgressed, if they got proud, uppity and arrogant, then Tallulah "went South"'. In later years she used to appear on radio talk shows and, in a broad southern drawl, she would entertain her listeners with stories about her old Black Mammy whom she loved so, and about Daddy and the Coloured People.

She never spoke of her own half-brother, and perhaps several other half-brothers and sisters, in these homely anecdotes. The half-brother in question was called John Quincy Bankhead. He lived with his mother in a shack somewhere behind the family mansion and was four years older than Tallulah. One day she suddenly realised that he was the spitting image of her grandfather, with the same tall frame and the same features, only his skin was darker. When she mentioned this resemblance to John Quincy, he replied in a very matter-of-fact way that 'all Bankhead men, both coloured and white, was always tall'. She then asked her father to tell her more, and he smiled conspiratorially and said of course there was a blood tie, for after all 'boys will be boys'.

From a young age Tallulah had learnt that she could draw attention to herself by being outrageous, and as she grew older, especially once the acting jobs were no longer on offer and her beauty was on the wane, this outrageousness took

★ For this account of Tallulah, I have relied for the most part on the biography by Lee Israel, *Miss Tallulah Bankhead*, 1972, and on her own ghosted autobiography, *Tallulah*, 1952.

over from everything else and knew no bounds. Tallulah loved to expose herself at parties, lifting her skirts and dropping her knickers, or showing off the effects of a recent breast implant. She lay on top of a grand piano and sang a drunken song, wearing nothing but a string of pearls. She was again naked when she hit a police officer who had come to the door of her apartment to complain about a particularly noisy party. When Eleanor Roosevelt came to tea, Tallulah made a point of talking to the President's wife while sitting on the lavatory, with the door open.*

Tallulah had a natural affinity for all sorts of drugs and stimulants. In later life she consumed vast quantities of the new amphetamines and barbiturates, and paid her doctors hundreds of dollars a week to give her injections of an opium derivative called Demerol, but during her early years she had a preference for marijuana and cocaine. She was part of the wealthy white jetset who would come uptown for the drugs, the music and other forbidden excitements.† According to Pop Foster, she was a frequent visitor at the notorious Daisy Chain club and there were stories about a hunchback called Money, who was able to supply her with as much cocaine as she wanted. People remembered seeing Tallulah at the Hot Cha on 52nd Street, when the blind pianist Eddie Steele was playing. She would sing songs with him and sometimes would lead him to the dance floor and they would dance quietly in each other's arms.

However, there was already a rather ominous note creeping into all this 'fraternising'. When Tallulah's respectable southern father, Daddy Dearest, heard reports that his daughter had been seen in Harlem, she immediately arranged for the film producer Walter Wanger to reassure her worried parent with

---

* While attending a party in the early 1960s she announced, 'I'm going to take a suppository and do not become alarmed at anything that might happen. I will soon become incoherent and leave the room, but let the party continue!' (Israel, p. 303).

† According to the brothel madam Clara Winston, 'Around 1939 everyone was jammin', jumpin'. Wealthy society white folk came up. Best of everybody. Your biggest stars of that time. Vanderbilts, the Goulds, Tallulah's been all over Harlem, that's my darling.' Pop Foster, Detroit Red and many others who were interviewed by Linda Kuehl talk about Tallulah and the wild life she lived.

a confident string of lies. 'Tallulah showed me your letter,' he wrote. 'I think it is scandalous that her sole trip to Harlem should be so misinterpreted. She was sent there with her director, Mr Cukor, to see conditions, as there is a Harlem night-club scene in her present picture. But after her visit it was decided the atmosphere was too vulgar.'

Throughout the 1930s Tallulah and Billie must have often come across each other, but it was in the summer of 1948 that they became close friends and perhaps also lovers.★ Tallulah was performing in Noël Coward's *Private Lives* on Broadway, and Billie was appearing with Count Basie and his Orchestra at the nearby Strand Theater, where in spite of the July and August heatwave, some of the largest audiences that New York theatre had seen in years turned up.†

Tallulah came to the Strand Theater every night of the week. She would sit in the front row, 'as if this was the only show in the world'. After the show she and Billie and the comedian Stump Daddy would go to the White Rose bar to get drunk together. And they'd get Billie's boxer dog Mister drunk as well and would laugh at his gentle confusion.

Because her Cabaret Card had been taken away from her since her time in jail,‡ Billie could no longer sing in New York clubs that held a liquor licence; she had lost her easiest means of earning a living. She was forced to undertake endless tours from one city to the next and for several months Tallulah followed her whenever she could. She was in Hollywood in December 1948 when Billie was arrested after a fight broke out at Billy Berg's, and she was still in Hollywood in January 1949 when Billie was arrested again and charged with possession of opium.

★ As Detroit Red put it, 'Tallulah was a lesbian but she was such a nice person!' In her later years Tallulah tidied up her image and concentrated on men. She paid for the services of a string of young gay men whom she referred to as her 'caddies'. Their duties included squeezing toothpaste onto her toothbrush and spraying her with Chanel No. 5 while she lay in the bath.

† Billie had only come out of jail four months previously and she was sure that people came to see her because of her notoriety and to judge for themselves if she was back on drugs.

‡ She was in the Alderson Federal Reformatory for Women from 28 May 1947 to 16 March 1948.

The circumstances of this second arrest were very dubious, but as a convicted narcotics user and felon, Billie was in serious trouble. She was in a panic, but Tallulah was very supportive and, when Billie threatened suicide, she even paid for a psychiatrist.

Tallulah also took the trouble of contacting J. Edgar Hoover, to see if he might be able to help. He was a family friend as well as Director of the FBI. She opened her letter to him with these words: 'Knowing your true humanitarian spirit, it seemed quite natural . . . to go to the top man. As my Negro Mammy used to say, "When you pray, you pray to God, don't you?"' Tallulah went on to explain the nature of her relationship with Billie and her understanding of the singer's personality.

> I have met Billie Holiday but twice in my life, but I admire her immensely as an artist and feel the most profound compassion for her . . . My intention is not to condone her weaknesses . . . She is essentially a child at heart whose troubles have made her psychologically unable to cope with the world in which she finds herself . . . However guilty she may be, whatever penalties she may be required to pay for her frailties, poor thing, you, I know, did everything within the law, to lighten her burden. Bless you for that.★

The two women never met again. In 1952, Tallulah was paid the vast sum of $30,000 for her ghosted show-business memoir,† which was serialised in thirty American newspapers and in the *Daily Express*. The book was dedicated to Daddy Dearest and, although it was full of boastful

★ As a fellow southerner, Edgar Hoover was a close friend of Tallulah's father. He had a particular hatred of what he saw as the 'subversive' black press and he also pursued a lifelong vendetta against people like Billie. However, he appreciated the letter and replied, 'Your kind comments are greatly appreciated and I trust you will not hesitate to call on me at any time you think I might be of assistance to you.' There is no indication that he did anything on Billie's behalf.

† The book was ghosted by Richard Maney, whose 'arch, florid, literate style' supported the Bankhead legend. It became a bestseller. Israel, p. 290.

eccentricities and coy suggestions of wicked behaviour, it said nothing of Tallulah's early sexual preferences, her fondness for illegal drugs, or her strong connection with Harlem and the jazz world. Her friend Billie Holiday was not mentioned once.

Three years later, when Billie was putting her name to her own ghosted life story, *Lady Sings the Blues*, a copy of the manuscript was sent to all the well-known people who might not want to appear within its pages. Orson Welles, who had been a friend of Billie's when she was in Hollywood in 1942, made no objection, but others were less amenable. As Billie's editor admitted when Linda Kuehl spoke to him, 'everybody vanished' under the real or perceived threat of a libel suit.★

In *Lady Sings the Blues* Billie spoke of Tallulah at some length. She described her as a 'dear friend' who recommended a psychiatrist at a time of trouble, and who sometimes came round to the house to eat spaghetti. Tallulah's response was an immediate warning to the book's editor: 'Darling, if you publish that stuff about me in the Billie Holiday book, I'll sue for every goddamn cent that Doubleday can make.'

Billie responded with a calm and heartfelt letter to Tallulah. 'I thought I was a friend of yours,' she said. 'That's why there's nothing in my book that was unfriendly to you, unkind or libellous . . . Read it again. There's nothing in it to hurt you. Straighten up and fly right, Banky. Nobody's trying to drag you.'†

But Billie never received a reply to her letter, and the 'offensive material' was dutifully removed from the manuscript.

In later years Tallulah suffered from 'several psychotic episodes in which she became very southern and very proud'. She was often heard to complain about how the Negroes

---

★ During the time when Billie and Orson Welles had been seen together a few times in Hollywood, Billie received threatening telephone calls, telling her that she was jeopardising his career. She was also warned that if the relationship continued, she would never be given a chance to appear in pictures (John White, *Billie Holiday: Her Life and Times*, 1987, p. 78).

† Quoted in Ken Vail, *Lady Day's Diary*, 1996.

were 'not what they used to be'. The peace strikes, the sit-downs, the new militancy had made them unacceptable as far as she was concerned. 'I used to think that if I were ever in real trouble, I would run to Harlem for friends and shelter,' she said. 'Now I'd be afraid to go up there alone.'

Tallulah Bankhead died in New York in 1968. Her last discernible words were 'codeine–bourbon'. According to Billie's friend, the dancer Detroit Red, Tallulah's sisters sent her body to Virginia to be buried, 'so Negroes couldn't come to her funeral . . . because she was a friend of Billie's and of all the Negroes in Harlem and her sisters didn't want no Negroes hanging around'.

TWENTY-ONE

James 'Stump' Cross

'This is Stump Daddy talking.'

James 'Stump' Cross was a comedian and tap dancer who worked with his partner Harold 'Stumpy' Cromer. He said that in their comedy routines, 'We never did anything off-colour. I always felt that a good human laugh is better than a guffaw.' Between 1937 and 1945 he often appeared in the same shows as Billie and said, 'From there we never lost contact with each other . . . although after 1942 she and I strayed. I went into the army and she was on heroin.'

Linda Kuehl interviewed 'Stump' in January and June 1972. They met, as she put it, 'in my pad' and obviously got on very well. At one point Stump says, 'But we're gonna get it all, we gonna work on it straight. I'll relate it to you and you'll put it down. I think you're sincere!' So this is Stump talking:

It was 1936 and I just came to New York from Philadelphia. I was a Philadelphia boy. And it was my good fortune to be in front of the Alhambra Grill on 126th and 7th Avenue and there was this cab that had a slide-open roof and this lady was standing up through the roof and smoking a cigarette and looking *so happy!*

At that time there was no cigarette I knew could make you *that* happy!

I said to the cab driver – his name was Billy Wood – 'I'm late, man! I've gotta get to the Cotton Club! The show is in seven minutes!'

So he said, 'Lady, can I take him?'

And the smiling lady with the cigarette said, 'Yeah, you take him! Take him, baby!'

And the cab driver said, 'Come on in, Stump! Lady, this is Stump from the Stump and Stumpy Show! And this is Lady Day, this is Billie Holiday!'

And she looked down and grinned at me with the prettiest smile. Oh, that smile melts you; you gotta go when that smile comes! And she said, 'Hi there, Stump Daddy!' And that was my name to her from then on.

She was at the Hot Cha while I was at the Cotton Club, but then we worked together at the Club Ebony with Count Basie and then at the Strand Theater. I was with her from 'Lock Away My Heart and Throw Away the Key' through to 'That Old Devil Called Love'.

I was one of her boys. One of Lady Chatterley's lovers. She used to say, 'I don't go *anywhere* without Stump Daddy!' And she wouldn't leave until she heard my voice. I was a sort of charm. We were sweethearts in a sense. We loved each other so.

I loved her because of the way she said, 'Good morning, Stump Daddy!' and because of the way she dressed and the way she dragged her fur around. She dragged her minks from Broadway to Kelly's Stables, to the Royal Roost, to Birdland. She wore out more minks than anyone I knew.

Lady was handsome. She strolled through the street and she was such a charm. She had the most charming face; a face that grew and grew into a beautiful thing, and her voice grew with it. Oh, her face, there's none like it! Her face – a sculptor could tell you more – it was such a beautiful, pure little face! A little turned-up nose, beautiful eyes, luscious mouth, very regal chin and neckline. She was a Lady! She was Queen Bess! Her taste started with those little flowers in her hair and all of a sudden as time went by she became wise as to what to wear and how to wear it.

Lady was always part of the band. She was a band singer. She had little melodies* that she'd give to each musician, 'Here you are . . . Here you are . . . Now, come, sing with me!' It was so pretty, like she was sending out sparks. She never scrambled. She never hurried. Ben Webster stands up and goes, 'Bahdooodooo . . . deedoobahdoodende . . . dah!' and she's close to the mike and it's Singing Time! She starts pumping with her right elbow and she'd tap with her left foot, like she was grinding it out and she has those lights on her that go from magenta to pink to green. Going off, she'd nod just to the side with a pretty smile and she walked off regal! The other broads used to come to watch her, to try to steal from her, but they could never get her thing. Oh, to see her eyes when she sang 'You're My Thrill'!

Lady inspired everybody because she had a knack with a lyric. She knew the verses to every song that everybody ever sang! She'd sing anything of *Carmen*, anything that knocked her out. She had no great knowledge of music or reading musical notes. She just knew it! She'd look at a music sheet. Put it down. Walk away. Have a drink. And come back three minutes later and sing the whole thing! She was singing arias, in her style. Between the lyric and the drink, I don't know what happened; it must have come from somewhere. There must have been a Lyric Angel who came down from the clouds and said, 'Here, Lady, you get 'em!'

Lady's favourite tune was always the next song she was going to sing. She loved 'Gloomy Sunday', but she got tired of it; it was so real to her that as she sang it she would *see it* and it would get to her. She loved it,

---

* He calls them 'dribbles'.

but she hated it – Lady being Lady and the things she'd been through. She hadn't been that far south, but she's from Baltimore: the men, the speakeasies, you know . . . With her vivid imagination, when she sings a song like that, the tears come down.

To Count Basie she was William. She'd call him Bill and he'd say, 'Yes, William!'* Louis Armstrong was The Landlord – like he owns jazz and any room he's in, that's jazz! – so he's The Landlord. She'd say, 'Come on, Stump Daddy, let's go see The Landlord!' He would make her day, just to hear him play. And she would interpret what he played on trumpet into her thing. She would do any tune that he did. She said he had more soul than any singer.

She had a beautiful personal touch with people, like they loved her immediately and she loved musicians no end. I don't think Lady ever found a musician she *didn't* love! She always found good in them. And there were so many musicians that loved her. They were playing through their hearts and crying out to Lady! They would be calling to her, through the piano, the trumpet and the trombone.

She had a knack for picking a piano player. She'd say, 'You! You're going to play for me!' And the next recording date, this cat would be there. Like 'A Sailboat in the Moonlight' and the piano did 'ding-a-ling' and she'd just go her way and you'd just play the melody and she's got you in her Lady Day Magic Bag. That little tinge she had, that little whine, it was like an echo in the night from Valhalla.

Behind the pimps and the parasites – like Jimmy Monroe, like John Levy, like all those guys who really robbed her heart – behind all of them there were these virtuoso piano players that loved her secretly. Men like

---

* When he was interviewed, on 3 November 1971, Count Basie said of his relationship with Billie, 'We were tight. Much tighter than that. I loved Billie an awful lot. I loved Billie as far as love could go . . . She'd deliberately try to do something to get me angry. Something silly. Otherwise she was always on the job. Never juicing, always singing, never out of her mind.'

Eddie Heywood,★ who used to cry when she sang. So did Sonny White, but she loved him for playing for her, so it was two-sided.

Sonny White was so beautiful and I think she threw him a curve. He was a little chubby man, a brown, pretty man, a dear boy. He was a cherub. And he loved Lady. He knew all about her life and her thing, but he played for her regardless. I've seen him come off the stage and break down. She'd just sung 'You're My Thrill' or whatever, and Sonny White would walk away and hide in a corner and cry.

Lester Young adored her. He loved Lady like he loved spring, summer, winter and fall and every day that broke at dawn. It was not a love-love thing, it was just a passion. She inspired his playing and he loved being around her so. I don't think she realised that he was deadly in love with her and that he loved her for ever. He'd look at her – the look in his eyes when he played for her! He'd play his whole soul. But he wasn't her type of man.† He wasn't manly. The kind of guys with big Cadillacs, big Packards or whatever, they represented something to Lady. I imagine her father must have been like that. I imagine he was that type of man.

In 1938 it was a Basie time,‡ it was a coke time. Cocaine. Oh goodness, yes! Basie's an avid cokehead. Basie snorts whatever you've got! George Raft and all them used to do it. Happy Dust, it was called, and you'd buy a bottle like that for twenty dollars, and this was great coke. I don't think opium thrilled Lady too much. Opium is a relaxed ritual, when you have nothing to do tomorrow, so today we smoke. She didn't like laying on her side and hugging this thing that smells like burnt

---

★ Pianist, composer and arranger, born 1915 in Atlanta, Georgia, died 1989. He arrived in New York in 1937 and recorded classic sides with Billie from 1943.

† 'She loved the wrong kind of people and they never returned the kind of love she gave because Lady gave her whole being,' Stump said.

‡ 'When Lady was with Basie they snorted, yeah, Basie, Sweets [Edison], Buck [Clayton]. Lester was just a pot man and Johnnie Walker Red or any gin at all' (Stump).

chops, and pretty soon you're in the dream world and you have to cover the doors with wet towels. She dug it. She did it. But she was someone who wanted to get high *fast*.

We were staying up until early in the morning every morning, not leaving one another until we saw that each one got home, and I mean *in bed* got home. Or maybe we'd just continue and stay with each other at Lady's house, or at Lester's, or at Sweets' house, or at my house. There was camaraderie. We'd go to the oddest places – like a corn joint where they'd sell white whisky with orange peel in it: pure alcohol mixed with water and slices of orange that cut into the alcohol. We would go there and sit all night and remember tunes and sing them to each other.

I first met Tallulah in New York, and she loved me and called me The Being. I don't know what this meant, but everyone understood I was The Being. And she'd say, 'Dahling, I'm looking for The Being, not you, not any of you other peasants', and I would come out and kiss and hug. And then Tallulah, Lady and I were bosom-buddies. You couldn't separate us, except for the job. Tallulah came to the Ebony★ every night, just to see us. And then we opened at the Strand with Count Basie and she used to come and sit in the front row, centre, as if this were the only show in the world.

Tallulah and Lady were like sisters. Lady called her Lula. They used to carry me piggyback.

Tallulah would come thundering down the stoop and she'd say, 'Stump, dahling, will you please announce me!'

I'd say, 'Miss Day! Here comes Talluh!'

Lady would say, 'Lula! Come here, Lula!' in her cute little voice, because she sang as she talked and her voice was always a melody.

Tallulah would come and say, 'Next week, dahlings,

★ Club Ebony was set up by Billie's manager/boyfriend John Levy, and because he had a special relationship with the New York police, it was the only licensed club in the city where she could sing *without* her Cabaret Card.

it's Connecticut!' And we were off to her house just outside Greenwich on Long Island. And we would paint the little room downstairs. Tallulah would say, 'I think it should be green this week!' and the three of us would paint the room green.

Or we'd go to the White Rose bar at 52nd and 7th Street, and there they had a chair saved especially for Lady. No one sat in that seat! It was Lady's seat. Tallulah would tell her, 'Sit there, Lady!' And she had such a grand way of sitting at the bar, dead-centre, surveying it all.

Tallulah and I got Lady's boxer dog Mister drunk, and then Basie's little white Pekinese whipped Mister because he was too high to fight. Mister was a comfortable Boxer, a gentle Boxer. Mister was the best hangout dog on Earth. He didn't believe in playing, and all he believed in was Lady. He would sit backstage where he could hear Lady's voice and, as long as he could hear her voice, he was happy. Mister was a junkie, he was always high, Lady would shoot him up.★ The bartenders would feed him while he was sitting at the bar, or maybe Lady would leave him in the dressing room, which he detested. But he couldn't do anything about it and so he would wait patiently until she got back and, when he hears her footsteps, he'd get up and look at her. Oh, he was a phenomenal dog! He was never on a leash, not ever.

In 1942 we were in Hollywood together. Lady was in between romances. She had just left Jimmy Monroe and I think John Levy was on the way, but not completely, and she was having herself a wonderful time. I was doing *Ship Ahoy!* with Frank Sinatra and Eleanor Powell, she was touring with Jimmy Dorsey and Tommy Dorsey, and Duke Ellington had just put

★ 'Lady had this thing, anxiety, like, "Make 'em wait. I'm Lady, I'm from Baltimore, Green Willow Street, and if they can't wait for fifteen minutes" . . . and all the time she's trying to find a vein and that's what makes her late. And they're trying to stuff things up her nose.'

on the *Jump for Joy* musical.★ We were lovers then, true lovers. We had the best love affair in California. One night there was an earthquake, and as the earth shook, I told Lady to stand between the doors to feel it and she said, 'Freaky, freaky, Stump Daddy!'

In Hollywood we lived in Clark Annex across the street from the Clark Hotel. Lena Horne lived on the top, Lady and I lived at the bottom, and Humphrey Bogart lived on one side and Orson Welles lived on the other side. Orson Welles would come every night to see *Jump for Joy* and he would go down on one knee before Duke Ellington. He was our air-raid warden in the street and Humphrey Bogart was our boy, he was the thing.

Everyone in Hollywood invited Lady: Lana Turner, Ava Gardner, the group, the would-be singers. Ava tried her darnedest to get Lady to sing in *Showboat*, but Lady thought it would be a waste of time.

My rapport did not go as far as John Levy, not in any direction. John Levy was a pimp, a hustling man, an evil-doer. He was self-living, with no sense of anyone around him. It was all *his* world, and you were welcome just so long as you were serving him. Lady was being treated so wrong by him and she was loving it at the same time. She would dissipate herself because he wasn't there to take care of her, as he should have been. He was off at the racetrack, or with racing people, or with his ex-women.

John Levy detested Tallulah with a purple passion, and Tallulah loathed John Levy. She loathed any man around Lady Day, because she can only take men like little pawns and put them there and put them there. Tallulah would never say hello to John Levy, or even acknowledge that he was in the room.

★ An all-black musical, 'a sun-tanned revue-sical', in which there was to be 'no shuffling, no dialect, no blackface comedy'. Ellington said it was an attempt to give 'an American audience entertainment without compromising the dignity of the Negro people'. Ellington insisted to the comics that they go on stage without blacking-up and they 'came offstage smiling and with tears running down their cheeks' (Ward and Burns, pp. 295–6).

At Billy Berg's, John Levy told Tallulah she can't be backstage.

I said, 'Now wait a minute, John, you've got this out of proportion!'

He said, 'She is not to be backstage. This is a show here, Lady, and I don't want Tallulah back here!'

Tallulah said to me, 'Stump dahling, I'll be in the front row, waiting as you come on. Come and kiss me and I'll see you after the show.' And to John Levy she said, 'You, my good man, are a bloodsucker!' And she slammed the door right in his face.

And all the chorus girls looked at him and he was made so small, and he walked away slowly. And we died, we died of laughing. And Lady laughed until she cried, she was so happy. You see, she realised these things, but she could do nothing when a man talked his magic to her. She was a romantic. She was a very romantic lady, and those men would tell her beautiful stories about who she *really* was and what she'd be and how grand she was. It was like telling a bedtime story to a little girl, and she loved it, because she reached out for love.

Joe Glaser★ was the same type as John Levy. A pimp. I don't think those two had a clean thought towards anybody; it was always about using you, squeezing you like a lemon, wringing you dry. I don't care if Joe Glaser had eight, nine, ten baths a day, he was still unclean – to me anyway. There are nice pimps, but these two were horrible little vermin. They managed because they had a strong arm and a gift of the gab. And Joe Glaser had no problems. He had gangster connections. The word was out, 'Don't meddle with Joe Glaser.' He had an office in Chicago, one in Miami, one in California; so the whole territory was covered with ex-Chicago boys.

★ Nat Nazarro (Stump's agent, who represented comedians and actors) and Joe Glaser 'were bullies who controlled a whole dynasty of black actors and singers and band leaders . . . You're accumulating money, but you're not counting. They tell you a beautiful story, beautiful pipe dreams, and they're raking it in with your talent.' Glaser, who represented Louis Armstrong, became Billie's agent in 1936.

There wasn't any humour between Lady and Joe
Glaser. He was very mild and meek with her, he'd got
to handle her with kid gloves. He couldn't mess around
with her, he couldn't afford to. He'd say in his very
high voice, 'Gee, Billie, that was wonderful!' And he'd
kiss her on the cheek. She'd say, 'Thank you', and she'd
go about her business or to a pusher or to a stagehand
or to an elevator guy, because she liked these kind of
people.

Chin Fu, the chef of the kitchen at the Onyx Club,
was her favourite and he was a sweetheart and a sweet
little man. He made a whole Chinese thing for her one
time. The whole dinner thing, as he would do in China
or Peking or whatever, and nothing like he'd do ordinary.★ And all the doormen loved her, the whole fleet
of them from Kelly's Stables clear down the Street.
They'd hold the shit for her that somebody gave them
and they'd come backstage and say, 'Hey, Lady, somebody left something for you.' Her favourite doorman
was Chick, a big, heavy-set fellow and very jovial, and
whenever he had a break he'd come in and she'd always
buy him a drink and he'd drink with us and talk with
us. The gay boys, they loved her, they cherished her,
and if someone stole her squirrel mink or one of her
coats, we'd have it back to her in ten minutes. She was
a wonderful mixer; she could cut anybody on mixing
because she could mix with all sorts of elements, all
sorts of people. She was like Count Basie and Duke
Ellington. They were lowly-born people who rose above
all this thing into a beautiful niche that they cut out
for themselves, and there's Lady and Count Basie and
Duke Ellington and they stood in that little niche, with
elegance.

★ Stump Daddy said that Chin Fu 'also got the opium for Lady's husband',
Jimmy Monroe.

TWENTY-TWO

Greer Johnson

'Baby, will you hold this for me?'

Greer Johnson arrived in New York in 1943. He was twenty-three years old and, according to his own account, 'very young, very green, very southern and very stupid'. He got a job in public relations, which he hated, and then did some work as a theatrical press agent. He later became a critic of classical music and dance. He died in Los Angeles in the late 1970s, killed by a car that mounted the pavement where he was standing, waiting for the 'Walk now' traffic sign to tell him it was safe to cross the road.★

When Linda Kuehl turned up at Greer Johnson's New York apartment on West 46th Street, he was playing one of Billie's records. He explained that he had not put the record on especially for the interview; he listened to Billie frequently, because he always heard new things every time. He said he

---

★ The account of the sudden end of Greer Johnson's 'neat, clerkly life' appears in Elizabeth Hardwick's book *Sleepless Nights* (1979), Part Three, pp. 24–39. The two were childhood friends who lived together for a while in New York. She wrote about her '*mariage blanc*' relationship with this 'red-cheeked homosexual . . . whose holy habits ruined his sex life'. She also described the various meetings the two of them had with Billie Holiday. She provided a very different interpretation of Billie's personality and circumstances from the one offered by Greer Johnson when he was interviewed by Linda Kuehl in August 1971.

was particularly fond of the late recordings when she was 'going into a kind of freedom . . . and singing the ultimate possibility in the jazz lyric'.

He'd also hunted out two photographs of Billie: one of her as a baby, which Sadie had given to him, and the other a beautiful portrait study, which was part of the famous series made by the society photographer Robin Carsons in 1946. Greer Johnson had organised that session and so he was able to choose a picture for himself.

Another unexpected memento from the past that he'd found was a rather battered tape recording of Billie singing 'Oh Come, All Ye Faithful'. Apparently one Christmas she and Sonny White had gone to a studio on 6th Avenue where you could walk in and pay a fee and make your own recording – and that's what they had done. The quality of the tape was bad and you could hear that she was very drunk. He said he would play that later when he and Linda had finished talking.

It was clear that Greer Johnson was already quite drunk when the interview started. He kept repeating himself and changing and adapting the same story every time it occurred to him again. He would suddenly get angry and then forget the cause of his anger and drift off into a vague nostalgia. He said that the disappointments of his own life had taught him a compassion that he did not know 'in those early sentimental days, when I was awfully young and awfully everything else', because 'When you are young you don't understand people's pains and commitments and addictions . . . but I hope I understand now.'

He was born in Lexington, Kentucky. According to Elizabeth Hardwick, he was terrified of his businessman father, who was a 'large, fair man in black clothes' and stiff-collared white shirts. He told her the story of how, as a two-year-old, he had once 'toddled' into his father's office to be confronted by this huge apparition of masculine authority sitting behind a roll-top desk. He was so terrified that he screamed. 'I screamed like the girl I was,' he said.

The town of Lexington had its own racecourse and there

was a dance hall called Joyland Park out in the open fields,
beyond the final perimeter of the houses. In *Sleepless Nights*
Elizabeth Hardwick described how the 'great bands' would
arrive at Joyland Park in the summer: 'Ellington, Louis
Armstrong, Chick Webb, sometimes for a Friday and Saturday
or merely for one night. When I speak of the great bands
it must not be taken to mean that we thought of them as
such. No, they were part of the summer nights and the hot
dog stands, the fetid swimming pool heavy with chlorine,
the screaming roller coaster, the old rain-splintered picnic
tables, the broken iron swings. And the bands were also part
of Southern drunkenness, couples drinking Coke and whisky,
vomiting, being unfaithful, lovelorn, frantic. The black musicians, with their cumbersome instruments, their tuxedos, were
simply there to beat out time for the stumbling, cuddling
fox-trotting of the period.'

The musicians would arrive in their laden buses and fill
the air with music before disappearing into the landscape,
bound for some other southern town. Most of the white
audiences were only aware of the music as a noisy back-
drop, or as Elizabeth Hardwick put it, 'something inevitable,
effortlessly pushing up from the common soil'. But for the
young Greer Johnson, it was different. He said that when he
first heard jazz, he immediately felt at home with it.*

He already had a copy of Billie Holiday singing 'Strange
Fruit', and he began to collect all the jazz records he could
find. He remembered going into Main Records Company
on Main Street and ordering everything that was available
on the old Okeh and Vocalion labels. The man in the shop
gave him a very quizzical look, because why would a white
boy from a good southern family want to listen to stuff like
that?

When Greer Johnson moved to New York, he and
Elizabeth Hardwick shared rooms in the Hotel Schuyler on
45th Street. She said the Hotel Schuyler was 'more than a
little sleazy and a great deal of sleazy life went on there'. It

---

* Elizabeth Hardwick said he had 'a passion for jazz or maybe for blackness,
even though he was hesitant with black men'.

was also very dirty and was occupied by a shifting population of residents who seemed to have been stranded there
by mistake and never got round to leaving.

In the interview, Greer Johnson spoke a great deal about
Elizabeth Hardwick and the people they met together and
the places they went to. He described her as 'a kind of
delicate-looking blonde', but said nothing about their relationship, beyond implying that it was amicable. Elizabeth
Hardwick was much more outspoken; according to her, the
friendship 'was a violent one and we were as obsessive, critical, jealous and cruel as any couple'. She hated what she called
Greer Johnson's 'coercive neatness' and despised his habit of
carefully laying out his suit each night, in preparation for going
to work the following morning. She also despised his obsessive need to brush his 'perfect teeth' after dinner, no matter
where they were or what else was happening. He shared his
passion for jazz with her, but even that was tainted by 'the
methodical, intense, dogmatic anxiety of his nature'.

The gay young man and his beautiful blonde companion
lived very close to 52nd Street, which, as Greer Johnson said,
'at that time was very much a jazz street and you simply
went from club to club. You could buy a seventy-five-cent
beer and stand at the bar for a very long time, and hear a
great number of great performers without being bothered.'

One night they were at the Onyx Club with Elizabeth
Hardwick's soldier boyfriend, George Jeston, and Billie
Holiday was the main attraction. According to Greer Johnson,
she looked 'incredibly beautiful and very much fixed up in
a long gown and make-up, the famous gardenias in her hair'.
Looking back on that same first impression, Elizabeth
Hardwick described Billie as 'large, brilliantly beautiful, fat'.*

---

* Elizabeth Hardwick went on to say: 'She seemed for this moment that never
again returned to be almost a matron, someone real and sensible who carried
money to the bank, signed papers, had curtains made to match, dresses hung
and shoes in pairs, gold and silver, black and white, ready. What a strange,
betraying apparition that was, madness, because never was any woman less a
wife or mother, less attached; not even a daughter could she easily appear to
be. Little called to mind the pitiful sweetness of a young girl. No, she was
glittering, sombre and solitary, although of course never alone, never. Stately,
sinister and absolutely determined.'

During the interval Billie swept down the steps from the tiny bandstand and stood close to them at the bar. She ordered drinks, taking the money out of a little jewelled coin purse. Greer Johnson longed to meet her, but was too overawed to speak to her himself. He persuaded George Jeston to introduce their party. 'Not knowing Billie, I thought she would be impressed by the uniform because there was a war on.'

Billie's response was polite, formal and non-committal. Elizabeth Hardwick told her that she had heard her singing some years ago at the Joyland in Lexington. All she got as a reply was, 'Yeah, I remember your town.'

But then Billie turned to Greer Johnson. She looked him in the eye and decided straight away that she liked the person she saw there. Just at that moment she was being called back to the stage. 'Ladies and gentlemen,' said the Master of Ceremonies, 'I give you – Miss Billie Holiday!' As she got ready to go, she presented her little jewelled purse to Greer Johnson and said, 'Baby, will you hold this for me?' And of course he was glad to. As he said in the interview, 'You know, I don't know what was in that coin purse. It could have been twenty thousand dollars, or two dollars, or anything else . . . At this time, mind you, I knew nothing about Billie or drugs, or drink, or her habits, except that I was completely and totally slain by her.'

When she had finished the set, she returned to the bar and told him she had been invited to the Westside to sing and to initiate some sort of civic project. She asked Greer Johnson if he would escort her.★ It was the start of a friendship that lasted until her death. As Greer Johnson said, 'From that point on, Billie never failed to trust me or to ask me

★ He said that on this first occasion the police warned him against being involved with Billie, and later he was often warned and threatened when he was in her company. He did his best to fight for her and, when she was subjected to racial abuse at the Plantation Club in St Louis, he wrote an article for the Walter Winchell column, in which he complained about how 'in the city which gave jazz to the world, an outstanding figure of the jazz world should be ridiculed for the colour of her skin'. A few days before this incident, a member of Benny Carter's band was severely injured in the same club, from a blow to his head with a pistol.

any time for whatever she wanted, nor did I fail to try to give it to her.' He followed her as well as he could, through the drugs★ and the drinking, the courtroom trials and the imprisonment, the acclaimed performances at Carnegie Hall and Town Hall, as well as the often chaotic appearances at dingy little nightclubs outside the city.

He never doubted that Billie was a 'musician of enormous importance' and 'way ahead' of everyone else. He felt it was unfair to condemn her as a victim of the drug culture, as if she was the only one taking drugs at that time. And he said there was nothing special about her sexual behaviour, either; everyone was doing the things she did. No, the problem was her huge talent; it isolated her. 'I really think she was destroyed by the enormity of her gift, which she did not know how to develop, where to place it; nor was there anybody to receive it.' He felt it was terrible that even now, in 1971, 'As far as I know, and I've seen any number of lists of Great Black Women, I have never seen her name on that list.'

Greer Johnson remembered how, in the early 1940s, Billie had asked him to take her to a dance performance by Katherine Dunham at the Martin Beck Theater on Broadway. 'I want to know what the Negroes are doing, Baby. Will you take me?' she said. And so he bought two tickets for the opening night.

He remembered that she dressed very demurely for the occasion, wearing a sweater and skirt with a turbaned hat and glinting, hooped brass earrings. They were surrounded by an all-white audience, and throughout the first part of the show people kept turning their heads to stare at her. During the intermission he went to get her a drink and, when he gave it to her, her hands were trembling.

'Everybody's looking at us,' she said.

He tried to reassure her. 'No, Billie, everybody is looking at *you*! And for good reason, because you're so wonderful to look at!'

★ He said, 'She was completely open with me about what she was taking. I saw her roll up a dollar bill and sniff cocaine, shooting heroin, chain-smoking marijuana. She never hid it from me.'

'It's because everyone is saying, Who is *that woman*, with that white boy!'

'No, they're not! That's not it!'

After the show was over, Billie took her friend to a very black club in the upper reaches of Harlem, where his was the only white face. Everyone greeted Billie and stared at him. They sat there until Greer Johnson was so tired he could scarcely keep his eyes open. Suddenly Billie said to him, 'OK, Baby!' and she took his hand and led him out onto the street where she hailed a cab. She gave the cab driver some money and told him, 'You take this man back to his hotel and don't stop till you get there!'

Greer Johnson sometimes used to visit Billie in the apartment she shared with her mother above the Braddock Hotel on 99th Street. He never stayed overnight, because 'they didn't ask me and I'd have been afraid at that time', but he did feel that once he was inside the door, he was 'family'. He met Sadie there about three times and she was always busy cooking or 'running around the apartment'. He considered her to be a 'relatively stupid, sad little woman who had been caught in a relationship and it produced a Phoenix and she didn't know what to do with a Phoenix'. And he said, 'At no time did I have any feeling from Sadie that she had any inkling whatsoever of the greatness of her daughter. I didn't think Sadie had any feelings for Billie at all.'

Billie's attitude towards her mother was very ambivalent and 'a disturbing thing to watch really', because she would be tender and caring one moment and abrupt and aggressive the next. To illustrate this ambivalence, Greer Johnson described meeting Billie at her mother's funeral. He had gone there with a 'charming and lovely boy' called Frank Harriott, who wrote articles for *PM*.* Billie arrived in a limousine and, when the Mass was over, they all went to the

---

* Frank Harriott wanted to write a novel about Billie. Greer Johnson arranged an interview at the Braddock Hotel, which became an article called 'The Hard Life of Billie Holiday'. He said the article was 'full of naïveté, which was Harriott's, not mine. It caused a great deal of comment at the time and he got a contract for a novel out of it. He wrote two chapters and then died.'

burial plot. 'I stood with them while they threw flowers into the grave, or whatever it is they do during the thing. After that we all went to a bar in Queens. She showed very little emotion except, "Let's have a drink!" '* With hindsight, Greer Johnson said he could understand such apparent coldness because 'I don't think whatever Billie felt, she would have shown.' He said he had the same sort of emotional confusion in relation to his own mother, who was currently in hospital and gravely ill. He thought he was fond of her, but if someone contacted him on the phone and told him she was about to die, he might do nothing more than pour himself another drink.

He remembered the time when he and Elizabeth Hardwick were invited to a sit-down dinner at Billie's, somewhere else in Harlem. They arrived at six-thirty or seven, to find the house partially boarded up with sheets of corrugated iron. A sign fixed next to the front door explained that the property had been raided for drugs and no one was to enter. A white policeman was standing on guard by the door.

'We're going in here. We have a dinner date with Miss Holiday.'

'This is raided property! The best thing for you is to turn round and go back downtown!'

'We are not here to buy drugs, or get drugs, or sell drugs. So, if you don't mind, we have a dinner date with Miss Holiday!'

Reluctantly the policeman agreed to let them in.† Dinner was not yet ready because their hostess was busy curling her hair with hot tongs, and anyway she always enjoyed the prerogative of lateness. One of her own songs was playing on a gramophone and her boyfriend, the trumpeter Joe Guy,

---

* Elizabeth Hardwick was also at Sadie's funeral. She wrote, 'At last [Billie] arrived, ferociously appropriate in a black turban . . . Sadie and Billie Holiday were a violation, a rift in the statistics of life. The great singer was one of those for whom the word *changeling* was invented.'

† Elizabeth Hardwick wrote, 'Our frozen alarm and fascination carried us into the void of the dead tenement. The house was under a police ban and when we entered, whispering her name, the policeman stared at us with furious incredulity.'

and his brother were there among the cigarette smoke and the shaded lamps and the bottles of liquor. Eventually they were served braised meat with onions and rice, and Greer Johnson said they had the 'most fabulous dinner you could imagine'.★

In return Billie said, 'Baby, you never have me to dinner!' and asked to be invited to the Hotel Schuyler. A date was made and Greer Johnson and Elizabeth Hardwick had to wait outside on the street for her, 'just to make sure she was not in any way embarrassed or insulted'.

Billie arrived with the bass player John Simmons. He had been a junkie for years and some people said he was the one who first introduced her to heroin. Greer Johnson didn't like John Simmons at all, because he kept making harsh jokes about Billie's desire to be in the company of white people in a white neighbourhood. He mocked her for straightening her hair and putting on pale make-up to lighten the tone of her skin, as if she wanted people to think she was white. Billie ignored his taunts. Among the things she wanted to listen to that night was her own recording of a Gershwin song called 'Things Are Looking Up'. She said she thought it was the best thing she had ever done.†

In Greer Johnson's opinion, Billie was 'extremely bright, bright and sharp. She was as sharp and intelligent a woman as I have ever known, and I have known some very intelligent men and women. Nothing escaped her ever, except at those times when she was so knocked out, which she often

---

★ Elizabeth Hardwick described the evening: '[Billie] filled even a black hotel room with stinging, demonic weight . . . She was living with a trumpet player . . . He was as thin as a stick and his lovely, round light face, with frightened, shiny, round eyes, looked like a sacrifice impaled upon the stalk of his neck.'

† Elizabeth Hardwick also described this same evening: 'Once she came to see us in the Hotel Schuyler, accompanied by someone. We sat there in the neat squalor and there was nothing to do and nothing to say and she did not wish to eat. In the anxious gap, I felt the deepest melancholy in her black eyes, an abyss into which every question had fallen without an answer. She died in misery from the erosions and poisons of her fervent, felonious narcotism.' Greer Johnson had a photograph of Elizabeth and himself in a nightclub looking 'obviously high', with Billie and Joe Guy and 'other strange Mafia-type people'.

was, that she wasn't interested. Then she was asleep, but that's true of anybody, right?'*

For his part, Greer Johnson was determined to give Billie status and dignity. He wanted her to be treated like Marlene Dietrich or Lotte Lenya, singers who were increasingly able to reveal their humanity and their frailty in their songs. He felt her voice was the perfect vehicle for singing arrangements of the Schubert and Schumann song cycles. On one occasion he arranged for her to meet the harpsichordist Ralph Kirkpatrick,† who took her to listen to Bach's Partitas being played by Wanda Landowska. Greer Johnson said that when he heard about this, 'I must say I did a double-take; the picture of Billie together with little, funny, almost bent-over Wanda . . . I asked Billie, "What did you think of her?" And she said, "Well, all I know is those little hands sure ran up and down the keyboard like a bitch."'

In 1946, Greer Johnson told Billie he thought 'It was time for a jazz artist to do a recital the way anybody in classical music does a recital.' She liked the idea and so he organised Lady's Town Hall Concert. Together with a friend called Robert Snyder, he 'put up every cent of the front money', planned the programme, sent out 3,500 flyers and invited every music critic he could think of to attend. The concert

---

* This assessment is dismissed out of hand by Donald Clarke, who says in his biography *Wishing on the Moon* that Johnson was 'obviously prejudiced, he was clearly crazy about her'. And yet Clarke accepts the judgement of John Simmons, who was very damning of Billie in the interview he gave. This is in spite of Linda Kuehl's description of meeting John Simmons in Los Angeles, 'living with his mother . . . teeth missing, greyed, sleeping away much of the day, although still quite electric in his understated way and attractive. Undoubtedly John, like most men, had more trouble with Billie than suited his image and had to prove himself as a male and as a musician when he was with her, and we must read between the lines. She was the instant artistic legend and she was a provocateur with men and stronger than most of them.'

† Greer Johnson describes Kirkpatrick as 'a classical music critic, and in my opinion the greatest living harpsichordist'. In a separate interview Kirkpatrick said Billie came to his apartment in 1943, and 'While she put away the better part of a bottle of rum, I played Bach for her. Her face registered everything; no manifestation of the music seemed to escape her. I am not sure if she knew who Bach was, but I could have used her as an infinitely sensitive precision instrument to monitor my performance of the G-minor English Suite, using the subtle variations of expression on her face to show me with uncanny infallibility what was coming off and what was not.'

was scheduled for five-thirty and he had to get Billie ready a full hour and a half before, which wasn't easy. On the way to the Town Hall, she suddenly decided she needed another dress, so they stopped off at a 'not particularly elegant dress shop' called W. R. Burnett and he waited while she chose what she wanted. He said he was hysterical with worry when they finally arrived at the Town Hall, but still she was just on time.

The performance was a success; they had to turn a thousand people away and could have done the concert three times over. Greer Johnson said the audience was extremely polyglot and very attentive. 'I don't think any jazz artist ever had such a reception.' Billie obviously enjoyed the formality of the occasion and liked the idea of 'something orderly and meaningful and being billed as America's Jazz Artist'. 'She sang with more apparent pleasure and ease than on 52nd Street,' said one reviewer. 'Her dignified bearing and her wonderful poise helped to keep the large, quiet, intelligent audience enthralled,' said another.[*]

Greer Johnson was also determined to get Billie photographed by the society photographer Robin Carsons, who was in his opinion 'the best man in the business', someone who would be able to capture her serious qualities as an artist. Robin Carsons said there was nothing he would 'rather do than take pictures of her' and she agreed to pay for the cost of a session. And so, on a cold autumn afternoon they arrived at Carson's apartment.[†] A very prim New England secretary called Miss Spencer was there to let them in. A fire was burning in the grate and liquor began to flow. Billie had brought several suitcases filled with dresses and make-up, and a 'pretty little singer' called Ann Cornell had come along to help her change from one outfit to the next.

The secretary became increasingly nervous because they began to run so far over time that the next client had to be

---

[*] John Hammond and Leonard Feather. Quoted in Clarke, p. 242.
[†] Elizabeth Hardwick said she came along to the session, but Greer Johnson doesn't mention her as being present.

turned away. But still the hours went by, and everyone was laughing and joking and Billie was relaxed and beautiful. Robin Carsons was keen to do her justice and, although he had taken numerous pictures, he still felt he hadn't got the image he was seeking. He said, 'Now look, I've got some good shots, but they tend to be conventional and they tend to be pretty, but this is not all I want from this woman. There must be some way to get what I feel about her.'

Billie had meanwhile changed into a black sequined dress and had a bunch of artificial gardenias pinned to the side of her head, and she was 'feeling absolutely marvellous'. Greer Johnson suggested that she go over by the fireplace and sing 'Strange Fruit'. At first she said she couldn't possibly – just like that, with no musical accompaniment – but then she agreed to do it. She sang a cappella and Robin Carson's camera never stopped. Later she chose four prints, and Greer Johnson was able to have one for himself.

He remembered how once, towards the end of her life, he came into Billie's dressing room and she was very drunk and depressed, and she tripped and fell on the floor and burst into tears. 'Baby, fuck it! I've had enough!' she said. 'Honest to Christ, I'm never going to sing again no more!'

'What the hell do you think you can do if you don't sing?' he asked her.

'I don't give a fuck!'

'Fine! And then what will you do, Billie?'

And she got up off her knees, dusted off her dress, smiled a blurred alcoholic's smile and muttered, 'I'll sing again!'

And Greer Johnson said, 'You're damn right you will!'

TWENTY-THREE

Jimmy Rowles

'Oh, I loved her! Oh, how I loved her!'

Jimmy Rowles had to get himself ready for this interview. He had to get himself a couple of drinks, because if he is going to talk about Lady Day, he is going to need to feel good.

A few years ago he was disgusted with a lot of things. He was taking drugs and drinking heavily; he needed a pint of gin or vodka in the morning, just to find the energy to get out of bed and get started. He used to sit on the floor in the middle of the living-room and he'd put on the record *Lady in Satin*, which Billie made towards the end of her life.

He'd put on the record and sit there, and the full orchestra with all those strings would be playing, and her familiar voice would soak into him and he'd pray with all his heart that she'd come back and sing – just for one day.

'One day, one day, it would be nice!' he says. She could come to sing at the Forum Theater in Hollywood and he would make sure he got a good ticket for the show and he would be right there, close to the stage, watching her every movement, luxuriating in her sound, being happy again. 'I knew it wouldn't come through, but I used to pray anyway. And sit and curse and carry on. Funny thing, man!'

As Jimmy Rowles speaks about Billie, it's as if she has stepped silently into the room where he and Linda Kuehl are sitting, the tape recorder catching his words.* It's as if Billie is standing there right in front of him and watching him, a milk glass full of gin in her hand and the same wistful smile on her face, which has hardly changed since the first photograph of her was taken when she was four or five years old.

And as Jimmy Rowles speaks, you begin to understand that he really did love to be close to this woman, to be part of her world, under her spell. He says, 'I remember her turning around and looking and laughing, and maybe you'd play some tune and she'd hug you and say something like "I love you!" And if she said "I love you!", boy, you heard it! She used to growl it out! . . . And she liked to have you tell her you loved her. Of course I told her! I told her all the time! Everybody used to tell her. You couldn't help it! She'd do something and you'd have to say, "Oh Jesus Christ, how I love your ass!" She'd say something, do something, sing something, and all over the place people would be saying, "How I love her!" It just came out of people.'

Jimmy goes back to when he first met Billie, in Hollywood in May 1942. He was a young white boy, fresh from college and 'still green, but starting in on getting a little darker'. He was playing piano in the Lee and Lester Young Band† when he heard that Billie was coming to work with them at Billy Berg's Trouville club. He couldn't believe it. He couldn't wait for her to arrive.

And suddenly there she was. Jimmy says, 'I was in awe of her. When I first met that girl, she was one of the most

---

* Jimmy Rowles was born in 1918 and died in 1996. An obituary by John Fordham in the *Guardian* described him as 'a subtle, laconic and all-but-psychic pianist, who elevated the art of creative jazz accompaniment to the status of a miniaturist wonder of the world'. Linda Kuehl interviewed him on 23 August 1971, at the Montecito Hotel, Hollywood.

† The band leader was Lester's brother Lee (short for Leonides). He played drums and, according to Jimmy Rowles, 'He speeds something terrible. He'll start out slow and wind up in a horse race. And that was a drag because if he had been any kind of drummer we would have had some hell of a band. Nobody ever said a word about it.'

beautiful women I had ever seen. She was big, but she didn't seem big. She was just strong, you know. Her skin was like satin, like the tune "Satin Doll". Her skin was flawless. And she was graceful. Watching her was like watching a dream walk through the room. Even if she was jumping around with slacks on.'

The band used to rehearse together every morning and she came to every rehearsal and he got to know her style. 'She liked pure harmony; she didn't want to hear anything that would distract. She would stray ahead with her intonation and if you played something atonal like a chord, and threw it at her all of a sudden, she'd say, "Don't *do that*! Don't play that fucking chord! I can't hear my note!"'

But it was Billie's sexuality that most impressed Jimmy Rowles, and it was her sexuality that he keeps referring to all through the interview. He says, 'I wouldn't know anything about her sex life. Whatever she wanted to do was all right with me . . . But sex had a lot to do with it, because she was a sexy singer. She sang from her crotch. You bet she had the greatest crotch in life. Now that I look back, I'm sorry I missed it.'★

Billie never had female dressers or make-up girls to help her get ready for a show; she just liked to be there together with the band, joking, drinking, smoking, putting on her make-up, while all those men were milling around her. 'Lady Day was like one of the cats,' says Jimmy Rowles. 'She had no complexes, no personality problems. She was open from the beginning. She was always the same.'

Very often she'd be naked, and at that time she had her hair dyed red and her pubic hair dyed red as well.† 'And she'd just stand there with just a pair of shoes on, and it got

---

★ Jimmy Rowles also had his own theory on Billie's sexuality. 'She's a masochist. She digs punishment. She was unfortunate enough to be mentally arranged so she had to have a cat that beat the shit out of her three times a week, to keep her happy.'

† Arthur Herzog remembered coming to see Billie after a show and she ran around to embrace him, even though she didn't have a thing on. 'The maid looked horrified and Billie said, "Oh, he sees me like this all the time!"' Elizabeth Hardwick, writing about that same period of time, said, 'Sometimes she dyed her hair red and the curls lay flat against her skull, like dried blood.'

so that I loved her all the more because she was so gorgeous, beautiful . . . and every night I saw her body, every inch of her body.' When she was in the dressing room she'd often call Jimmy Rowles over and say something like, 'I want the chords to this tune, I want to sing this tune', and he'd scribble down the chords and 'whatever she wanted to sing, we had to make sure we knew it.'

When Jimmy met her, Billie still hadn't started on heroin, so she was just smoking reefers and drinking gin. Jimmy thought she was probably more happy than she had ever been, or ever would be again, because things were going so well and on top of that she was working with Lester Young. Jimmy knew that when Lester played for her 'She felt as if she was in her mother's arms; she was always happy when Lester was playing for her because of what he did for her, because he was there with her. The two of them were perfectly matched. They belonged together.'

At first Jimmy presumed that Billie had come to Hollywood 'to fuck Lester',★ but a couple of days after Billie arrived, she moved in with the other tenor player, 'Bumps' Mayer. He was 'very even-minded, relaxed, nice, never any trouble unless things got real mean and then . . . he might kill somebody. He could take care of himself, that's for sure. He was just a big strong bull, a docile bull. He had the deepest voice you ever heard, a down-in-here voice, and it was beautiful to hear him talk. He never got mad and they got along well together. He handled her very nicely.'

Jimmy Rowles remembers the first time he spoke to Billie on her own. It was about a week after she'd arrived in Hollywood and they had just finished rehearsing. He was sitting at the end of the bar and he saw her come in. He called to her, 'Lady, can I buy you a taste?'

'So she sits down beside me. I bought her gin and Coke. Can you imagine drinking that shit? I didn't know what to talk to her about, but I remembered a tenor player called

---

★ In fact Lester Young was happily married to his Italian wife, Mary. Jimmy Rowles described her as 'a small dark girl who he called his Teddy Bear'.

Dick Wilson, and for some funny reason I asked her about Dick Wilson.'

'She put her drink down. She asked me, did I ever know Dick Wilson? And she said, "I'm going to tell you something. I was going with Freddie Green and I was true to that motherfucker. But every time I saw Dick Wilson, I just had to take him out and fuck him!"'

Jimmy Rowles was bowled over. 'She just about wiped me out. I couldn't believe that chick! The first time I had heard anything come out from a chick like that! Crazy chick! She had me then. What can you do after that? You have to love her!'

He was also fascinated by Billie's relationship with Lester Young and tried to understand whatever it was that bound the two of them together.* 'The way he and Lady Day got along was really strange. They'd go together like that praying mantis that devours the old man when they're through making it. That's my own image for them. He was a weird guy anyway. If there ever was a unique individual, this man was it! And his language! You couldn't understand him unless you worked with him for three months.† . . . Lady was never all over him, like always sitting together. She went her way, he went his. But she'd say, "Well, Pres! I can smell him! I know he's here and so it's good!"'

Jimmy Rowles would watch Billie come out of her dressing room after a show was over, 'And she's rough, and I mean rough!' And then Lester would appear from behind a pillar, pigeon-toed, with his mincing walk and his high whispery voice. Jimmy Rowles says they had the funniest way of meeting: she'd be hugging him and then she'd move back.

---

* Billie and Lester couldn't work out Jimmy Rowles, either. In a conversation that was recorded during a rehearsal with Art Shapiro in 1955, Billie said of her first impression of him, 'That damn little boy was *scared*. He was a little piss [a kid] and he was a grey [white], you know, and me and Lesta put the eye on him [got his measure] right away.'

† Going on with his explanation of Lester's language, Jimmy Rowles says, 'Chicks were hats. He'd look at the cat and look at the chick and say, "I see you're wearing a new hat. Skull cap? Homburg? Mexican hat dance?" They were discussing her pussy, you see. He'd say, "How's 143?" and that means a head job. "A little 143 is good for a cold!"'

'They were like goldfish or something. And they went through their little trip. They had the funniest way of looking at each other. It was like brother and sister, but another thing. He was so strange, he was like a visitor. And she was, too. And you put the two of them together and it's pretty wild. But they'd just touch and get their guns off and it was cool, until the next time they'd bump into each other around the club.'

Lester would say, 'How are you, Miss Lady Day? Lady Day?' Puffing out his pale cheeks and bobbing up and down in a long dark coat, a milk glass full of old Schenley bond proof whiskey clasped in his hand, and the flat black porkpie hat fixed to his head as if it grew there.

And Billie would say, 'Hey, Buppa Baby,★ you mother-fucker!' and they'd be smiling and weaving and touching and parting, until the next encounter took place later in the night. Jimmy Rowles says it was 'like accidental joy. And Billie was happy all the time.'

The stories continue. One time Billie had a birthday party. 'Bumps' Mayer was on his way out by then and Billie's first husband, Jimmy Monroe, was just out of jail and had come back to claim her.† Jimmy Rowles had nothing to say against Jimmy Monroe and didn't want to put him down, but all the same he was 'a little disappointed' when he first met the man, because Jimmy Monroe was only 'a teeny fella, a pimpy cat, high collar, a real conk, all that shit, a greasy little motherfucker'.

But at least Monroe was better than most of Billie's other men. According to Jimmy Rowles, 'The trouble was, Billie was a fool for cats. She'd go from one to another. She went through the whole zoo and finally she got to the leopard cage.' By this he seems to be referring to Billie's manager, John Levy, whom he calls 'that hoodlum Mafia cat'.‡

★ Everyone called Lester 'Buppa' at this time, because that was what nephews and nieces and his younger brother Lee had called him since childhood.

† This must have been in Los Angeles in April 1943, when Billie was working at Club 331. Jimmy Monroe was in jail on drugs charges from May 1942 until February 1943, and the two of them did attempt a brief reconciliation.

‡ He says, 'John Levy was stronger than Billie and he had her nailed. My idea would be that he used her as an implement to make money.' According to Jimmy Rowles, Billie's arrest in January 1949 was a set-up job, and John Levy

Anyway, here is Billie at her own birthday party, dancing around in a tiny room. Her records are playing on the gramophone and three or four white girls are there as well. Suddenly the door opens and in comes a man called Leo Watson, whom Jimmy Rowles describes as a 'powerful little cat, strong like a gorilla and with a reputation for wildness'. Billie goes on dancing and, after a few drinks, Leo Watson gets louder and louder, and after a couple more he starts swearing.

Billie turns to Jimmy Monroe and she says, 'You get that son-of-a-bitch out of here!'

So Monroe tries to talk to Leo Watson, which Jimmy Rowles says is 'like trying to have a conversation with Gargantua, and he didn't get nowhere'.

Meanwhile Billie is dancing and getting high and watching what is happening, and Leo Watson is getting louder and louder. Suddenly Billie picks up a batch of her own records, and she smashes them down on Leo's head, almost knocking him through the floor. 'Then she grabbed him, and the blood is coming out of his head and his hair is sticking up and he's screaming and he's bleeding, and she picked him up and said, "Open the door." And they threw open the door for her, and she threw Leo Watson clear across the hall and he hit the wall, boom! And she slammed the door and came back and put another record on, and started dancing and snapping her fingers.'

Jimmy Rowles also tells the story of the New Year's Eve celebrations at Billy Berg's club in Hollywood.★ 'It was about a minute to twelve, place was really packed and another band was playing, and there's a curtain there closing off the kitchen and Lady Day spent a lot of time there with a one-legged chef. And all of a sudden there is this terrifying noise, this screaming, and she's cursing and she's throwing plates and tearing the kitchen apart, and it's a big rumpus.

(cont. from pg. 168) arranged with the Federal Narcotics men to have her 'smashed in Frisco. He planted that shit.'

★ This incident took place on 31 December 1948, a few months after Billie was released from jail. Bobby Tucker and John Levy, the bass player, both give their version of the same story.

'And from behind the curtain comes a cat I've never seen before, an *ofay*, and he's got a white shirt on, no tie; and in one hand he's got a basket of biscuits and he's got a twelve-inch butcher's knife buried in his left shoulder, about a quarter inch above his heart. And the blood is gushing out and his eyes are glazed, and he's coming at me and he's in shock, and he's two feet from me and he's going gagagaga! And I say, "Holy Christ!", and I went right under the piano backwards clear across the stage!'

Jimmy tells another story about Billie getting badly beaten by John Levy, who was 'jumping up and down on her stomach, beating the shit out of her . . . So she aches and burns and her crotch hurts, which is great because that's where she sings from. So she starts to think what she's going to sing, and she thinks she's going to sing "My Man"! And she's not even made up yet and Billy Berg is saying, "Jesus Christ, you'd better go down there and get that mother-fucker off her so she can get up here to sing a tune."'

But neither Jimmy, nor Billie's other pianist Bobby Tucker, is brave enough to go, and so they sit and wait until she emerges, just a few minutes before she is set to sing. And Jimmy is sure that 'By the time she gets to the bandstand she hates the world. She's madder than a bitch, and she turns to Bobby Tucker and says, "Strange Fruit", but that's the end of her show, the last tune she sings.' Bobby Tucker tries to argue with her, and she turns her anger on him and slams the lid of the piano down and he just gets his hands away in time, as it goes *bam*! And she says, 'Strange Fruit', and he says, 'OK!'

And then the year is 1954, and Billie has changed and her voice has taken on a drawly edge and she has slowed up, although as far as Jimmy Rowles is concerned, 'She is still Lady Day and whatever she wants to do is all right by me. I don't give a shit. If she wants to go to Tokyo, let's go! That's the way I feel!'

They are making a record in Hollywood for the producer Norman Granz and they are working in the Radio Records Annex, just off Santa Monica Boulevard. Jimmy Rowles has the task of going to the hotel to get Billie ready for the next session. 'I first had to go get her up,' he says, 'and that was a job because she'd stayed up all night. And then I'd give her a bit of juice to get her heart started. So she's had three or four drinks — and I mean drinks! She whacks out a pint of booze, it was either vodka or gin, but probably gin, and she says, "Now I'm going to eat breakfast!"'

'So now she's trying to get her shoes on and her feet are swollen and she can't get them on. And she goes into the next room and tries to get dressed. Now I've seen this woman buck-naked so many times it means nothing, but she's still coy. And she's got this corset she's trying to get on, and she calls me in to tie her up while she's holding herself together. And she says, "Don't peek!" And she's loaded, and I'm laughing and I say, "Oh, you're too much!"'

By the time she got to the studio, Billie was ready to go and it was 'cool and fun and a lot of laughs'. Her old friends Harry 'Sweets' Edison and Ben Webster★ were doing the recording with her, but Jimmy Rowles felt the sessions didn't go as well as they could have done, because Norman Granz was not a musician. 'He was rather irritating in a way. He was like a stranger off the streets that came in and hung around . . . And he couldn't understand it took us some time to get the chords together . . . He wanted to go, "One, two, three . . . Why don't you play 'How High the Moon'? All right! Set the keys and let's go!"'

And Billie used to get 'a little salty', because she wanted it to be right. 'What the fuck's going on?' she said to Norman Granz. 'Give us a couple of minutes to figure out the fucking chords on this tune!'

★   ★   ★

★ Webster was known as The Frog. Jimmy Rowles remembered being in a club when Ben Webster was playing stride piano. 'He's emptied many a bar playing stride piano and he's doing "Little Girl, Little Girl, You're the One for Me!" Bum, bum, bum on the stride, and Lady is over there and she's saying, "Ben Webster, get off that piano. You black son-of-a-bitch, you can't play that motherfucker!" and he's going bum, bum, bum, and he just keeps on playing. Aw shit! They loved each other! They came up together. She was just a little girl and came up to 52nd Street and he was already there.'

Jimmy Rowles remembers meeting Billie in the late 1950s when they hadn't seen each other for a while. He was playing at the Roxy Theater in New York with Evelyn Knight, and after the show he was going to a Chinese restaurant across the street, when he saw Billie with her Chihuahua Pepe on a lead. He says that Pepe 'just wanted to get down and chew all the garbage, and she's cursing at Pepe and everybody's stopping and saying, "Look at that terrible coloured girl!"*

'And I'm standing behind her and she says, "What are you doing here?"

'"I'm at the Roxy, playing for Evelyn Knight."

'"That fucking bitch! She's doing the Roxy for ten thousand dollars a week and I'm still doing the fucking Apollo for one hundred and fifty! Fuck her! And fuck you!"'†

When Jimmy Rowles tries to protest, Billie calls him a 'motherfucking white *ofay*'. And all the time the dog is still busy with its nose in the rubbish, and she is screaming and cursing, and people are standing and watching and wondering whether this is the moment to call the police. 'Oh, I loved her! Oh, how I loved her!' says Jimmy Rowles.

The last time he saw her she had changed. 'She was less humorous, more desperate, so strung out on that shit and drinking so badly . . . She was fighting, doing anything she could to feel good, because when you fuck with that strong shit, when you mess with that Chinaman, he drains the meat off your bones and you don't have much energy, you don't have nothing. You have to drink twice as much, smoke twice as much, sniff twice as much shit, to get to where you all of a sudden remember feeling how you should be . . .

'She was fighting it out. But, on the other hand, she'd have her good days when she didn't need to do that. When she'd feel good. But there would be mornings when she'd

---

* Mae Barnes had a similar encounter. 'It was 4 a.m. and nobody was out on the street, and I was coming from the Bon Soir and who should I see but Billie. I almost knocked her down with the car. She was out there with two Chihuahuas, trying to find a cigarette. Down on her knees. Four o'clock in the morning. She was wearing a robe.'

† She had a point, since she could not make really good money in New York without a Cabaret Card.

have to knock off a pint just to get dressed. I've done that myself. You keep going because of necessity, and your feet are swollen up with your shoes on. She was just beat. That's all. I was young. I didn't realise she was that sick. I knew she was thin, but Louis was taking care of her. He was really taking care of her.*

'She said, "Louis is out of town. You have to take me home."'

'She said, "You gotta feed me. I wanna go to a Chinese place."'

So Jimmy Rowles took Billie to a Chinese restaurant a block away. They sat down to order, when 'all of a sudden a young coloured cat walks into the kitchen with a tray, and she flipped. She started throwing things and swearing, yelling. "Did you see that?" she said. "There's not a Chinaman on Earth would let a black motherfucker into his kitchen! Or a white motherfucker! This ain't a Chinese restaurant! This is a bunch of shit!"'†

Eventually the manager calmed her down and the food was brought, and Jimmy Rowles took her back to her room and tucked her up in bed. '"Here's your shrimp," I said. "Here's your *foo yong*. You've got it all here. Now goodnight, you lovely bitch. Eat your food. Drink your gin. I'll see you tomorrow."'

'She's in bed, her titties are sticking out. And she gets all coy. "Louis is out of town, you know," she said.'

Jimmy Rowles did not take up the offer, even though, looking back all those years later, he wishes he had. That's when he reassures himself. 'I'll fuck her after I die,' he says.‡

⋆ ⋆ ⋆

---

* Jimmy Rowles is one of the few people who seemed to feel that Louis McKay was doing his best for Billie.

† There was a reason behind Billie's fury. Earle Zaidins remembered being in Miami with her and 'We spent a whole night looking for a Chinese restaurant. And we went into one at 3 to 4 a.m. and sat down and the Chinese waiter said, "I'm awfully solly, but we don't serve coloured people!"' During the Harlem riots in 1943, the Chinese laundries put notices in their windows, saying, 'Me colored too', and their shops were left untouched.

‡ Donald Clarke uses this story to end his book about Billie. As Farah Jasmine Griffin points out in *If You Can't Be Free, Be a Mystery*, it is an odd decision to use such a 'locker room narrative' as the closing pages of a biography that she describes as being 'fundamentally decent . . . but deeply flawed by its author's obsession with every minute detail of Holiday's sexuality and drug use'.

And then, right at the end of a long interview, Jimmy Rowles is back to the beginning again, back to Hollywood in the late spring of 1942 when he had just met Billie and they were working together for the first time. One Sunday afternoon he and his wife Dorothy went to a club where all the bands were playing; Count Basie, Jimmie Lunceford, Duke Ellington – everybody. Billie was there and she came to sit at their table. And Jimmy Rowles remembers how Nat 'King' Cole got up to play and 'He was playing real good, and Buck Clayton was playing and he was playing real good, and Lady was screaming at him, "Go on! Play it! You blue-eyed son-of-a-bitch! You motherfucker! Let 'em have it!"'

And over in a corner Jimmy Rowles could see Lester Young sitting by himself and saying, 'Isn't that nice! Isn't that nice!' with a glass of whiskey in his hand. And then Lester got up and 'he started blowing and he wiped them all out!'

'It was wild!' says Jimmy Rowles. 'It was really wild! Those that were there will remember!'

TWENTY-FOUR

Bobby Tucker

———

'You're not going to have any trouble with me.'

I met Bobby Tucker in September 2003. He came to collect me at the Morristown railway station and drove me to the house his father had built with him years ago. It was directly opposite the house where he had grown up, and where Billie had stayed when she was first released from prison on 16 March 1948. He showed me his den downstairs, where he kept the evidence of his life as a pianist in the jazz world: the tapes and records and CDs, the books, papers and photographs, all relating to that now-distant time. On the wall there was a framed photograph of him with Billie and Jimmy Rowles, alongside more formal portraits of his parents and grandparents. There had been many teachers and educationalists on both sides of his family, although his father trained as a carpenter. Bobby Tucker told me that his father was so pale-skinned he was offered the chance of 'becoming a white man' and joining the union, but he refused because it would have meant renouncing his family as well as his background.

I sat with Bobby Tucker at the kitchen table while he talked about Billie Holiday and his love for her. There was a printed notice on the wall behind me that read, 'Since I gave up hope I feel much better.' Bobby Tucker was very quiet and self-contained, but when he spoke about fetching Billie from prison and how she told him he was the only one who cared, the tears welled up briefly in his eyes. Then he continued with his narrative. Many of the stories he told me were the same as the ones he had told Linda Kuehl when she interviewed him in January 1973. He said she came to see him three times and he liked her because of her perseverance.

Bobby Tucker remembered Wabash Avenue, Chicago, during the first week of May 1947. He had been playing piano for Billie the night before at Colosimo's New Theater Restaurant,* where she was billed as 'The Incomparable – Master Mistress of Song'. It was nine o'clock in the morning and the phone rang.

'You'd better get up here right away,' said a man's voice. Bobby Tucker had no idea to whom the voice belonged.

'What's the matter?'

'I can't tell you,' said the voice. 'You just get up here!'

Bobby Tucker was staying at a hotel called the Evans, while Billie was at the more expensive Pershing.† When he got there, the stranger he had spoken to on the phone was waiting for him in Billie's room.

It is easy to imagine that hotel room. The heavy curtains drawn against the intrusion of daylight from outside, and the air in the room smelling sweet and sour and stale. Glasses half-full of whisky and ashtrays overflowing with dead cigarettes, and perhaps a bunch of gaudy flowers still in their cellophane wrapper next to a pair of lacy knickers and a single high-heeled shoe. And there is Billie Holiday sprawled

---

* The club took its name from Old Man Colosimo, who was shot dead on the premises by Al Capone.

† Billie's current boyfriend was the trumpeter Joe Guy, who was a heroin addict. Bobby Tucker said, 'By this time she was so strung out, sex was a thing in the background. Joe was an easier way to cop and someone to get high with.' Billie was known to be using heroin in 1946 and it was getting in the way of her reliability with work, but she was not yet under surveillance by the Federal Bureau of Narcotics. She always made sure Bobby Tucker never saw her taking drugs because that way, as she said, 'He may *think* a lot of things, but he don't *know*.'

across a sofa with one shoe off and one shoe on. Her slippery evening dress is twisted above her knees and on her face there is the look of puzzled concentration that comes to someone who is right on the edge of sliding out of consciousness.

Bobby Tucker said that a man called Jimmy Ascendio was beside her. He was the one who used the phone. He used to be 'in the fight business', but recently he had been acting as Billie's 'road manager', which meant he was her connection who got hold of the drugs for her, while making a profit for himself.★

Jimmy Ascendio explained to Bobby Tucker that Billie 'got hold of some bad stuff'. Another man, with the wonderful name of Boss Moss, had also taken some of the same bad stuff, and the hotel valet was with him right now, getting him to walk the streets until he felt better.

Jimmy Ascendio said, 'We can't let her go to sleep, because if she goes to sleep, she'll never wake up.'

Bobby Tucker filled the bathtub with cold water and helped to drag Billie's limp body to the tub. He said, 'She was fighting', but they managed to throw her into the tub and heave her out again. And then 'We walked her and we slapped her and all she wanted to do was sleep.'

It took Billie about four hours to revive, but as Bobby Tucker said, 'She was strong, strong as a bull.' Following this incident they had a day or so off and then they went on to the next booking, a week at the Earle Theater in Philadelphia, along with Louis Armstrong and his Big Band.

Bobby Tucker first met Billie in 1945 or 1946. He would have been about twenty-six years old at the time and she was about five years older. He happened to be walking down 52nd Street when he saw his childhood friend from Morristown, the musician Tony Scott, who said, 'I've been looking for you.' He took Bobby at once to the Downbeat

---

★ Bobby Tucker didn't think that Ascendio was a user; he was just a connection. He died in 1949 as the result of 'an accident with a horse'.

Club where Billie was supposed to be playing. It was her first night and it was 'desperation night' because she had no music, no bass player, no drummer, and John Simmons, another of her junkie friends, had just punched her pianist Eddie Heywood in the eye, so he had stormed off and wouldn't be coming back.

Billie was introduced to Bobby. 'I've heard about you,' she said. 'Will you play for me? . . . You're not going to have any trouble with me!'

Bobby Tucker said, 'And so I went in and I knew those recordings inside out because of my idol Teddy Wilson. So when she asked for this or that it was *so* easy, because I used to play those things for kicks. So she felt relaxed, but then, she's so easy to play for. She didn't fight you. She could find a groove wherever you put it. She could swing the hardest in *any* tempo, even if it was like a dirge . . . Wherever it was, she could float on top of it.'

Bobby Tucker played for Billie for the next four or five weeks. They were supposed to do the first show between nine-thirty and ten, but she never went on before midnight. Sometimes she would be in the club and hidden away in the 'cubbyhole' of her dressing room, and sometimes she simply had not turned up yet, but as Bobby said, 'She was more unique than probably any other performer, because she could damn well do whatever she wanted to do . . . She had that charisma.'

During those early weeks he felt as if he was stealing her money because, 'She didn't kill me at all, not at all . . . To me there was no sound. It was a flat thing.' But then his friend Tony Scott told him how to listen and appreciate Billie's qualities by explaining, 'When Ella [Fitzgerald] sings "My man he's left me", you think the guy went down the street for a loaf of bread. But when Lady sings, you can *see* that guy going down the street. He's got his bags packed and he ain't *never* coming back.'

So Bobby Tucker began to listen to what Billie was singing and how she was singing it and, once he had started to listen, he couldn't get away from it. He said she had a very small voice and she couldn't belt, but she could tell a story, that's what she could do, and she had a thing about how she *felt*. He thought her quality might be her pain; at least that was the nearest he could get to explaining it.

Bobby Tucker spoke a lot about Billie's lack of confidence, about how she didn't think of herself as a good singer and was always amazed that people wanted to come to listen to her. He understood that this lack of confidence was related to her own particular form of honesty. 'She was basically so honest,' he said. 'She'd be honest even if it meant she had to lie. You'd ask her the same question and twenty minutes later you'd get an entirely different answer, but it would still be *her*. It was how she felt at a particular moment that mattered.'★

He described how she would walk out onto the stage and stand there until everyone was quiet. 'It was not an act. She was not trying to prove anything to anybody. She was just being *herself*.' And it was her fear, rather than her sense of the dramatic, that made her want to be illuminated by only a pin spot, leaving everything else in darkness. That way 'There's not really an audience, it's like a living-room.' He remembered the occasion when she was being presented with an award at the Tijuana Club in Cleveland, 'And when they announced her, they turned up the house lights and it was like broad daylight and she literally froze; her voice was shaking, she was trembling, she couldn't stand to look at the people.'

Bobby Tucker was devoted to Billie. It didn't matter to him that he had witnessed some harrowing scenes of violence and chaos; it was her kindness and her gentleness that remained with him.† Certainly she could be coarse in her language and her first and last word was always 'bitch', but mostly she was rude or angry because her sense of justice

---

★ There is a curious parallel to be found in the numerous photographs of Billie. As Bobby Tucker said, 'Lady could look like any of her pictures . . . and on every one she looked different.'
† When Linda Kuehl asked him about Billie going with girls, he replied, 'I won't say she didn't experiment, but if I just put in a driveway, it doesn't mean I'm a mason.'

was under attack. He said, 'She didn't like to see a small person being abused. She didn't like to see their dignity squashed.' Bobby Tucker said Lady was one of the first to 'up the establishment'. 'One of her best friends might be the attendant in the ladies' room and this would really be a friend, and this friend wouldn't take back seat to the First Lady or the Queen of England.'

There were many occasions when she would defend someone she felt was helpless or was being looked down upon. That was why she often attacked people in authority, whether it was a record producer, a club owner or anyone else behaving badly. Bobby Tucker remembered one New Year's Eve. Billie was 'like Queen Victoria', standing at the bar drinking a triple brandy and white crème de menthe, when a merchant sailor came in and said to the bartender, 'Since when did you start serving nigger bitches?' 'And she just worked his face over with the end of that glass.'

Looking at photographs of Bobby Tucker from this time, you are confronted by a delicate, pale-faced and serious man with an air of gentle fair-mindedness about him. Billie must have seen him as someone she needed to protect, not just from the drugs and the zeal of the narcotics agents, but also from the hazards of life on the road. Bobby had been married since the age of eighteen and she didn't want that marriage to be jeopardised. He remembered how on one occasion she woke up the house detective in a hotel where they were staying at five in the morning, saying something must be done quickly. 'My pianist has a *woman* in his bed.'

He said, 'She never raised her voice with me, the whole time I was with her. She never bawled me out. I'd play the wrong key and it still didn't make a difference. But if anybody else did it, she'd go out of her mind.' But he also had a strange authority over her. 'She wouldn't fight me,' he said. 'I would stop her from doing things, like if she wanted to get violent with somebody. I'd grab her and hold her and say, "All right, you cool it", and she'd try to break loose and she's as strong as a mule, but I'd tilt her to one side so she couldn't plant both feet; and she'd relax and she'd try again and I'd say, "Aha!" and she'd finally break up laughing.'

In March 1947, just a few weeks before the drama with the bad stuff in the hotel on Wabash Avenue, Chicago, Billie's agent Joe Glaser had persuaded her to take a cure for her drug addiction at the private Park West Hospital in New York. In theory this might have been a good idea, but in practice it was the beginning of a disaster. No attempt was made to cure her during her three-week stay, and apparently one of the nurses simply provided her with drugs. According to Billie, the stay in the clinic marked the beginning of her real troubles because it was from this moment on that the narcotics agents began to follow her every move.

As Bobby Tucker said, 'It wasn't until she went to Philadelphia that she started getting surveillance by the narco people. But Philadelphia's known for that. Very rough city. Very rough.'* They were playing at the Earle Theatre in Philadelphia on a contract that was to last from 12 May to 16 May. On the night of the final performance, Billie's hotel room was raided by the police. Bobby Tucker and Jimmy Ascendio were there packing things up to go and, when they searched the room, the police found a package wrapped in a lady's stocking under the bed. This package contained a spoon, two hypodermic needles, one eye-dropper, sixteen unused capsules and nine half-empty capsules, which were all shown to contain heroin hydrochloride. The two men were arrested.

When Billie arrived at the hotel with her driver, she was warned of the raid and managed to escape, even though the police shot at her car as it sped away. The next evening she opened at the Onyx Club, which had changed its name to Club 18. Two days later, on 19 May at 5 a.m., she was arrested at the Hotel Marden on West 44th Street in New York by Agent Ryan of the Federal Bureau of Narcotics, on behalf of their Philadelphia office. She was then taken to

---

* Philadelphia was also the city where the Federal Bureau of Narcotics had its most powerful base. As Harry Anslinger said in his book *The Traffic in Narcotics*, 'Pennsylvania has formed an excellent Bureau of Narcotics . . . There is a need for such special narcotics squads in all the larger cities' (p. 301).

room number 32 at the Grampion Hotel in Harlem, where Joe Guy was found and arrested.*

According to Agent Ryan, 'When we entered the room a window was open about six inches. Outside the room we found a capsule and a half, approximately 1½ grains of heroin.'†
Billie and Joe Guy were taken to the Federal Bureau of Narcotics' offices, where Billie admitted that the capsules found under the bed in Philadelphia were hers. Joe Guy was held in custody and she was charged with possession and released on bail. She returned that evening to perform at Club 18. Five days later, during the intermission at Club 18, she and Bobby Tucker were whisked away by car to Carnegie Hall to make a surprise appearance at the Jazz at the Philharmonic concert.

On 27 May, Billie contacted the Assistant US Attorney to say she wanted her court case to be dealt with as soon as possible. She appeared before Judge Cullen Ganey Jr at 4 p.m. that same day. She had no legal representation‡ and she simply asked to be sent to a hospital for a cure to her addiction. Instead, she was charged with violation of section 174 of the US Narcotics Act, 'that she did receive, conceal and facilitate the transportation and concealment of drugs'. The judge told her, 'I want you to know you are being committed as a criminal defendant . . . You will get treatment, but I want you to know you stand convicted as a wrongdoer.' She was sentenced to a year and a day at the Federal Reformatory for Women in Alderson, West Virginia.

---

* For more details of this arrest, see p. 215.
† Agent Ryan testified under oath in the case brought against Joe Guy in September 1947. Guy himself testified that he used 1½ grains of heroin a day, but when his case was brought to court in September 1947 he was found not guilty.
‡ There was no clear case against Billie, since she could not be directly connected with the drugs in the hotel room, but Joe Glaser told her not to get legal help, and he made sure she had no access to the proper legal channels. A letter signed by two probation officers, based on an interview with Joe Glaser, stated that 'he cooperated with the Federal Narcotics agents as he had no recourse except to have [Billie] "forced" to take proper treatment [for drug addiction].' As Nicholson says, 'The trial became a travesty of justice when she waived the right to legal representation. Her sentence of one year and one day had disastrous consequences for her career' (p. 159).

With regard to the others involved in the arrest, Jimmy Ascendio did spend a time in jail, but Billie spoke up for Bobby Tucker and he was not charged at all. 'I didn't even have a hearing. Lady killed that as soon as she came back.' He said Billie also 'took the rap and saved Joe Guy', even though he had basically confessed that the heroin at the hotel belonged to him.

Billie was sent to prison when she was at the height of her fame. She had been earning around $50,000 a year, although Joe Glaser maintained that all the money had been squandered by Joe Guy. According to her admission documents, she had just $6.34 in her possession when she arrived at Alderson. Her age was incorrectly given as twenty-eight (she was in fact thirty-two), and the document included an IQ assessment, which stated that 'She rates best in language and vocabulary, poor in factual knowledge. Has done singing and housework. Quit school to go to work. Seems inconsistent in her reasoning.'★

Billie was given an injection of morphine for her train journey to West Virginia and was admitted to the prison hospital at 9.30 a.m. on 28 May. Her medical records stated that she appeared 'nervous and weak', and she was given a little Nembutal to help her sleep and a further shot of morphine. For two days she felt 'nauseous', but she apparently 'went through the drug withdrawal with the minimum amount of discomfort'. After eight days she was moved from the hospital to the prison.

She proved to be a model prisoner, just as once, long ago, she had proved to be a model inmate in a Baltimore reform

---

★ Nicholson (p. 160), quoting from Billie's medical file No. 8407-W. There is the complex issue of *how* addicted Billie really was. Apparently she was menstruating when she was admitted and the majority of women who inject heroin do not menstruate. There is also the ease with which she stopped using any drugs. When I consulted Ditti Smit van Damme, who works at a drug clinic in Holland, she told me that this description of Billie's process of withdrawal is that of 'a person who uses heroin only incidentally or at weekends'. In *Lady Sings the Blues* a very different and much more dramatic account is given. 'They don't cut you down slow, weaning you off the stuff gradually. They just throw you in the hospital by yourself, take you off cold turkey and watch you suffer' (p. 133).

school. She was initially given the job of brass cleaning and 'This and everything else she attempted she did thoroughly and without assistance, preferring to work alone. Except for one reprimand for the use of profanity she was quiet, well-mannered and appreciative of suggestion . . . She never asked for aspirin, stating that she wished to get away from anything associated with narcotics . . . She was neat and clean personally . . . and very interested in her appearance.

'When she went into the clinic she was surrounded quickly by fans both colored and white and it was interesting to see how she changed in deportment, brightened and acknowledged their welcome. When speaking to officers she often spoke of the importance of being cured so that she could return quickly to her "public" before she was forgotten . . . She played cards and sewed during most of her leisure hours.'

In November 1947, while Billie was in prison, the record producer Norman Granz organised a benefit concert for her to cover her many debts. But Joe Glaser decided that this would be bad publicity and insisted that all the monies raised were donated to charity. Apart from this intervention, Glaser kept his distance and did nothing to help his client.*

Bobby Tucker was the one person with whom Billie had regular contact during her time in prison. He said she sent him letters every week, knitted sweaters for him and his young son, and 'made little things like they make in jail, little belts . . . The only way she knew there was a world outside was because I wrote to her.'

When Billie was released, Bobby Tucker was there to meet her at Newark station at nine o'clock in the morning. He had her dog Mister with him to welcome her as well. He said, 'When she got off the train, she come up and grabbed

---

* Billie wrote to Leonard Feather from Alderson in July 1947 saying that she hadn't heard from Joe Glaser. 'I know he is a busy man but he has my money and I wrote these letters asking for some . . . Please ask him what he intends to do for some good publicity . . . I do think he should do something so that people won't forget me' (Nicholson, p. 161). He didn't even get round to telling her about the Carnegie Hall concert that was booked for 27 March 1948, ten days after her release. Billie was briefly persuaded to take another agent, Ed Fishman, but that ended in disaster and litigation.

me and she was holding me like this and I could see that she was completely out of it.'★ During her three months on parole she stayed in his mother's house in Morristown.

Ten days after her release, Billie appeared at a midnight show at Carnegie Hall. She checked into a hotel in Midtown, and Ernie Anderson, the promoter for the concert, said, 'I got the impression she was clean and was going to stay off drugs, that she was trying to stay away from Harlem and the drug pushers and ex-husbands who sometimes provided her with drugs to keep her in line . . . Meanwhile at Carnegie Hall the box office was going crazy. The senior Heck brother who ran the box office said we could sell more concerts by Billie that night. He even asked, "Why not? She could do another concert at 2 a.m. and another at 5 a.m.", but I wouldn't hear of it. Well, the gross we racked up set a new house record.'

Billie did two concerts, three weeks apart, singing thirty songs at each one. Bobby Tucker remembered, 'The night they opened, it was pouring rain and people were standing outside, waiting. She had the whole thing. Before she even opened her mouth, she had them. Ninety-nine per cent of them were Billie Holiday fans, so she really couldn't do anything wrong.' Bobby said that for him those two shows were the most wonderful things he'd ever done.

But he also said that Billie's sense of insecurity was worse than ever. She was amazed that people hadn't forgotten her, but she was afraid they had only come to see what a woman prisoner looked like. She felt that everyone was using her, that they didn't really care about her, except that she was a big celebrity, a star. Nobody cared, nobody really gave a damn. As Bobby Tucker said, 'A lot of people go to jail, but Billie took it personally.'

★ She was probably high on marijuana, which counted in those days as a narcotic every bit as dangerous and addictive as heroin. Talking to Bobby Tucker in 2003, he made no clear distinction between the two types of drugs. In another part of the interview, referring to Billie's addiction, Bobby Tucker said she told him she was getting sick and needed something.' We were on the south side of Chicago and she had a valet sent out and he came back with some reefers . . . We'd go to those backwoods places, little towns, and she'd always find it.'

It was after the second Carnegie Hall performance on 17 April 1948 that Billie started her disastrous affair with John Levy. Bobby Tucker couldn't think of one nice thing to say about this man. 'He was unscrupulous. He was doing business with both sides of the law and he didn't even have the guts to be a gangster.' The problem was 'John Levy was a sadistic pimp and Billie admired pimps. He was physically strong and he would holler and scream at people, and she liked that as well. He was a man who took over.'

He saw how Billie used to provoke John Levy, 'almost like a small child will do things to make you blow your top. Once you blow your top, they're satisfied. They feel they've beaten you. In her case it was like a little-girl thing.'★

There was the classic scene on New Year's Eve 1948, at Billy Berg's nightclub. Bobby Tucker gave a different version from Jimmy Rowles. He said the musicians were milling around Billie, joking and flirting with her, and maybe one of them patted her on the bottom or put an arm round her shoulder, and she pretended to be insulted, just because John Levy was there. 'She got into her act so that John could go into his act.' The whole thing snowballed within minutes, and John Levy produced a butcher's knife and managed to stab an innocent bystander who wasn't even part of the band.

Four days after this scene, Billie and John Levy were raided in their room at the Mark Twain Hotel in San Francisco. The narcotics agents caught Billie in the act of trying to flush an opium pipe and a small amount of opium down the lavatory.† According to Bobby Tucker, John Levy was an opium addict and the drug could only have belonged to him, but Levy managed to get himself off the hook by saying that he would go to New York and 'bring in somebody really big'. When he failed to return, Billie again took the rap. On this occasion she got herself a good lawyer and

---

★ It's the same pattern that she showed as a child in Baltimore, running after the men, shouting at them and challenging them until they chased her and punished her.
† See pp. 221–2 for a complete account of this incident.

avoided going back to jail, but it cost her a lot of money and endless trouble, and it further soured her reputation.

In spite of this she went back to John Levy for a while and that was when Bobby Tucker decided he had had enough. 'I really liked her and I couldn't stand the way he was treating her. If she asked him for fifty dollars, he'd say, "Don't ask for money in public", and he'd knock her down literally, with his fist in her face, in the stomach, anywhere.'

When Bobby said he was leaving, John Levy told him piano players were a dime a dozen and then tried to get him back with threats, saying, 'I have some guys. You'll never play piano again.'* But Bobby Tucker was determined, and anyway he had got himself a new job playing for Billy Eckstine. He wrote Billie a letter and she wrote back, saying she understood.

He worked for Billie one last time in September 1954 when she was doing some recordings for Norman Granz. Her ankles were swollen and he thought she was suffering from yellow jaundice. She could hardly talk and her singing voice was almost as hoarse as Louis Armstrong's, but still she sang for a couple of hours. During the recording she suddenly said, 'Move over', and insisted on sitting down on the piano stool right next to Bobby. 'I could hardly play,' he said.

---

* When I was saying goodbye to Bobby Tucker at the Morristown railway station, he suddenly told me the story of how Joe Glaser was paying off the police over a gangster shooting and how he gave John Levy $25,000 in a bag, to deliver to the police. But Levy died of a brain haemorrhage on his way there and, when his body was found, the bag of money had gone. This was in December 1956. When Billie was told the news she said his death was the best Christmas present she had ever had.

TWENTY-FIVE

John Levy, the Bass Player[*]

———————

'I came in on the tail end.'

This is John Levy, the bass player, talking:

A guy walked up to me and he said, 'You John Levy?'

'Yeah, I'm John Levy.'

'You're a manager?'

'Yeah, I'm a manager.'

'You ever managed Billie Holiday?'

'No, I *worked* with Billie Holiday.'

'You sure? Because there's a florist bill at the florist shop downstairs. They sent an orchid up to her every night and the bill's seventy-five dollars.'

Well, I *knew* the other John Levy, the pimp. I knew how he would order something and never pay for it.

———

* John Levy the bass player first worked with Billie as part of the Bobby Tucker Quartet at the two Carnegie Hall concerts in March and April 1948. He was then with her 'out of town, to the East Coast, Washington, Philadelphia and then out to Chicago and St Louis'. In March 1949, John Levy the bass player got tired of not being paid by John Levy the pimp. He stopped working for Billie after a one-nighter at the Pershing Ballroom in Chicago on 13 March 1949. He joined the George Shearing Quintet and became Shearing's manager. He was very successful and eventually 'we had Bing Crosby, Frank Sinatra, Peggy Lee and Nancy Wilson'.

But I said I would like to straighten this thing out, and so I went down to the florist shop. The florist looked at me and he said, 'That's not my man. My man's a big fellow. Looks like an Italian. A big Italian-looking fellow.'★

The other John Levy was a pimp and a hustler, and that was his game. He used to be in Chicago before he came to New York. He drived a big yellow Lincoln 31. Every night he used to drive through a park on the north side of Chicago, and he's driving seventy, eighty miles an hour and he's passing through all the red lights, and when he got downtown going through the Loop, the cops were waiting for him. He'd stop long enough for them to catch up with him and they'd pull alongside and he'd take out twenty dollars and hand it over and then he'd go on, driving seventy, eighty miles an hour. He'd get stopped three times, between the north and the south side of Chicago. He was paying out sixty dollars, every night.

John Levy the pimp was Billie's manager, but he knew nothing about the management end of things. Even in those days, even though I was just a musician, I could see she was being exploited. He only played Billie in places where he felt he could take out the most money, and he only cared that wherever she worked, he got the money. He took the money and bought a home in Long Island, and it ended up he had that home in *his* name. He used to get the money in advance. He would phone through to a club and say, 'She won't play for you unless you give me two weeks in advance, or at least one week in advance.' Then he'd pack up the dollars and fly back to New York, or he'd go to the race tracks at Hot Springs. Or he'd go back to his woman Tondalayo. He give her everything. She had a daughter by him. Billie was aware of these things. She knew Tondalayo.

★ John Levy the pimp did look like an Italian, even though he described himself as 'half-Negro, half-Jew'.

We never knew when John Levy the pimp was in town. He was gone all the time. He'd be there and then he'd leave and you wouldn't see him for two or three days, and then he'd come back and you'd see him in the club for two days. Usually you wouldn't see him on pay night, but he always paid Billie's hotel bills, because like any pimp or hustler, he makes sure a woman is taken care of as far as her *needs*. But after that, forget it.

In Philadelphia, Billie was staying in an old hotel right near the Academy of Music, and Bobby and I were staying in one of the smaller, cheap hotels nearby. Billie was in good form. She was big and healthy and in excellent shape and doing all right. I never saw her smoking pot, but she was drinking, and I could see the writing on the wall. Bobby and I would go by to pick her up to go to work. We had a ritual where we'd go to her hotel suite an hour or two before, to make sure she was together. If she wasn't in the mood, she would start drinking and get high before we ever got there. She'd get high on drugs and then she'd start drinking, brandy and Benedictine and crème de menthe.

I remember one time we went up to her room and John Levy the pimp had just left and she said, 'I can't go to work tonight! John beat the hell out of me!' She pulled her clothes off and we looked at her ribs and she was all bruised up. She said, 'I can't hardly breathe.'

So we decided to get some adhesive tape and we went to the drugstore and bought thick tape, and we bound her up as tight as possible and she went to work that night. We told her to see a doctor in the morning and the next day nothing was broken.

In that era all the female vocalists★ had to have a man who'll beat on them and take their money and misuse them. They seemed to thrive on that. Well, not

★ John Levy the bass player managed Nancy Wilson and said, 'She didn't have the beatings, but she had the verbal abuse and the misuse of her talents and her money, and she could sit there and see it and allow it to happen.'

thrive, but it was something. Why do some people take abuse from another human being? Why let someone do that to you? Nobody can answer that, but some people have to have this. Females call that love. I don't understand it, but maybe I've never been in love. I always felt a woman deserves the same feeling as a man, but you don't want to know about that. When you are writing my story I'll tell you about that.

For Billie, her manager must be her man or her husband. And she had to have a man who once in a while beat on her. In other words, 'I gotta have a man that is a *man*, and I gotta have a man that keeps reminding me of that! Otherwise I'm making more money than he can make and I'm more famous than him. So in order to assert his masculinity, he knocks me down, he slaps me down.' I call it the Frankie and Johnny Syndrome.

People didn't really know Billie. She was always trying to keep a hard front, but she was a beautiful person. She was a great woman. She had more feeling for everything and for people than anybody I've been in touch with. She wasn't selfish; she was generous to a fault. She always respected musicians. I don't think she ever said an evil thing to me or ever looked around to say anything, if anything went wrong musically.

Billie was a complete stylist. When you listen to her sing, you feel she has lived that experience and she is telling a story about it. I don't think anyone can express a story better than Billie. She didn't have a great range or any of that stuff, but most of the tunes she sang had good melody lines and good stories, and they're not easy to sing or play. She didn't sing a song unless she wanted to, or unless someone slipped her man some money under the table and her man *told her* to do the song; then she'd do it even if it wasn't right for her.

Bobby Tucker took care of the music. She pretty well had a repertoire, and most of the time we played the music and she wouldn't rehearse it, she'd just do it. I'd

stand out front and she'd be high, and she'd lean on
the bass and stand there and sing and she wouldn't move
from that spot. It was one of the most lucrative and
successful times in her life, as far as money was
concerned, but I came in on the tail end of the real
Billie Holiday.

She never had an entourage. Most female singers have
an entourage of females who are there with the dresses
and the hairdos, and the this and the that. The only
people I would see around Billie were the people who'd
come to sell her some shit. I always felt uncomfortable
with the dope peddlers and the users. They'd say, 'We're
going to sit here and we're going to shoot ourselves up
some heroin.' Or they might just be sniffing cocaine.
I'd go out of the room, I'd go any place. Bobby Tucker
was the same.★ We knew the people who were coming
around were just getting their claws in. We knew they
were spoiling her career.

We used to dress her. We'd go into the dressing room
before a concert, and Bobby and I would button her
up. There was nothing between us in that way. She'd
just walk in, take off her clothes and sit and talk to you,
rapping. It was never done in a vulgar way.

At first I was so prudish and such a square, but she'd
say, 'Sit down, motherfucker!† Where you going?'

'I thought you were going to dress!'

'So what!'

I thought she was beautiful. Very few people are
really beautiful or attractive, sitting there with no clothes
on, because very few of us have bodies that are that
beautiful. But with her it was done in such a way that
you really thought about the *inside* of the person, who
she really was. And she was well built and she looked

★ John Levy said, 'They didn't try to turn us on, Bobby and me. We didn't have
any. I was making two hundred dollars at most in a week. We were just
working musicians, so why turn us on? In those days they wouldn't bother
with people like us.'
† John Levy said, 'Even calling you a name, calling you something like that, it
was meant in a completely different way.'

good from my standpoint, as a man looking at a woman. She had some lovely skin. Her complexion when she came out of Lexington was great. She was healthy and she was so together, but she fell back into the same thing. If she was put in the right environment . . .

Billie was a female Duke Ellington. The only time I ever heard her put anybody down – and it wasn't really a put-down – was in the days when Peggy Lee and all the girls were trying to sound like her. And she'd tell them to their faces, it wasn't like she talked behind their backs. When Peggy Lee came around they'd just greet each other and Billie would say, 'Look, bitch, why don't you find some other way to sing?' Or, 'Why the fuck are you trying to sound like me?'

And Peggy Lee wouldn't take offence. She'd say to Billie, 'It's because I love you. I love everything you do.'

I remember Peggy Lee disliked me for years because she knew my name was John Levy and she told somebody, 'I don't like that John Levy the pimp on account of what he did to Billie.'

And I met Peggy Lee one day at Capitol Records and I said, 'I gotta straighten something out. You think I'm John Levy the pimp that managed Billie, but I'm John Levy the bass player, and I just played bass for Billie for less than a year. Seven or eight months maybe.'

Everything was cool then.

TWENTY-SIX

The Ecstasy of Paranoia

———

As Commissioner of the Federal Bureau of Narcotics, Harry Anslinger had no problem with heavy drinkers or with habitual consumers of the wide range of tranquillisers and barbiturates that were now legally flooding the market. For him, illegal drugs were demons that needed to be eradicated and he increasingly saw drug abuse as a 'cold, calculated, ruthless, systematic plan to undermine'.*

Anslinger felt it was crucial to emphasise that 'the drug addict is a psychopath *before* he acquires his habit'. He believed that an estimated 95 per cent of addicts were also criminals, and that a drug had 'more rapid and stronger effects on an individual with a flawed personality'. He concluded that it was therefore quite useless to send drug addicts to treatment centres or hospitals; harsh jail sentences were always the best solution.†

* For my information on the history of the heroin trade in America, I am indebted to *The Pursuit of Oblivion* by Richard Davenport-Hines, 2001, and especially Chapter 11, which deals with the career of Harry Anslinger as the first Commissioner.

† Anslinger said that treatment centres would 'elevate a most despicable trade to the status of an honorable business . . . and drug addicts would multiply unrestrained to the irrevocable impairment of the moral fibre and physical welfare of the American people' (Anslinger, p. 186).

If Anslinger had one particular obsession in the midst of all this, it was the way that the general public 'reacts respecting glamorous entertainment characters who have been involved in the sordid details of a narcotics case . . . There seems to be some sort of public approval of these degenerate practices.' Anslinger very much wanted to reverse this trend by having a celebrity punished in the way he saw fit. It would also guarantee excellent front-page publicity for his Bureau. He was greatly helped in his campaign by the newly proliferating breed of tabloid journalists, who could always sell more papers if they provided sensational material about acts of sex and violence, especially when carried out by famous people and fuelled by the consumption of narcotics.

Everyone who knew Billie Holiday has a different version of the nature of her addictions and the year in which she became a heroin addict. According to John Simmons the bass player, who was her boyfriend for a while, Billie didn't start shooting heroin until the latter part of 1942, or early 1943. Before then she was smoking weed, smoking opium, taking pills. It was when she began earning a lot of money that she became a natural target both for the drug peddlers who wanted to sell to her and for the men who wanted to become her boyfriend/manager/husband/pimp, and who encouraged her addiction in order to control her and have access to her income. As her friend Mae Barnes said, 'When Billie got on this heroin habit, she became meek and mild and couldn't help herself, and anybody could make her do anything . . . When she was drinking like a lush and smoking gage, she'd want to hear music . . . she'd rock and roll and carry on like hell and have a ball and move with the rhythm, but when she was on the heavy stuff she'd be listless and drop off.'

Billie's heroin addiction was never particularly dramatic, or at least she never boasted about her excesses as some junkies like to. Few people ever saw her injecting and it seems that whenever she stopped using heroin, either by choice or necessity, she always managed to avoid the usual traumas of withdrawal. On the two occasions when she was arrested, she adjusted almost immediately to being deprived of heroin, and several people who were close to her for long periods of time insisted that she was not using anything while they were with her.* She was clearly able to control her habit through sheer will power. As she grew older she apparently needed the drug less and less and she must have become what is called a 'chippy', getting by on a minimal dose.† On the occasions when she was under extreme psychological pressure during her last years, she tended to use alcohol to drown her sorrows.

According to the jazz critic Max Jones, who met Billie in London in 1954 and again in 1959, Billie was an 'odd amalgamation of naivety and experience', full of spontaneous streams of talk, full of laughter and rude jokes and not at all 'the tragic lady with morbid interests' he had been led to expect. He said her speaking voice was 'slurry, a little cracked in tone and meanly attractive' and that she had a prodigious ability to consume spirits. Together with his wife, they mostly talked about 'music, booze, sex, drugs, politics, gangsters, film actors, club owners, writers, and café society. Also about dogs or clothes and shopping.'‡ He said she knew that dope suppliers, including husbands and lovers, had leeched most of her earnings, and she realised that her immoderate use of all sorts of stimulants had shortened her life expectancy, but she wasn't maudlin about any of this. She said she had enjoyed the narcotics, the drinking and the men while they lasted and she accepted her habits as 'my own damn business'.

* This includes Roy Harte, who went with her on holiday to Cuba in 1943; Leonard Feather, who travelled with her to England; Memry Midgett, who was on tour with her in 1955; and her lawyer and friend Earle Zaidins, who was close to her towards the end of her life. When I spoke to Ditti Smit van Damme, a doctor specializing in drug addiction in Holland, she said that some very strong personalities can keep their heroin intake under control and can also move from 'snorting' to injecting at will.

† A study of jazz musicians made by the psychologist Charles Winick in 1957 showed that 'heroin use was concentrated in the 25–39 age group, after which it tapered off to very little. As one forty-three-year-old jazzman said, 'There were just longer and longer periods between the times when I took a shot. I guess you could say I diminuendoed out of it.'

‡ Quoted in Lesley Gourse, *A Billie Holiday Companion*, 1997, p. 41.

So why is it that the story of Billie's life has constantly been portrayed as that of a particularly hopeless drug dependency and a steady slide into artistic decline, despair and moral degradation? Why is it that even the briefest account of her on the back of a CD cover, or the caption to a photograph, will invariably include a mention of her heroin addiction, although others of her generation who were equally (or much more heavily) addicted are allowed to be cut free from the burden of their particular troubles?*

According to a long interview she gave to the black magazine *Ebony*, in July 1949, when Billie came out of prison in March 1948 she thought she had paid her debt to society for her wrongdoings and would now be given a fresh start. Instead, that was when her troubles started in earnest:

> I came out expecting to be allowed to go to work and to start with a clean slate . . . But the police have been particularly vindictive, hounding, heckling and harassing me beyond endurance . . . These people have dogged my footsteps from New York to San Francisco . . . They have allowed me no peace. Wherever I go, they track me down and ask me nasty questions about the company I keep and my habits . . .
>
> Recently the New York Police Department refused to issue me with a Cabaret Performer's Licence. The pretext used was my prison record . . . although many other nightclub employees with police records are licensed and working.
>
> I have been caught in the crossfire of narcotic agents and drug peddlers and it's been wicked . . . One of the narcotic agents seemed determined to make me the means of securing promotion. The peddlers made vile threats to me in an effort to make me a customer again.

---

* As jazz trumpeter Red Rodney said, heroin became 'the thing that made us different from the rest of the world . . . It was the thing that gave us membership in a unique club.' The long list of musicians who used heroin during this period includes Charlie Parker, Miles Davis, Fats Navarro, Chet Baker, Gerry Mulligan, Stan Getz and Bill Evans.

It is true that after her release from prison, Billie was constantly being brought before the courts of law on one pretext or another, and several people who worked with her attested to the fact that the police and other government agents were always at her shows – heckling, threatening, raiding her dressing room, making embarrassing enquiries at her hotel and spreading rumours at the clubs where she was booked to sing. Billie told the trumpeter Buck Clayton that the FBI agents, 'young ones with crewcuts . . . would come up to her and say, "OK, Lady Day, we know everything you're doing and when the time comes, we're going to get you!" Then they'd walk away. But they'd heckle her like that. She never knew when one was going to approach her, so she always had fights with the police.' Clayton said, 'She was very bitter about not being able to play, because they let other people play places, like Stan Getz – he got caught, but he got permission to play afterwards.'★

After her imprisonment Billie was four times arrested on drugs charges that could not be properly substantiated. On top of that, a number of individuals jumped on what seemed like a bandwagon of recrimination and brought civil actions against her. Ed Fishman, who was briefly her manager in 1948 while she was trying to break free from Joe Glaser, filed a $75,000 breach-of-contract suit against her, claiming that this was the commission he would have received if she had kept him on. Jake Ehrlich, the lawyer who got her off the second drugs charge in 1949, sued her for failure to pay his fees. And several club owners sued her, or threatened to sue her, for failing to honour a contract, no matter what her circumstances were at the time. She was also taken to court for causing grievous bodily harm when she threw a plate that hit a woman on the leg.

Billie was repeatedly denied her Cabaret Card, in spite of

★ The saxophone player Stan Getz was arrested in the 1940s, but after a brief stay in prison his career was not affected. As Billie said, 'Don't forget, I'm black and he's white.' Stan Getz worked with Billie at the Storyville Club in Boston in 1951 and said, 'I marvelled how strong she was for a person who had taken so many knocks from life, and at her honesty as an artist' (Chilton, p. 142).

applying for it to be reinstated on at least three separate occasions. The first time was in March 1949 when she was offered a rumoured $3,000 a week to appear at the Royal Roost club, just so long as she had her card. She tried to sue the New York Police Department, but lost the case. The presiding judge, Aaron J. Levy, said that the police 'deserved commendation' for their action.*

It also seems that the forces of law did a very thorough job in tarnishing her reputation and frightening off any clubs that might wish to hire her. Frank Holzfeind, manager of the Blue Note in Chicago, said he was surprised that she even turned up for a booking in 1949 because 'She came to the Blue Note thoroughly plastered with every stigma and accusation in the books, so much so that I doubted my reasons for signing her in the first place. That first night I just knew she wouldn't show up.' In the event, she was on time every evening and broke all previous attendance records at the club.† This story is repeated over and over again. On 15 November 1971, Frank Schiffman, the manager of the Apollo Theater, wrote a letter to Linda Kuehl in which he echoed the familiar prejudice, saying, 'I considered her a superb artist, but unfortunately a very sad woman who throughout her life was plagued by drug addiction. Our records indicate that she made her last appearance at the Apollo in September 1955. Her personal behaviour was excellent and she showed no evidence at the time of being adversely affected by artificial stimulants, but unfortunately the aura of stardom had diminished.'

Eager tabloid journalists all had stories to tell about Billie's

---

* Nicholson, p. 175. The Cabaret Card scheme came into force in 1939 as a means of controlling people, and especially potential Communists who were 'not of good character' and who might pose a threat to the security of the US. It became unlawful for a club to hire someone who was without a card. An appeal could be made every two years. Stan Getz did not lose his Cabaret Card because of drug offences, but Bud Powell and Sonny Stitt both did, although they got them back after a lawyer took on their cases. Thelonious Monk was without his for six years. Miles Davis was told his would be withdrawn if he made a complaint about police brutality after he was hit over the head outside the Birdland Club in 1959.

† Vail, p. 128.

excesses, because those were the stories that people wanted to read. As Barney Josephson, the owner of Café Society, put it, 'America at large didn't know much about her. I think the only way she could get onto the front pages of the white newspapers was by getting into some sort of trouble, like being arrested.' Strangers were quick to jump to conclusions, and many people presumed that Billie was high on heroin when it was more likely that she was drunk on whisky. For instance, a Second World War veteran gave a typical account of seeing her at the bar, 'obviously under the effects of heroin or some other drug which she must have shot up after her singing. Her words just dribbled out.'*

William Dufty, the *New York Post* journalist responsible for ghostwriting Billie's autobiography *Lady Sings the Blues*, had a lot to answer for.[†] When he was drawing up his contract for the book he agreed with his publishers that narcotics would be what they called 'the gimmick' that would sell it. And he did everything he could to give prominence to Billie's drug addiction.

When he began to write his book, Dufty combined the stories Billie told him with material that had appeared in earlier interviews. He added whatever extra spice he felt was needed, particularly in relation to Billie's lesbian experiences and her history of drug addiction. He was a skilled journalist and managed to provide Billie with a witty, world-weary manner of talking and presenting herself. It didn't matter that the voice was not hers, because the prose whizzed on the page, beginning with the famous first lines of the book: 'Mom and Pop were only a couple of kids when they got married. She was thirteen, he was sixteen and I was three.'

---

* Margolick, p. 94. This sounds more as if Billie was drunk. Heroin users have a sleepy way of talking, but blurred 'dribbling' speech is more symptomatic of alcohol.

† William Dufty ghostwrote a total of forty books during his lifetime. Apart from *Lady Sings the Blues*, he was most famous for *Sugar Blues*, which was about healthy eating habits and was inspired by his meeting with, and subsequent marriage to, Gloria Swanson, the star of the silent screen. *Sugar Blues* was dedicated to 'Billie Holiday whose death changed my life and Gloria Swanson whose life changed my death'.

William Dufty sent an outline and much of the first draft of the book to Norman Granz. He also enclosed an enthusiastic letter in which he said that he and Billie 'have worked for a week now, pulling stuff together. She has been dictating huge patches of terrific stuff. I have dredged the morgues and clip files . . . And the project has gone well.' But Granz was not at all impressed and his response was stern and critical. 'I must assume that the reason for writing the book is to sell as many copies as possible because of [Billie's] desperate need for economic aid . . . It may be that Billie wishes to tell her side of the story – in a sense to right the misconceptions that society may have about her . . . but I am not sure that it isn't working at cross purposes because so much mention is made of the narcotics and it might work against Billie . . . The fact that the publishers feel that the impact of the narcotics part is the most important aspect of this book, in a sense only confirms my suspicions, because it is a very saleable commodity.'★

But although William Dufty clearly made use of Billie's notoriety,† he was also very aware of where he felt the real blame lay. In a letter sent to a New York lawyer during a legal tussle shortly after the book's publication, he explained his interpretation of Billie's troubled destiny. 'She has been kicked around and harassed for years by the authorities. One of the reasons is that this song Strange Fruit made her well-known and controversial. At any one of a hundred points in recent years she could have gotten off easy if she had merely told the FBI or other government investigative authorities . . . that she didn't know what the song meant . . . that she thought it was about kumquats or something . . .

'At many points the FBI and other Congressional Investigators might have been delighted to expose this propaganda plot; how an innocent, big-eyed, barefoot little girl was used to inflame the saloon-set against lynching in accord

---

★ Norman Granz to William Dufty, letters dated 2 August and 19 August 1955.
† With a typical journalistic turn of phrase, Dufty used to refer to Billie as 'my late ex-wife-to-be', while she spoke of him more simply as 'that faggot'.

with the well-known aims and objectives of the Communist Party . . . But she didn't. She wouldn't.'★

It is possible to argue interminably over how much Billie was to blame for the troubles that gathered around her, but maybe here the last word should be given to the pianist Mal Waldron, who worked with her during the final two years of her life. 'Faults? Well of course she drank too much . . . She wouldn't stop drinking and she never did really stick the dope habit. But Lady Day had an awful lot to forget . . . Don't forget, if you are treated like a common criminal, after a while you begin to act like one.'

★ Letter to A. D. Weinberger, 21 October 1956.

TWENTY-SEVEN

Jimmy Fletcher

———

'She was the loving type.'

L istening to Jimmy Fletcher's voice, you don't get the sense that he is drunk or high; but he does sound very nervous and it obviously costs him a lot of emotional effort to tell the story he wishes to tell. The transcript of the interview runs to thirty-seven pages. I read it through four times as I tried to disentangle what was being said, and only then could I begin to fit the various sequences of events together. I suddenly realised that Jimmy Fletcher was struggling to tell the truth about the past, even though the truth was painful to him and he was still burdened by the way he felt he had betrayed his friendship with Billie Holiday.

Jimmy Fletcher had been trained as a federal narcotics agent and he was quick to condemn anyone who was caught up in 'that business' of narcotics. But he was also aware that in Billie's case it was her fame, her colour and her peculiar mixture of defiance and vulnerability that got her into such deep trouble. After all there were many others in the enter-tainment business who were not pursued so remorselessly, or punished so harshly once they had been caught.

Jimmy Fletcher was born in Princeton, New Jersey, at around the same time that Billie was born. He attended

Howard University in Washington and became an employee of the Federal Bureau of Narcotics not long after he had completed his studies. He seems to have been chosen for the job because he was a black man who knew how to move easily between the black and the white worlds. On top of that, he was good at mixing with criminals and was quick to establish friendships with a number of notorious gangsters.

Jimmy Fletcher was working in Chicago in the late 1930s when he got to know Joe Glaser, the man who later became Billie's agent. He said that at the time Joe Glaser was 'messing around with Al Capone's set . . . and he had quite an underworld record'. He was a manager of prize fighters and used to fix their fights. He had a string of whorehouses and a fondness for under-age girls, which landed him in court on two occasions. He also proudly proclaimed that 'nobody liked a bit of nigger pussy' better than he. He must have included Billie in that category because Jimmy Fletcher remembered seeing the two of them together 'way back in the thirties' at the Grand Hotel nightclub in Chicago. For years afterwards Joe Glaser often referred to himself as one of Billie's boyfriends.

When Joe Glaser became an agent for several important entertainers, he brought his gangster skills to this new profession. He was said to have a 'wonderful ability to lie with total impunity', and one New York club owner described him as 'the most obscene, the most outrageous and the toughest agent I've ever bought an act from'.★ But people felt that he was at least *openly* corrupt. There were others who were much more devious in their business arrangements.

Jimmy Fletcher also happened to be a friend of John Levy, whom he first met when he arrested him in 1934 or '35, on a pimping charge in Kansas City. When their paths next crossed, John Levy was a 'down-at-heels junkie' in Chicago and Jimmy Fletcher found him leaning against a lamp-post lost in a narcotic daze. Apparently Levy managed to break

★ Ward and Burns, p. 215.

his addiction to heroin;* after that he just smoked opium and 'secured any morphine that came through'.

John Levy became one of Jimmy Fletcher's informers and the two men saw quite a bit of each other when they both moved to New York in the early 1940s. Jimmy had no problem with John Levy's explanation that he was with Billie 'because I do everything I can to get rich', or that he 'sometimes felt like killing her'. He also accepted that once John Levy wanted to get rid of Billie, he 'set her up' a couple of times, trying to get her arrested while in possession of drugs.†

As a black narcotics agent, Jimmy Fletcher's main job was as a so-called 'archive man', mixing in the underworld to find out who was selling drugs and who was buying them, and who was ripe for prosecution. As he explained it, 'Being an undercover man you'd better not come in talking like a preacher. When you get in the underworld your language is just as rotten and filthy as the language of the whole lot sitting near you. And after you spend ten to fifteen hours a day in the underworld spots, then you know what's happening there, just as a sewer man would know what's going on in the sewers.'

As part of his work, Jimmy Fletcher often went to Clark Monroe's Uptown House on 52nd Street, and he and Clark used to 'run around all night together'. Billie was by then married to Clark's brother Jimmy Monroe, and so Jimmy Fletcher got to know her as well. In those days she was already drinking 'enough liquor for ten men and taking any drugs that came along . . . She would buy cocaine all the time. She was what was called "a snorting horse".' He remembered talking to her about heroin. She said she used it

---

* Throughout this chapter it is John Levy the pimp who is being referred to. Jimmy Fletcher said Levy cured himself of his heroin addiction when 'he went to a little place in Illinois . . . He was a heroin addict, but he was not a real junkie. He had never gone long enough to get hooked and he went back to smoking hop [opium].'

† Jimmy Fletcher described one occasion when Billie and John Levy had been smoking hop together in a hotel room, and Levy crept out while she was sleeping and informed the Federal Bureau of Narcotics that she was there. But Billie suspected something and, when the agents arrived, the room was empty.

occasionally, but she was not injecting. Anyway, she said, 'I never let it get me. I never let it happen. I can master it.'

Like a teacher in charge of a class of unruly children, Jimmy was always busy with his network of informers.* As he explained it, every drug user is a potential informer, and so what might be called the creative side of his work began each time he made a simple arrest of a person caught with drugs in their possession. 'You catch him and you ease his pain and tell him that if he cooperates, you'll tell the judge and that might get him a light sentence, or it might let him off with nothing on him at all . . . You tell him he needs to bring in five or ten cases – not friends or anybody he knows in the junk world, because the first thing he thinks is "How can I do this without getting killed?" – he needs strangers who won't suspect him. You suggest he gets someone to take him down to some district where he is not known . . . So then he comes back and he's got one for you and then another. And *then* you're getting somewhere!'

Jimmy explained that an agent is only as good as his sources of information: 'a cheap source brings you in flea cases, but an informer with a bit of personality can be *trained* and turned into a professional!' Apparently the standard fee for informers was five dollars a day and the pay was added to the agent's expense account.

Jimmy was always able to supply his informers with large quantities of drugs, so that anyone who didn't know his line of business would have presumed he was just a rather successful street peddler. He boasted that one time in Texas he was carrying a hundred ounces of heroin himself. As he explained it, he had to teach a new recruit to 'climb the echelons of peddlers', giving him quarter-ounces and then half-ounces to sell, 'until you're willing to get him on up to buying five, ten ounces'. At that stage in the proceedings it was necessary for Jimmy to consult his immediate superior and get permission from the Bureau's main office in Washington.

---

* Jimmy Fletcher said Billie 'was smart because she never sold anything, never handled it, and she didn't inform me and she wasn't an informer'.

Jimmy was sure, or at least he said he was sure, about the moral justification for the kind of work he was doing. He was very insistent that the people he caught had only themselves to blame, because 'you victimise yourself by becoming a junkie'. Nevertheless he was still painfully aware that what he called 'the law in general' was riddled with corruption and it was the little people who tended to get caught, while the fat cats could always avoid prosecution.

He described a New York 'shooting gallery' run by a 'very noted junkie prostitute madam' called Suzy West. This was a small first-floor apartment next to the Theresa Hotel in Harlem. The rooms were used by junkie-prostitutes who brought their clients there, and junkies could 'go shooting there all night, twenty-four hours of the day'. But Suzy West had 'such good connections and she sold so much stuff for the Italian bunch' that no one wanted to cause her any trouble. Jimmy said the police raided her establishment once a week, 'as regular as clockwork', but these raids were just symbolic, and every Saturday the police collected $500 from Suzy's, as a token of her appreciation. It was important, for the sake of the official records, that a certain amount of heroin was occasionally found on these raids, but then Suzy only needed to make one telephone call and a new supply was delivered at once.

By 1947 Billie had become a regular visitor to Suzy's and that was when the enforcers of the law were very keen to have her arrested; it was just a question of getting the timing and the circumstances right. According to Jimmy Fletcher, the Federal Bureau of Narcotics, the FBI and the local police departments had been keeping files on her 'from the beginning'★ and she was being constantly pursued by various agents who were keen to make a 'lovely big case' against her and were 'covering her ground, keeping her under observation, night and day'. But it was not just the forces of law that were involved, for Jimmy said there were also 'plenty of small-timers who never reached her stardom and, oh my

★ The FBI started their files on Billie in around 1940 after she sang 'Strange Fruit' at Café Society.

God, there is so much animosity between them, all the way up the ladder . . . Entertainers have all got enemies, jealous, envious enemies, and there were people who'd say, "Why don't you catch Billie Holiday? She's so high she can't sing!"'

The chance to fix Billie's arrest, and to be sure that she was sent to jail, came in 1947, when Joe Glaser decided that his client needed to be 'taught a lesson'. It is impossible to know what Glaser's real motives were; as he himself said, he knew hundreds of junkies; about one-third of the entertainers on his books were using either heroin or cocaine, and part of his job as an agent was to make sure they were protected. It is possible that he was in a situation where he was forced into making some sort of a deal with Harry Anslinger; or it might have been that he was busy with a personal vendetta against Billie and simply wanted to hurt her, especially since he knew she was terrified of ever being incarcerated again. Be that as it may, it is certain that Joe Glaser helped to engineer Billie's arrest, and he severely prejudiced her case by making sure that she had no legal representation when she was brought before the judge.

And so it happened that one day in the spring of 1947, Jimmy was summoned to his office for a 'confidential conversation' with one of his superiors. A message had come through from Anslinger saying that 'Joe Glaser wants a coloured agent to work on getting a case against Billie Holiday.' Jimmy was told that Glaser was very upset because Billie's mother was 'starving to death, in New England, I think it was, or New Jersey, while Billie was making $750 a week and spending it all on narcotics'. And that was presented as the moral justification for hunting her down, although numerous other reasons were produced later and they all contradicted each other.

Jimmy went to meet Joe Glaser for lunch at the Palm Tavern on 5th Avenue, and Joe Glaser told him 'the entire story . . . He confided about Billie being his girl and he'd like to save her, and the only way to save her is to have her knocked out by the government.' Joe Glaser went on to explain that he had spoken to Anslinger and had been given a guarantee that if he helped the Bureau to get Billie arrested, in return the Bureau would 'hook and crook' on his behalf – by which it was meant that his part in the whole affair would not be included in any of the legal reports.

The two men met again on several occasions and Joe Glaser was able to use his information as Billie's agent to say exactly where she was going to be performing and even whom she was planning to meet. He apparently kept repeating his mantra about how he 'only wanted to save Billie and this was *the only way*'.

And so the necessary machinery was set in motion and Jimmy's team of informers were told to be on the lookout. A man known as Stiffleg Baltimore was puffing with excitement when he turned up to say, 'Oh man, have I got a case for you! I just sold Billie Holiday thirty-six caps of heroin for eighty dollars!'* And then there was Sam, 'a storming-down, big-shot peddler pimp . . . who had done so much time in the penitentiary that he was pathetic'; he was eager to explain how much heroin he had sold to Billie over the last six years. But Jimmy didn't think that either of these leads was strong enough.†

At this time Billie was living upstairs at the Braddock Hotel on 8th Avenue with the trumpeter Joe Guy, who was known to be a junkie and bought an ounce of heroin every day from some connection in New York.‡ All the pimps and the pros hung out at the Braddock and the place was

---

* Jimmy Fletcher could have used this information as what was called 'a dated buy', but he would have needed two more such examples to make a case, and he wanted something bigger and clearer.
† She was buying two ounces a week from Sam, but all the peddlers were keen to 'take advantage of her. They'd catch her in a crack time. She's sick. She has to go on and what she really wants is a couple of fixes, but they wouldn't think of letting her have it that small and they'd sell her half an ounce for about a hundred and fifty dollars and many asked her five hundred dollars.'
‡ Billie's boxer dog Mister was said to be very skilled as a carrier, wearing a collar that was designed to carry an ounce of heroin. Joe Guy would buy his ounce, put it in the collar and tell the dog to go ahead. The elevator operator was in on the conspiracy and would carry the dog up in the elevator to the top floor.

raided quite regularly, especially since it did not have Suzy West's ring of protection.★

Jimmy had been involved in some of the Braddock raids and had 'caught Billie in the net' a couple of times, but then he had not been after her, so they had simply talked and made jokes like old friends. But now that she was a target, things were different. Jimmy arrived at the hotel with his colleague, a white man called Cohen, and they knocked on Billie's door, saying they had come to deliver a telegram.

'Stick it under the door!' she said.

'It's too big to go under the door! We'll take it back if you don't open!'

And so she let them in. She was on her own. Jimmy said he was embarrassed and wanted to leave the room as quickly as possible, and so he said to her, 'Billie, why don't you make a short case of this and, if you've got anything, why don't you just turn it over to us? Then we won't be searching all around, pulling out your clothes and everything. So why don't you do that?'

But Jimmy's partner Cohen didn't like this idea. He wanted a policewoman to be brought up to the apartment, to do a body search.

When Billie heard this plan she said, 'You don't have to do that. I'll strip. All I want to say is will you search me and let me go? All that policewoman is going to do is look up my pussy!'

And so Billie undressed in front of the two narcotics agents, while they stood at the door of the bathroom and watched her. Then she snatched a thin gown from the floor and put it over her shoulders, and she went to the lavatory and urinated, standing over the bowl, while staring at the two men.

'No, no, Billie, you don't have to do that!' said Cohen, trying to close the bathroom door to give her some privacy. But she slammed the door open and went on urinating,

---

★ The Braddock was a 'notorious hangout for prostitutes and pimps' and the army had asked for it to be declared 'raided premises'. There was a ban on racially mixed couples, and police even entered rooms to eject white persons. A policeman was always on duty in the lobby. See Brandt, p. 184.

forcing him to watch her, forcing both of them to see her nakedness and her defiance.

Jimmy said something happened to him during that encounter. 'She sealed our friendship. She sealed herself closer to me that morning, when we went to raid her' he explained in the interview.

Before he and Cohen left the room, Jimmy took Billie to one side. 'I promised her that I would talk this over with the US Commissioner.* I told her, "I don't want you to lose your job!"' It is not clear what her response was to this offer, or if he really was able to do anything to help her.

Jimmy remembered meeting Billie again in Philadelphia. He had been sent to catch her in a hotel room after a tip-off, but when he got there all she was doing was drinking spirits and there were no drugs to be found. The singer Sarah Vaughan had just been arrested on a drugs charge, and Billie started shouting about 'how the bastards had locked up her friend!' She grabbed hold of Jimmy and said, 'I want you to do me a favour. Go there and get Sarah out!'

Jimmy explained to Billie that his superiors were 'tickled to death' by all the big publicity they were getting because of the arrest, but still he did what Billie asked of him and he managed to get Sarah Vaughan let off. In the interview he was very proud of his ability to get his own way in such matters. He said it was because he always knew exactly how to make a report to the office.

The next time Jimmy saw Billie was at a party. She was so drunk she could hardly stand and she was on the arm of a wealthy white Ford plant executive whom she called 'My Daddy' and who was as drunk as her. And then Jimmy came across her by chance in a bar, and he sat with her and Chiquita (her Chihuahua) and they talked together for hours.†

---

* Harry Anslinger. Obviously at this point Billie was not going to lose her job, since they still hadn't got enough against her. I suppose what Jimmy Fletcher means is that she was bound to lose her job eventually, if the Federal Bureau of Narcotics went on hunting her.

† He asked her how she had managed to bring a Chihuahua out of Texas, because it was against the law to import them. She opened the front of her dress and 'she had nothing on but that gown and said, "Here's how I brought

And then there was another meeting. This was when Jimmy went with the entire office of fifteen or sixteen men for a birthday celebration at Club Ebony. He said the other agents were keen to hear Billie singing because they were all 'nuts about her sexually'. The picture girl at the club took photos of some of them hugging her.* Half the group went home early, but the rest stayed on drinking until the small hours, and Jimmy said that Billie 'was dancing with each and every one. And I had so many close conversations with her about so many things . . .'

After all this, it was just what Jimmy Fletcher called 'my bad luck' that he should be the one brought in for the next raid on Billie. A group of agents headed by a man known as Max G. had tried to catch her in Philadelphia.† They said they had found four ounces of heroin in her empty car and they attempted to arrest her when she arrived at the scene accompanied by three men. She claimed they could prove nothing about the heroin, and in the confusion that followed a fight broke out. Billie and her friends managed to bundle themselves into their car, but as they drove off, Max G. took out his .45 and 'shot a whole lot of bullet holes into it'. The car swerved and the fender was buckled, but the vehicle got away.

At five o'clock in the afternoon of that same day Jimmy was about to leave his office in New York. He had his overnight bag with him and he was planning to catch a train home to Washington, DC. He was already standing in the hall and waiting for the elevator when his superior, Colonel Williams, called out, 'Reeny, John, Philip? Who's back there? Are any agents back in the room there?'

'I hollered, "Yes, what is it, Mr Williams?"

(cont. from p. 213) him", putting the little dog between her tits with just his head sticking out – everybody was looking.'

* Jimmy Fletcher got these photos back later and 'melted them down' when he realised they could be used as incriminating evidence once Billie was under arrest. He told his chief 'a little white lie' about where he and the others had been that night.

† Jimmy Fletcher's story of Billie's arrest on 19 May 1947 and the events leading up to it is different in many respects from the other versions, but perhaps that doesn't make it less accurate.

'"Where are you on your way to?" he said.

'"Well," I mumbled, "I'm on my way to Washington."

'"Like hell you are! You find some agents! Call their homes! And you get to Newark, under that viaduct! Pick up on Billie Holiday and her group and stick with her till Monday morning!"

'I was reluctant,' said Jimmy Fletcher, talking about it so many years later. 'After all, when you form some sort of friendship with anybody, it's not pleasant to get involved with criminal activities against that person.'

But there was nothing he could do – orders were orders. He tried to find an agent to help him, but no one was available. He went to the Newark viaduct, but Billie and her friends had gone into New York by a different route. Jimmy had information that they might be heading for the Grampion Hotel, so he went there.

He found a green Cadillac parked outside the hotel. He had no torch with him, but with the help of some matches and a lighter he was able to tell it was Billie's getaway car because the fender had been damaged and then straightened out, and he could see the bullet holes made by Max G.'s .45.

Jimmy sat in his rented car and watched the hotel. He saw Billie leaving in a yellow cab and followed her to Kelly's Stables, where she was singing that week. He sat outside the club until five or six in the morning, when he saw her leaving in another cab. She went to Suzy West's place. He waited for her to emerge from there and then he followed her back to the Grampion.*

Jimmy knew that the Bureau was getting the warrants ready for Billie's arrest and that was why they wanted him to keep an eye on her. And so he watched her until Monday morning, then phoned through to the office and explained where she was to be found. As soon as a couple of relief agents† turned up, he drove his car back to the office, grabbed

---

* Billie claimed that the Grampion stole all her belongings when she was arrested. This information was going to be included in *Lady Sings the Blues*, but it was removed, for fear that the hotel might sue.

† According to Stuart Nicholson's researches, the hotel was raided at 5 a.m., by *six* officers.

his overnight bag and headed straight for Washington, DC and his lost weekend.

Billie and Joe Guy were searched and arrested when the police found a syringe containing heroin outside the door. As Jimmy said, 'They had nothing against her, no possession . . . They got her as a circumstantial witness, in being involved in the shoot-out and being present. The charge against her was as a fugitive from justice. That was the exact charge. She threw herself on the mercy of the court . . . She didn't have to throw herself. They didn't have enough of a case against her.'★

All the time that Jimmy was talking I kept trying to find clues to what he thought of Billie's character. At one point he said, 'She was the type that would make anyone sympathetic because she was the loving type'; by that he seemed to mean that she gave her love to people, as she had to him when they danced and talked, and that there was something in her manner that made her desirable to everyone who came into contact with her. He also said that she 'couldn't rate' as a prostitute because 'she was such a crazy girl. She didn't want to just go out with a man. She wanted to be with a man *all the time.*'

Just as the interview was coming to an end, Jimmy said that after the arrest Billie never called upon him for help of any kind, even though she must have known that he would have done what he could for her and might have been able to get her off the hook.

He said Billie did make contact several years later. This was in 1957 and she sent him a telegram from California, telling him that Bill Dufty had written the story of her life and she thought he would like to know. Jimmy found it nice that she wanted to tell him.

★ This is the same case that Bobby Tucker was referring to and that led to Billie being sentenced to a year's imprisonment at Alderson, West Virginia. It was because of this prison sentence that she was denied her Cabaret Card in New York. Apart from getting her into trouble in the first place, Joe Glaser was the only person who could have got her out of trouble, when she was released from prison, by getting her Cabaret Card restored to her. As Dolores Herzog said, 'Joe Glaser could cut corners when he wanted to. He could swing things, bring power to bear. He knew where the skeletons were buried, and if he wanted something done, he *had it done!*'

TWENTY-EIGHT

Colonel White and Friends

'A straight business thing.'

In the company of the narcotics agent Colonel George White and his two friends – one a lawyer and the other a doctor – you enter a world where it is almost impossible to disentangle the truth from the blatant lies, or the honest person from the bunch of crooks.

While telling their own versions of the arrest and subsequent trial of Billie Holiday on a narcotics charge in 1949, it seems that these three men were so at ease with the idea of corruption and double standards in their respective law-enforcement, legal and medical professions that they felt there was no need to explain the contradictions and unanswered questions that emerged as the case unfolded.

Each man had his own reasons for behaving as he did, whether he was motivated by financial greed, obedience to someone with higher authority or the simple desire to spit in the face of the idea of justice. As Colonel White said about his friend, the lawyer Jake Ehrlich, 'If I told him he was a conniving shyster-lawyer, he'd laugh and think it was a great compliment.'

Colonel White was proud to be one of the most successful narcotics agents in the business. He was also proud of his reputation for heavy-handedness.★ He said he believed in being firm, and when he was arresting someone he had always found it better to punch them in the stomach straight away, rather than hesitating and maybe having to shoot them dead a few moments later.

When Colonel White was being interviewed in 1971, he was full of nostalgia for the good old days of the 1940s and '50s, when the job had been so much more fun and crooks would buy three or four kilos of pure heroin at a time because, as he put it, 'they understood the meaning of a good investment'. They might then cook the heroin with milk, but they didn't fool around with it, didn't kill anybody with it, didn't mix it with anything really dangerous like rat poison or horse tranquillisers.

In those happier days, Colonel White had been on friendly terms with many of the Italian hoodlums and Mafia men; people like Joe Adonis. He used to meet up with them regularly and they would talk and play chess together. Of course they understood that sometimes he had to arrest one or two of them and maybe punch them in the nose in the process, or even testify against them in court, but still it was what he called 'a straight business thing'. And when they were arrested, White was sure to have 'something substantial' against them. This meant that either they would agree to turn informer and bring in some good connections for him, or they would be brought before a judge and jury and found guilty, no matter what sort of a lawyer they had employed to fight their case.

Colonel White explained that the Federal Bureau of Narcotics used to have a book in which it listed the names of all the national and international drugs traffickers who were considered to be major public enemies. The task for people like him was continuously to widen the net of contacts and informers and every so often arrest those who were chosen as targets for prosecution.

★ According to Jimmy Fletcher, White was 'a rotten supervisor, I can tell you. He was a drunkard. Worked coast to coast and everyone from Port Authority down to Seattle knew him as a drunkard. And mean, mean to defendants.'

Of course there was a file on Billie Holiday, but Colonel White said she was not considered an important target, since she had never been a dealer or an informer. She was simply a 'sometime addict' who was known to have used marijuana, heroin, cocaine and opium and who was hurting nobody but herself in the process. Colonel White realised that it was not usual to put such a person in jail, unless there was some other reason for it.

But that was exactly the problem. Although Billie was not a 'public enemy', she was what Colonel White called a 'very attractive customer' and it was obvious that she could provide the Bureau with some very good publicity. And after all, if she did get into trouble, he felt she had 'brought it upon her own house' because she was so ostentatious. 'She flaunted her way of living, with her fancy coats and fancy automobiles and her jewellery and her gowns – she was the big lady wherever she went and a good deal of resentment was generated.' On top of that, Billie was not a very stable personality, and as a 'prominent person' she was under an obligation to be extra-circumspect in the way she lived her life.

Ever since her release from Alderson women's prison, in March 1948, Billie had been in the public eye, but from the way the popular press described 'the unforgettable lamenter of Strange Fruit in the million bucks worth of silver blu' mink', it seemed that her conviction in a drugs case and her 'episodes of violence' were much more interesting than her talent as a singer.

Once Billie could no longer work on the New York club circuit because of the loss of her Cabaret Card, she was forced to take on a hectic schedule of performances, which had her zigzagging across the country, sometimes performing as many as five times a day, seven days a week. Three Carnegie Hall concerts in March and April were followed by a Broadway show, four weeks at the Ebony Club, one week in Philadelphia, three in Chicago and then six at the Strand Theater on Broadway. This sort of pressure had been continuing unabated when Billie opened at Billy Berg's club in Hollywood on 15 December 1948. On New Year's Eve there was the drunken brawl in which John Levy stabbed a man in the shoulder and Billie screamed and threw dinner plates.

On 3 January 1949 she was charged on three counts of assault and released on bail. Ten days later the charges against her were dropped, although the woman who said she had been wounded by a dinner plate took out a private lawsuit later. On 13 January Billie started a four-week engagement at Joe Tenner's Café Society Uptown★ in San Francisco. The publicity surrounding her latest arrest had proved very good for business and the crowds were so keen to come and see the 'notorious blues singer' that there was standing room only.

Colonel White explained that during the first week Billie was at Joe Tenner's, he and two of his officers picked up 'four or five little coloured prostitutes' on a minor drugs charge. And they all complained to him, 'Why do you pick on little people like us, and let Billie run around and use drugs? And everybody knows she uses stuff and yet you pick on poor little things like us! Why don't you bring her in? ... Show us that you move against the rich as well as against the poor!'

Apparently this was when the first seed of an idea was planted. A few days later, when Colonel White and his men were 'at a loose end' in the office, they had the sudden inspiration to 'polish it off . . . to kick her over . . . to make the arrest'. Colonel White said he realised that an outsider, or indeed Billie herself, might think it was a pre-arranged plan that had finally grown ripe and ready for execution, but he insisted this wasn't the case. As far as he and his men were concerned, arresting Billie was done on a whim and was a way of passing time.†

★ Colonel White explained that Joe Tenner was on his list as a drugs dealer with Italian hoodlum connections. While Billie was performing, heroin was on sale in the club as well as from Joe Tenner's house, which was just around the corner. Colonel White said that later the place went 'down, down, down and went to the dogs and got very shabby . . . Then one day the agents shot the lock off the door.'

† According to the lawyer Jake Ehrlich, his 'good and honourable friend' Colonel White arrested Billie 'because of some dealing he had with John Levy'.

In those days a search warrant wasn't needed for an arrest, just so long as the case was brought before the State Court and not the Federal Court. And so this little group of determined law-enforcers set off to the Mark Twain Hotel in San Francisco's red-light district, where they knew Billie and John Levy were staying. They checked with the hotel receptionist that their two suspects were indeed at home, and then they went on up and knocked on the door of room number 203.

Colonel White couldn't remember if he and his men went through the familiar ritual of pretending they had a telegram to deliver, or if they simply kicked the door open. As they entered, John Levy picked up a glass bottle that had been turned into an opium pipe and a small quantity of opium wrapped in paper, and he handed them to Billie. She fled obediently into the bathroom, threw the bottle and the packet into the toilet bowl and tried to flush them away. In her haste she managed to topple headlong into the bathtub, but was not hurt. Colonel White fished out the incriminating evidence and announced that he was arresting John Levy and Billie and taking them to the county jail.

In the interview White said there was no indication that the opium had been used, and when he and his men searched the room they found no other drugs and not even any alcohol. He said Billie was wearing heavy silk pyjamas and she was sober and clear-headed. She didn't swear or complain; she just sat there, very quiet and passive. Colonel White said he examined her arms and found old needle scars, but no new ones.

John Levy was wearing white silk pyjamas and did all the talking. He was known to be an opium user and he was also known to be a police informer. He now mentioned the names of some of the officers he'd 'worked for' and suggested that he could 'turn the tricks' on some very important people in the narcotics business if he was released and allowed to go back to New York, although he was very vague about the names of the people he could bring in. Colonel White found John Levy smooth and persuasive, even if he was not particularly charming. 'He was a smart man who'd do anything to extricate himself from trouble. He gave the impression of being more of a shrewd businessman than a pimp – as pimps go, on a scale of ten, I'd have given him a seven . . . If he had given information, we might have settled the whole thing and let them both go, there and then. If he had just called up somebody in New York or Chicago to get them on an airplane and bring some stuff out, everything would have been fine.'

Instead, Billie and John Levy were freed on bail, in time for her to do her usual three shows at Café Society Uptown that evening. They appeared together for a preliminary hearing on 3 February. Their lawyer, Jake Ehrlich, was a good friend of Colonel White's. He also happened to be a good friend of Joe Tenner's, and Tenner had agreed to pay the legal fees out of Billie's forthcoming earnings at his club.

As Colonel White saw it, 'Most criminal trials are not after justice at all, they're not after the truth. Lawyers speak a different language than ordinary people and their concerns are: "Can I prevent the jury from knowing what really happened? Can I obscure and confuse and misdirect the issue?" The whole thing is a show.' White thought that perhaps Jake Ehrlich 'got together' with the District Attorney and the two of them agreed to drop the case against John Levy, who immediately packed his bags and got out of the State of California as fast as he could. And when White asked the District Attorney why this man had been allowed to go free, the answer was very simple: 'We could have indicted Levy if we had wanted to, but Billie Holiday is the name and we want to get some publicity. Levy to us is a nothing guy!'

Since Jake Ehrlich was employed by the club owner Joe Tenner, his first consideration was to ensure that Billie could complete her lucrative engagement at Café Society Uptown. There were also several later bookings that she needed to fulfil, otherwise she was in danger of being sued for breach of contract.

The contracted engagement at Café Society Uptown was

completed on 22 February.★ Billie then went on a tour of one-nighters that took her through northern California to Los Angeles and Chicago, ending up with a three-week engagement at the Club Bali in Washington.† The Club Bali had three record-breaking weeks, ending with a grand finale celebration on 7 April, Billie's birthday. The following day she was in Baltimore and then Chicago, Detroit, Milwaukee and back to San Francisco, where she was described by the *San Francisco Chronicle* as looking 'large and luscious in a dazzling white-beaded gown'. When she appeared on stage with a black eye, after having been beaten up by John Levy, that same newspaper observed, 'Billie Holiday, the torchanteuse, is singing these nights with more than lumps in her throat; she had lumps elsewhere, too, after being beaten pretty brutally one night last week. She knows some lovely people!'

By now Billie's trial had been set for 1 June. Five days before that date Colonel White and Jake Ehrlich arranged for her to be sent to a psychiatric hospital called Twin Pines, where she was put under the care of Dr James Hamilton. The idea was to make sure that she had no drugs in her system when she was tested at the trial, although as far as one can tell there is no evidence that she was using *any* drugs at the time.

So here comes the third member of this curiously crooked team. When Linda Kuehl interviewed Dr Hamilton, what he said was remarkably contradictory. He said that when Billie was brought to him she showed no signs of being addicted to heroin or to any other narcotics.‡ All he needed to do to keep her calm was to give her 'enormous amounts

---

★ On 10 February three zealous policemen turned up at Café Society Uptown and arrested Billie for a second time during the intermission of her show. They took her down to the county jail for more questioning and rebooked her on the old charge of opium possession.

† It was while she was in Washington that Billie was offered a substantial sum for a three-week appearance at the Royal Roost, provided she could get her Cabaret Card back, but her appeal was turned down by the Supreme Court.

‡ According to Dr Hamilton, 'If she had been addicted to heroin, she would have gotten diarrhoea and withdrawal symptoms, but she didn't, so after five days it was perfectly apparent to me that she was not addicted.'

of booze', which, if he remembered rightly, was about nine fluid ounces a day of crème de menthe and brandy. He said, 'She took command of the hospital. She set the hours she wanted to eat and she had her drinks when she wanted them . . . I mean a psychiatric hospital cook doesn't usually act as a bartender. I arranged this for her because that's the natural thing to do. And I can do as I damn well please!'

On being asked what he thought about Billie's state of mind and character when she arrived, Dr Hamilton said, 'Billie came to me to be cured of nothing. She was a beautiful, strong, dynamic kind of person in a jam, and my natural instinct was to try to help her . . . She was royalty . . . I couldn't find a diagnosis category. This was a superior woman, who interested me very much . . . an unusual person, almost an operatic tragedy figure who had this aura.'

So far so good. But then a little later Dr Hamilton continued with his diagnosis, saying, 'What drives Billie? I don't like to use this word, but she's really a psychopath; an impulse-driven, strong, talented, but not dependable woman.' He looked at the notes he had made when Billie was in his care and added, 'She'd had a lot of tough breaks in her life, and the tough breaks were part of the racial problem.' Summing up his whole encounter with her, he concluded, 'It was kind of fun. It was real fun to see this unusual person!'

The trial opened as arranged on 1 June. Billie still had the black eye, but no trace of drugs was found in her system.★ Her lawyer put forward the case that her manager John Levy had conspired with the narcotics agent Colonel White to have her arrested. A photograph was produced as evidence; it showed Colonel White and John Levy sitting companionably together

★ The legal problem for Ehrlich was that Billie had been charged with *possession* of the drugs that were thrust into her hands as the agents burst into the hotel room. Dr Hamilton said he was 'primed' by Ehrlich to state that Billie was not addicted to any drugs, the moment he was put on the stand. The prosecution objected, and Dr Hamilton was severely reprimanded 'as if I had been the worst guy in the world . . . to expose the fact that this woman was not an addict', but in spite of that he got the jury on his side and this led to Billie's acquittal. At one stage in the proceedings Ehrlich told the jury, 'We're trying a human being here! We are not trying her for the colour of her skin!'

at a table in Café Society Uptown.★ Billie had been told to 'act dumb' when she was questioned, and she simply said that John Levy was her man and she loved him so. On 3 June she was acquitted.

According to Jake Ehrlich, the whole fiasco could be blamed on John Levy. 'He was turning Billie over to White. There's nothing wrong with that, that's his business . . . Levy wanted to get rid of her. He had cleaned her out of money. She was at the end of the road. Oh, sure she was!'

Jake Ehrlich claimed that he had really wanted to save Billie. It was not just because she was his client, but because 'Here was a woman who was so great, she had so much heart. She was like a child with nobody to guide her . . . I wanted to acquit her more than I wanted to acquit anyone. Levy and those others were making a living off her body and to me the lowest scum on God's green footstool is a pimp.'

Such protestations were fine and dandy, but soon after the trial was over Levy invited Ehrlich and his wife to come to meet him in New York, so that the three of them could celebrate the victorious outcome. And only a year later Ehrlich was busy taking 'this great woman' to court, for failure to pay his legal fees. He knew that in the end all the money she had earnt had been appropriated by John Levy, who had agreed to pay her legal costs with it. But as he said, 'This was a legal manoeuvre. Billie was the principal. She was my client. Services were given to her!'

This story has an epilogue. In 1974 the Mark Twain Hotel in San Francisco decided to dedicate rooms number 203 and

★ When William Dufty was going through the manuscript of *Lady Sings the Blues*, checking it for possible libels, he contacted Ehrlich and asked if he still had a copy of that photograph, because, 'in a fit of pre-publication nerves, Doubleday has questioned the use of the episode because . . . it was referred to in the testimony, but never admitted in the record . . . They seem to feel that the implication of a frame . . . would in some way inflame Colonel White into suing Doubleday. Since this goes to the heart of the trial and your strategy, it seems worth fighting about.' Dufty never got a reply and the scene was omitted from the book. I can't work out if Colonel White agreed with Jake Ehrlich to get Billie let off the hook, or if he was genuinely surprised when the photograph was produced as evidence.

204 as the Billie Holiday Suite. Apparently the rooms are 'tastefully decorated with relics of the era', and this includes framed newspaper reports of Billie's arrest, her trial and subsequent acquittal.

TWENTY-NINE

Carl Drinkard

'We were like a family.'

The interview with Carl Drinkard must have gone on
for many hours over several days because the typewritten transcript of the tapes covers more than 130 pages.
Linda Kuehl doesn't say when she first met him, but among
her other papers there is a letter that suggests they became
very good friends. This letter has no address or date, and
it is written from a prison somewhere. Carl sends Linda
his love and calls her his honey and his baby. He asks her
to contact a friend of his who might write an affidavit
for his forthcoming trial. He says he has just heard that
Billie's last husband, Louis McKay, has shot somebody,
and he wants to know if this is true and 'Did he kill the
guy?'★

Carl Drinkard was Billie's piano player on and off between
1949 and 1956. Their relationship began in Washington, DC
in the summer of 1949, when he was twenty years old and
close to finishing his studies at Howard University. He was
living with his mother and earning between eight and fifteen

★ Louis McKay was indicted by the Nassau County Police in Mineola, for
shooting a man in the chest. The man did not die and McKay's plea of self-
defence was accepted. This took place around 1972.

dollars a night, playing at a small upstairs club called Little Harlem.

Then one evening he was telephoned by Al Suder, the manager of Club Bali, the most lavish place in Washington, where all the big-name singers appeared. Billie Holiday was in town and she had said she wanted Carl to accompany her. A man called Coolridge Davis had been booked for the job, but 'he played big fat piano in the Fats Waller bag' and she didn't want that; she wanted Carl.

Carl told the Club Bali manager that he was flattered. He said he considered Lady to be the greatest jazz singer in the world and, like everyone else in the business, he was in awe of her. But he couldn't do it.

Just at that moment there was a noisy commotion on the stairs leading up to the Little Harlem club and 'here comes Lady Day up the steps'. She marched over to the piano and said, 'You! You're coming with me!'

She was wearing the blue mink coat that was reputed to be worth $17,000, and when Carl looked at her he said to himself, 'Truly, if I didn't know who this woman was, I'd know she must be *somebody*!' He said she had a way of carrying herself very erect so that she seemed tall, even though she wasn't that tall. And she always stared straight ahead, looking neither to the left nor the right, and that made her seem independent and full of confidence, even though as soon as you got to know her you knew how insecure she really was.

Carl could not resist her authority and so he agreed to go with her. Billie began by taking him to a bar called the Crystal Cabin. She ordered herself a double brandy with a crème-de-menthe floater and she got him a double gin, which was what he asked for, even though it was more than he could manage because he was hardly a drinker at that time.

'You don't have to worry about my music,' Billie said. 'If you can play "The Man I Love", you can play for me. I'm the easiest thing in the world to play for.'

They then went in her car to the Club Bali, which was

packed with people all waiting expectantly for her to re-appear after the intermission. In the dressing room she tore off the first five numbers from her music book and gave them to Carl. 'Let's go on!' she said, and there wasn't even time to look at the tunes.

He remembered how he had to walk through the hushed crowd to reach the stage. And there he saw Art Tatum, the idol of every jazz pianist in those days, sitting at the horse-shoe bar. In spite of his blindness, Art Tatum felt Carl passing close by and reassured him, saying, 'You just do your best! Nobody can expect more than that!'

Then the compère was announcing, 'And now, ladies and gentlemen! The Club Bali takes pleasure in bringing you the one and only Lady Day . . . Miss Billie Holiday!' And with that, a great roar of pleasure rippled through the room as the audience watched her going up the little flight of steps that led onto the stage. The pink spotlight followed her. She carried her head high, so that you could feel what Carl called 'the magic of her proudness'. She turned to her new pianist and he gave her the opening of the first song.

And then she began to sing, standing very stiff and not looking at the audience, but staring beyond them, her arms bent at the elbows, her hands clenched into tight fists and ready to punch the air. Carl Drinkard remembered that she was wearing a long, heavy gown of the type that her manager John Levy always bought for her, and it was sequined from top to toe 'like the suits that warriors wore to the Crusades'. He said she always knew how to carry herself in a gown like that, with just enough movement to be seductive, without ever being gaudy or vulgar.

The first set went smoothly and when it was over Billie said, 'From now on, Carl, you belong to me. You're going to be *my* piano player!' And it was true. He did belong to her for several years. He was with her on her first European tour in 1954; he played for her at the Carnegie Hall in 1955; and he made recordings with her in 1956. Then they drifted apart, although in the interview he never explained why.

Carl was used to snorting heroin in those days, but he

was not what he called 'a needle junkie' when he first began working for Billie. He knew all about her habit and what he called her 'checkerboard career with heroin, going back and forth on the needle'.★ He'd sometimes 'pick up a package for her', but she did her best to protect him and warn him off the drug. 'She did not endorse the use of heroin, except for herself . . . She used to preach to me day in and day out. She'd say, "Carl, don't you ever use this shit! It's no good for you! Stay away from it! You don't want to end up like me!"'

In the interview he wanted to make it clear that when he did become a junkie, it was not Billie's fault. This happened in 1952 in Chicago. For a short while he was playing in a band along with Miles Davis and 'a little drummer' called Jimmy Green. Every night after the show the three of them would go to Jimmy Green's house and they'd get high together. Carl said, 'The two of them were shooting and I was snorting', and they began to tease him, saying, 'If Carl doesn't stop wasting this stuff, we're going to take it from him!' That was when he decided to join the club and 'Miles Davis put that needle in my arm and helped me wreck my life.'[†]

So Carl became a needle junkie and he must still have been a junkie when he was interviewed by Linda Kuehl, because that would explain his rambling stories and his endless fascination with the details of getting a fix, or failing to get a fix.[‡] It would also explain his curious detachment from

---

★ Carl Drinkard said that Billie was more secretive about her habit when she was still with John Levy. 'Every time John would go out of the room she'd reach into her stash – her roll of money tucked in her stocking (along with what she called her "widdle wazor blade") and she'd pull out a packet, roll a match book up and snort.' Things changed when she was with Louis McKay.

† In 1954, Miles Davis cured himself of his heroin addiction. He returned to his father's farm in East St Louis, locked himself in a two-room apartment and stayed there without food or drink, 'struggling to keep from screaming with the pain that tortured his joints'. And then, after seven days, 'it was over, just like that' – more or less.

‡ It makes me think of my old friend, the American writer Mason Hoffenberg, famous for his excesses and for his co-authorship of the book *Candy*. Mason was a junkie for many years, until he moved over to alcohol. He told many deadpan junkie stories, including the one about turning up at the surgery of a London doctor who was providing him with a prescription for heroin – something that was still legal in England in the 1960s. A very white-faced

the chaotic scenes of violence and despair he was talking about. On one occasion he described a quarrel between Billie and John Levy, which culminated in her smashing a portable TV set over Levy's head. At this point in his narrative Carl remarked absent-mindedly, 'It was the first portable TV I'd ever seen.'

When asked to explain the nature of his relationship with Billie, Carl said that Billie had a magnetism that could make anyone love her, if she wanted them to. But he insisted that his love for her was never sexual, even though they often shared the same living quarters and even the same bed. He was so young when he first started to work for her, and so relatively inexperienced, that he felt he was like the son she never had. He never called her Billie, always Lady, and he felt she appreciated the dignity of the name. 'God knows, to me she was the great Lady Day!'

Like a child with a wayward parent, Carl tried to watch over Billie as well as he could. When I look at a photograph of the two of them arriving at London Airport in 1954, it does seem as though they might be related, although that might be just because they both have the same tired and puffy faces and the same distracted stare that makes them appear like creatures from another planet.

For Carl, Billie always appeared exquisitely beautiful when she was fully dressed, but terrifying in her nakedness. He said her legs were too short, her breasts were too baggy, her arms were too long, her hips were 'insane', and she was either too fat or too thin, depending on her intake of drugs and drink. Perhaps this is why he hated her lack of modesty and her way of welcoming complete strangers into her dressing room when she was wearing nothing more than a pair of high-heeled shoes. But it could also have been because her skin was 'tattooed like a map' with needle scars and he saw the signs of his own condition mirrored there.

Carl said that of course all of Billie's men were pimps and

(cont. from p. 230) nurse arrived at the door and explained that the doctor had just died of a heart attack. 'Yeah, whatever,' replied Mason, 'but what about my prescription?'

for him there was nothing odd in that. 'A man could give her money and jewellery and she didn't give a damn. She'd grown up in that pimp–whore environment and she expected this. She felt and believed that if a woman was making money, the man should have it.' He described how John Levy treated her as a 'valuable commodity . . . and she represented everything he had attained at that time'. When he bought her mink coats and fine jewellery, he did so with the knowledge that he could always use these items as 'collateral' if he was short of cash. Levy made sure Billie was kept working so hard because 'that was how the money kept coming in', and even when she behaved badly he was 'too smart to walk out on her, but would lay and lay until she had calmed down. Then he would take her home and that would start another chapter in their torrid love affair.' On one occasion John Levy explained his belief that 'You gotta keep your foot up them bitches, Carl, otherwise they'll get lazy on you.'

In 1950 and 1951 there were about four months when Billie was not on tour from one city to the next, and during that time she lived in a house on Linden Boulevard in St Albans, New York. John Levy had bought the house using her money, but he kept it in his name so that, when he left, the house went with him. Nevertheless, for a while it was a place that seemed more like home than most of the places Billie had ever known.

The house had three bedrooms, as well as a kitchen and dining area. Billie had the walls decorated by a 'guy called Jay' who was apparently the inventor of flock wallpaper, so he covered the walls with swirling patterns in fuzzy brushed nylon. The house was never completely furnished and Billie had no record player, but the radio was kept on at all times, although nobody bothered whether it was playing music or reporting the latest news headlines.

Billie had Chiquita her Chihuahua and Carl her pianist to keep her company. John Levy used to come and stay occasionally, but as Carl said, 'he was usually gone' with his gambling commitments, a club in New York, numerous property deals and at least two other women to keep him busy.

At home in St Albans, Billie and Carl followed a daily routine. She tended to wake up between ten in the morning and noon. She never bothered to eat breakfast, but would begin the day with a large glass of Gordon's gin and Seven-Up. As Carl explained, 'When I say she had gin for breakfast, I don't mean just having one double. It started in the morning and it went on all day long until she went to bed.' If she had no need to go out, she didn't bother to get dressed, but would potter around the house wearing slippers and Japanese silk pyjamas or 'satinish-type lounging robes'. She liked to wear an apron to give her a feeling of domesticity.

Carl said that Billie enjoyed doing things around the house herself. She might begin with a bit of cleaning and then she'd take up some knitting or crocheting, 'which was how she'd spent a lot of time while she was doing that year in West Virginia'. For a while she was busy making a tomato-red woollen sweater for Carl, but then they quarrelled about something and she transformed it into a jacket for the dog instead. The main event of the day was the preparation of 'a really good dinner', which Billie cooked in the vague hope that John Levy might turn up to share it with them. She never had much interest in eating and it was 'only during the very late hours that she would even consider food at all', but she liked to cook. Her speciality was recipes using ground topside of beef: dishes like meat loaf or Cornish Hens. Carl said, 'Her seasoning was perfection', and she could spend hours chopping and kneading and fiddling about in the kitchen.

Such work was regularly interrupted by more gin, a cigarette, a quick snort of heroin, because 'she was sniffing at this time, she didn't use the needle', or simply the wish to stop everything and talk. Billie could talk for hours, mostly drawing on her own memories and anecdotes about people she had known. She had the habit of inventing stories and, once she had thought them up, they took on a life of their own, until they seemed to have all the validity of real experiences and she herself never doubted that they were true. As Carl said, 'She was a pathological liar and she'd repeat herself and change the details, and she'd tell a story so many times a certain way that she'd begin to believe it herself. She'd tell it the way she'd think was most impressive and, even if it lost all semblance of truth, that didn't seem to worry her at all.'

Although she had a lot of famous friends at the time, very few people ever came to the house. The only frequent visitor was a man called Freddie Bartholomew, who had been a child star years before, when he played the film role of Little Lord Fauntleroy.*

As long as John Levy was not there, Billie dominated the conversation, but in his presence she made an effort to sit quietly in a corner, drinking gin and looking demure and obedient. Things would go well for a while, but eventually trouble was bound to break out. Although Levy wanted to appear as a tough guy, Carl said that Billie was by far the stronger and could always beat him when it came to a real fight. John Levy would be huffing and puffing and going red in the face, and you could tell that he was terrified of her.

According to Carl, at this time Billie was earning about $5,000 a week. Carl was paid about $150. Billie got whatever it was felt was necessary for her needs, and John Levy kept the rest. Apart from his deals and obligations, he was also a compulsive gambler and so most of the money went on paying his debts.

Carl said that 'Billie didn't care about money for money's sake; she'd let John run for four or five weeks without saying a word. All of a sudden, knowing he had fucked up about twenty to twenty-five thousand dollars of her money, she would enquire about it. John couldn't stand this. Lady was not supposed to question him about it.' The enquiry would

---

* Bartholomew was married to a woman called Maely, who later became the wife of William Dufty. Carl described Maely as a 'very big woman, fat and sloppy-looking, a pretty swift talker and an opportunist'. Billie called her a 'fat funky jive bitch who is just hanging around trying to get something going for herself', while Arthur Herzog said she was 'a very aggressive publicist and she became a Billie Holiday sycophant. So no one liked her much . . .'

be a cue for Levy to fly into a hysterical rage and go red in the face.

Carl remembered the occasion in 1950 when they were appearing at the Earle Theatre in Pennsylvania. John Levy had spent all of Billie's earnings in advance of her performances, and at the end of a show two men 'were standing there just at the stage door and they were very well dressed, but you could see they were hardened goons'. Carl knew who they had come for, but remembered that he said to John Levy, 'Listen, John, there's a couple of guys down there and they look like killers and I don't know who they want to see.'

It was when Billie heard about the men and the money that she hit John Levy over the head with the portable TV. She also once cut him with a knife and tried to slash his throat with a piece of broken mirror, but she missed and cut his chest instead. John Levy sometimes managed to hurt her too, but as Carl explained with his deadpan detachment, it was only her next man, Louis McKay, who was 'the real true man she always dreamed of, who was . . . really strong enough for her. He could knock her unconscious with a single blow of his fist.'★

According to Carl, the main problem between Billie and John Levy was drugs. Levy was addicted to opium, but he was 'scared to death of heroin, because he knew it had a tendency to bring the Feds on him'. He also took pride in the fact that he was intimate with all the big gangsters, 'and heroin to them was a lowly thing. The gentlemen gangsters used cocaine and opium.' John Levy wanted to 'gorilla' Billie into giving up heroin, although Carl suspected that in fact

---

★ In praising Louis McKay's strength, Carl said, 'I don't think I could have hit her and knocked her down, unless I caught her off-balance, like I did at the Rendezvous Lounge.' He described how Billie would taunt Louis McKay until he attacked her. 'She put her face as close to his as she could and said to him, "Motherfucker!" The next thing I knew, Louis hit her on the jaw — *Bop!* — with his fist and caught her before she could drop. He picked her up and walked her into the dressing room; nobody had any idea she was out cold . . . Two minutes later here comes Lady, prancing out of the dressing room as though nothing had ever happened . . . looking as though she'd just stepped out of a shower.'

he was 'playing a two-prong game' and supplying the drug to a friend of his called Pensicola, who then sold it on to her.★

Louis McKay had a different approach. As Carl put it, 'Of all her men, he was more considerate as far as her stuff was concerned than any of the others.' When he started with Billie in 1952, Louis McKay realised at once that she was looking for a man who could advise her 'like her own mother' and that above all else 'she needed guidance'. That was why, instead of letting her buy the drugs from street peddlers, McKay arranged to obtain large quantities of heroin himself, which also gave him much greater control over her.

Louis McKay would buy a kilo or more at a time, 'especially when they were getting ready to go on the road, so we wouldn't have to connect in small towns'. Carl said that everybody was more or less happy with the arrangement. Carl was convinced that Louis was also 'as hooked as a dog', but he managed to keep his habit private, and anyway 'he was handling all the money so when he told us he had bought half a kilo it could have been a kilo.' And if Louis McKay ever showed signs of addiction, he always said it was Billie's fault, because she was sprinkling heroin powder in the food she cooked for him.

Just like his predecessor, Louis McKay had a family of his own as well as two or three other girls. 'But if ever Billie loved a man, she loved Louis. She called him "Daddy" and she did her best to please him . . . Louis used to play around on her, but I think he was fairer to her than any other man that I knew her to have.'

Both Billie and Carl seem to have treated Louis McKay like a father whom they hoped would be kind to them, by giving them as much heroin as they needed. 'We were like a family,' explained Carl, with something close to nostalgia. 'There were no secrets between us, but I knew that in a dire

---

★ According to the singer Marie Bryant, John Levy put his wife Tondalayo 'on the strong stuff' in order to have more control over her. She said it wasn't Billie's addiction that bothered him, but the fact that she 'wouldn't turn tricks for him'.

situation I could never count on her . . . We were like a family and there was no telling what trouble she might get into if she was left on her own . . . She was weak. She was like a little girl needing guidance. She had a morbid fear of going to jail and she could not stand pain.'

So there they were, the two of them, waiting for Daddy to come home with gifts. But when Louis McKay was away for days on end, they were left to their own devices and it was here that Carl was able to get into the swing of his endless junkie stories. There was the time when they were waiting for Louis, and every day Billie sent Carl out to the pawn shop on Long Island with a new piece of jewellery. 'It started out with a ring. I pawned the first ring and the next day I pawned another ring. We were shooting up just as fast as I could pawn the rings . . . She gives me another ring; it is a cluster ring with a ruby at the centre, and when the man saw it he said, "My God, you don't see rings like this any more!" '

When the rings had gone, Carl took the blue mink coat, but the man in the pawn shop said, 'Oh my God, I don't think I can deal with this!' And so Carl had to drive for miles into an all-white area until he reached a man who dealt in furs. And the man almost cried when he saw the beauty of the coat and the name Billie Holiday stitched on the lining in gold thread. He gave Carl $3,000 for it.

On another occasion they were again waiting for Louis to turn up and Carl was sent out with $200 to see what he could do. He found 'a raggedy dope fiend dashing along the street faster than a motherfucker, and I know he's a dope fiend by his walk'. But on that particular night everything went wrong and Carl ended up being arrested by two white policemen and thrown into jail.

Carl explained that, for him as a junkie, 'Getting straight means getting normal, when you're not sick. There's no such thing as getting high after your first fix; you can throw that fucking high out of the window.' But he was aware that, for Billie, it was somehow different. Not only could she shift from injecting to snorting without any apparent problem, but 'Up until the very end, Lady seemed to have gotten a peace of mind and a certain kick from drugs. It was not just to keep from getting sick; she actually enjoyed using drugs.'

Even when she was having a 'bad patch' and couldn't get the heroin she needed, she was not like everyone else. 'Most addicts would lie on a bed, sweltering and yelling and wallowing in their own pain, but she would just sit quietly in a tub of the hottest water she could draw and sit and sit, even if it took her all day and all night and all next day. She'd say, 'I'm not getting out of this fucking tub until somebody brings me some dope!'

And so the stories go on, tangling around each other. And then Carl was no longer working for Billie. And then he was in a jail in New Jersey somewhere, and he was walking the yard with a friend when it came over the loudspeaker: 'Jazz singer Billie Holiday arrested in her hospital room for possession of narcotics in New York.' He looked at his friend, who was a little trumpet player known as Be-Bop Sam, and he said, 'Lady's going to die!'

Carl said that even though Billie had presented the image of being somebody who was incapable of dying, he had always known it was possible for her to die like everyone else. But he doubted if she realised it, even then.

THIRTY

Melba Liston

'Strangers down South.'

In the early summer of 1950, Billie was getting ready for a four-week tour of one-nighters that was scheduled to wind down through the southern states, ending up in New Orleans on 23 July. The trumpeter and bandleader Gerald Wilson had put together eighteen musicians, including one woman, the trombonist Melba Liston.* For the purposes of the tour, this group was turned into the Lady Day Orchestra, with the name painted in bold letters on the roller blinds at the front of the bus that had been hired to carry them from one show to the next.

John Levy was still Billie's manager, even though Melba Liston said it was clear they 'didn't get along too well'. He was supposed to be 'handling the business' and he had also promised to act as the guarantor for the musicians' wages. Promotion for the tour was being arranged by a chauffeur and part-time burglar called Dewey Shewey, who had no previous experience of this kind of work.

---

* The trombonist and jazz composer Melba Doretta Liston was born in Kansas City in 1929. She worked with several bandleaders during the 1940s and '50s, including Gerald Wilson, Count Basie and Dizzy Gillespie. She was a naturally shy person and said that life on the road could be very difficult for the only woman in the band.

After three weeks of rehearsals in Philadelphia, Melba Liston said that everything was 'pretty well set'. The songs had been chosen and the songbook was 'all written out'. Billie was in good voice and she was going to sing all her favourites. They even rehearsed 'Strange Fruit', although she said they didn't get round to performing it because there didn't seem to be any point, since they weren't booked to play for mixed houses.

Baltimore was their first engagement and on Saturday 24 June they were to be playing in the ballroom on Sparrow's Beach, down by the seafront and close to the docks. Different bands and entertainers were booked there every week during the summer. People would gather on the beach and swim and drink and have picnics during the day, and then the music would begin in earnest with the approach of evening.

Whenever Billie came home to play, the news spread fast. Her old friend Pony Kane was by now working as a cleaner and general helper in Alice Dean's whorehouse and she remembered hearing Willie Diggs boasting to people, saying, 'Guess what? I knew her! She used to live in this house! She used to live right there, with us!' Everyone who was still around from the old days was eager to get tickets for the show.

Some of them remembered seeing Billie arrive in her green Cadillac, with a shivering Chihuahua tucked like a handbag under her arm and her manager John Levy sitting tense and angry at her side. They both tended to wear dark glasses, even when the sun was not shining, and in the surviving photographs Levy always looks as though he is on his way to a funeral.

The Lady Day Orchestra opened with some dance numbers for about forty-five minutes and then it was time for Billie to make her way to the bandstand, walking through the crowd that cleared a thin pathway for her. Maybe she was wearing the high-heeled, sling-back suede shoes that Pony Kane admired so much, the white flowers like a pool of light in her hair and her dress glittering as she moved.

The ones in the audience who knew Billie when she was

a young girl still called her Eleanor★ and she must have turned her head every time she heard the sound of her old name, looking to see what memories were brought flooding back by familiar faces from the past. 'Hey, Freddie! You shut up and sit down! . . . Dee Dee, you motherfucker! You still working in that fucking fish market? . . . Where's Diggs? Or can't the bitch leave the pool table for long enough to come and see me?'

And then there she was, standing on a rough stage platform, without the luxury and solitude of a perfectly aimed pinpoint of pink light to follow her every step and to drive away the eyes of those who were watching her. The crowd surged around as close as possible to see this miracle of worldly success, who had been hatched out of their same nest of poverty and confusion.

She signalled to the orchestra that she was ready to begin. What was her first song of the evening? 'I Cover the Waterfront' perhaps, because this was a city where the ships came in from far-away places and sailors tumbled into the clubs and bars and whorehouses to spend their money and then slept off their exhaustion, lying like flotsam along the beach. As Billie's cousin John Fagan said, 'When she sang "On the Waterfront" [*sic*], it had a certain meaning for those of us who lived on the Point. The Point consists of an area which is south of Lafayette Street and it went all the way down to the waterfront. It was a very nice community to live in, even though we were poor. And this is the area she came from.'

The people who knew Billie before she left for New York could see that the years had moved on, and they could hear how her voice had gone slower and darker and was no longer that of a young girl. But her presence was as hypnotic as ever. She was singing the long introduction to that song about a woman whose sailor-lover has abandoned her, but still she waits and hopes for his return.

★ Billie told Max Jones, 'Of course if I go to my home town of Baltimore, someone will shout out "Eleanor!" and nobody answers. I'm looking round and think, "Where the hell's Eleanor?"' (Max Jones, *Talking Jazz*, 1987, p. 244ff.).

Away from the city that hurts and knocks,
I am standing alone by the desolate docks,
In the still and the chill of the night.
I see the horizon, the great unknown,
My heart has an ache, it's as heavy as stone,
Will the dawn coming on, make it last.

I cover the waterfront,
I'm watching the sea.
Will the one I love
Be coming back to me.

I cover the waterfront, in search of my love,
And I'm covered, by a starlit sky above.

She might have followed with 'Fine and Mellow', and
with the words 'he wears high-draped pants, stripes are really
yellow', the image of Skinny 'Rim' Davenport in his fine
suits and hats, and the many other pimps and hustlers she
knew and ran around with, might float into her mind. All
those men who had enjoyed her singing and her company
and who had given her the freedom to be 'one of the boys'
in return.

And then, turning to gaze at John Levy's luminously pale
skin, his unsmiling face and beetling black eyebrows, she
could sing 'My Man', telling the world how she would 'like
to dream of a cottage by a stream . . . where a few flowers
grew and perhaps a kid or two', then explaining with the
next verse that each time her dream is broken and her life
returns to despair, when her man 'gets hot and tells [her]
not to talk such rot'. And always at the back of her mind
as she was singing, she must have had racing thoughts about
the money that was disappearing faster than she could earn
it, and about this tour and Dewey Shewey and whether he
had sorted out the promotion.

She sang into the hot night with the sound of the sea
whispering beneath the sound of the music and people's
voices. And when the show was over, she and John Levy

must have made their way to the York Hotel, which was
run by a man called Sammy and was the only black hotel
in the whole city. Unless they had chosen to go to Tom
Smith's Hotel, but as Pony Kane said, that was only a 'black
rooming house, nothing fancy'.

Perhaps there was a lot more talking and drinking and
quarrelling to be done before Billie was ready to sleep. Melba
Liston said that John Levy had the idea that Billie would be
able to break her heroin addiction in the South, simply
because it would be hard to obtain the drug down there.
But that meant she would need to drink very heavily to
keep her nerves at bay and to keep going.

The following morning they were ready to set off, heading
for the New Dance Pavilion on Carr's Beach in Maryland.
The next day they were booked to appear at the Pier Ballroom
in Ocean City. Then they would go through Virginia, visiting
the southern states that Billie had avoided since her days of
touring with Count Basie and Artie Shaw.* They were also
booked to appear at the Mosque Ballroom in Richmond,
Virginia, the Highway Boxing Arena in Newport News,
Virginia, and the Municipal Auditorium in Norfolk, Virginia.
Then they were supposed go on down to North and South
Carolina, Florida, Georgia and Louisiana.

This was strictly segregated country and they were playing
to all-black audiences. Melba Liston said they played a lot
on a ferry that went 'from one side of a lake to the other',
the bus containing all their equipment going back and forth
with them. And they played in 'barn-like' ballrooms on the
beaches and in dancehalls that were really tobacco ware-
houses, with tobacco leaves hanging from the high wooden
beams and the air sharp from the pungent smell.

In order to transform some of these places for the night's
entertainment, they'd often just rope off a space for dancing

---

* Talking about what it was like to tour the South in the 1930s and '40s, the
drummer Jo Jones said, 'We went through hell, baby! What kind of hell? When
you can't get a meal, when you can't sleep . . . Miss Billie Holiday didn't have
the privilege of using a toilet in a restaurant or in a filling station! . . . How
did she take it? Fuck it! She'd go in and sing! Go and fuck 'em! She did what
she did till she died.'

and then Billie would 'do her stuff, doing what she did'. And if ever a few white people did turn up to listen because they had heard her records and were curious to see her, they were led to a specially cordoned-off white area, away from the rest of the audience.

Soon after the tour began, Dewey Shewey was arrested and carted off by the police, and it then became apparent that he had done nothing about advance planning or publicity.* Very few bookings had been organised and no radio networks or local newspapers had been contacted. Sometimes Billie and John Levy would drive ahead to the next city to try to get things going, or Levy would attempt to make the necessary contacts on his own. But it was often too late and she would end up playing to a small crowd of shuffling strangers who had no interest in the Lady Day Orchestra and its unfamiliar northern music.

Gerald Wilson said that the band really enjoyed it when Billie travelled with them on the bus because she was 'such a trouper' and she made everybody laugh. He said they 'all loved Billie enough to keep on trying, in the hope that the tour would turn successful' although it was nothing but trouble from the moment it began.

As Melba Liston explained it, 'We were all strangers down south, and the people didn't take to us too good . . . We were playing black places, but we were foreign to them. It's a territorial thing; northern blacks were something else to southern blacks, at least to the people we were playing for. We didn't talk the same language.'

The Lady Day Orchestra was 'kept together as a family' by its own sense of isolation. The music they heard on the radio was 'very slow, very sombre, very sad' and even the records on the jukeboxes in the restaurants were quite alien. 'We stayed together and played records together and jammed,' said Melba. 'We tried to be gay, but the music was so bad.'

As the only other woman on the tour, Melba Liston was

---

* The whole tour was such an odd, mismanaged affair that it sometimes seems as if John Levy planned it, just to show Billie that 'she was finished' and to get rid of her afterwards. Which is what he did.

asked by John Levy to stay with Billie in her hotel room, to keep an eye on her and see nothing happened. 'He would get nervous she wanted stuff and he didn't want her to have it!' And so this shy twenty-one-year-old woman, who 'didn't have any experience' and who wasn't used to what she called 'night-life people', did her best to reassure Billie and keep her calm.

Melba Liston remembered how Billie would wake up in the morning and 'She wasn't feeling too good. She'd cry a little bit . . . and then she'd have her coffee and sit up in bed and have her bourbon with it and talk a while.' She talked about her childhood and the chaotic life she had lived in Baltimore, maybe with certain memories reawakened by the recent visit there. Melba said she didn't understand half of what was being said to her, but it didn't matter because 'I thought she was really great. I loved her. Lady was an easy person to like because she was a very warm person; you couldn't help it. If she liked you, she liked contact. I'd see her and she'd always hug me.'

Melba felt that the two of them were kindred spirits — one sad soul with another. She said that Billie called her 'my little girl' and tried to warn her against 'getting messed up in life'. It was only later, looking back on this time, that she realised how for a while she became the daughter Billie had always longed for.

Although Billie was low-spirited, Melba Liston said she wasn't 'laid up or generally irritable.' She kept going and kept on having fun. After the coffee and the bourbon and the tears, she'd get dressed, go out and walk around, and go to the restaurant. Then she'd often put some music on the jukebox and dance and persuade others to dance with her.

Melba Liston found the whole tour far too wild and frightening and did her best to keep out of trouble, hiding in a corner and reading her book. She was what she called a timid child and didn't like violence. She tried to stay as far from John Levy as she could and was terrified when he and Billie quarrelled. She remembered how once they had a fight in the front of the bus and she was so afraid she hid under a seat and crouched there, waiting for the storm to pass.

Billie was venting her fury at the whole mismanaged tour. She said she should never have agreed to come down south with the band, and she was sick of the whole thing and didn't want her name associated with such a disaster. During one of her rages she managed to tear down the heavy roller blind on which the 'Lady Day Orchestra' was written and then she ripped it apart. As Melba Liston said, 'Billie was strong . . . She had to be pretty strong to do that.'

There was another bad fight between Billie and John Levy in a hotel. Billie split his head open with a Coca-Cola bottle, while he managed to cut her with a knife. They were both taken to hospital, but Billie was ready to work that night. 'It didn't show on her,' said Melba Liston.

The days were passing and there was hardly any money coming in. The Orchestra hadn't been paid and neither had the bus driver. And then somewhere in the Carolinas – it was either Greensboro or Greenville – the bus driver announced that he had had enough and walked out on them, leaving them stranded on the bus.★ At this point John Levy said he was going to fetch some money, so he disappeared too. According to Melba Liston, he took Billie with him, but in *Lady Sings the Blues* Billie maintains, 'Mr Levy walked out and left me and my goddamn band stranded in the Deep South without a dime.'†

Whatever the real details of the story, it is certain that Billie disappeared and the entire Lady Day Orchestra of seventeen men and one woman was left stranded without a driver and without money, and with nowhere to sleep except on the upright seats of the bus. But it wasn't just the discomfort that

---

★ The bus driver on these tours was always a white man. This meant that when they were in the South he was the one who could go into a restaurant to get sandwiches without trouble. And he could be sure of being served at the petrol stations.

† In *Lady Sings the Blues* Billie also says, in a voice that doesn't sound like hers at all, 'Mr Levy had invested a little of his own money in this project, so he was playing Simon Legree all the time . . . Somebody once said we never know what is enough until we know what's more than enough. They could have had me and Mr Levy in mind' (p. 155).

Melba remembered. Every night a group of policemen would come and beat against the side of the bus with their long sticks, threatening that 'if anything went wrong in the town, the guys were responsible'.

Melba Liston said the whole situation frightened her so much that 'she was going to pieces'. But she was luckier than the others, because after three days she and Gerald Wilson somehow managed to get a train to Kansas City. From there she made her way home to the West Coast.★

The other members of the band waited another five days until the bus driver finally returned. He announced he was driving to New York, but although that was exactly where most of the men needed to go, he refused to give any of them a lift. And so they were forced to gather up their instruments and make the difficult journey north on their own. Some were able to wire their families to send money out; for others it was not so easy.

Although John Levy had arranged the whole disastrous enterprise and had agreed to be financially responsible, nothing had been put in writing and, when the tour collapsed, the blame and the cost fell on Billie. After all, it was her voice that had taken them along and it was her name that had made it all possible. A number of members of the orchestra felt they had no choice but to put financial claims against her for their loss of earnings and the extra expenses. As Gerald Wilson said when he was interviewed, 'It was one of those things.'†

And so these debts and legal expenses were added to the mountain of debts and legal expenses that had accumulated ever since Billie was released from jail. Over the past two years she had earnt more than ever before and yet she had

---

★ After this experience Melba Liston gave up performing. She worked with the Los Angeles Board of Education for four years until Dizzy Gillespie persuaded her to come to New York and join his band in 1955.

† According to John Nicholson, 'Billie was left [in South Carolina] without a dime and had to beg John Levy for money to get home. When the money came through, she pulled out with a promise to send for her stranded band when she got back to LA. The band waited in vain and the whole sordid affair was left for the Musicians' Union to unravel' (p. 180).

nothing left to show for it. John Levy and Billie parted company, but he took much of her 'collateral' with him, including the house on Long Island. She was also committed, for weeks to come, to contracts that Levy had signed on her behalf.

In spite of the trauma of the tour, Melba Liston stayed close to Billie and said they used to talk on the phone maybe once or twice a year, just to catch up on news. They also bumped into each other occasionally, once Melba had moved back to New York in 1955. Their last meeting was at the airport in 1958. Melba was 'going out some place' with her agent and her all-women quintet and Billie was just coming in.

Melba said that even then, even though Billie was sick, she 'was looking beautiful and she was dressed real nice!' She remembered that Billie gazed at this little group of female musicians and then addressed the agent in a voice filled with maternal authority. 'Now, you take care of my children!' she said.

THIRTY-ONE

Memry Midgett

———

'What tune is this, Memry?'

Throughout the 1950s Billie was leading a fugitive life, on the move more or less all the time. Three weeks in San Francisco, one week in Los Angeles, back to New York for a single performance, over to Boston the next day, up to Alaska, down to Detroit. One night she might be singing in a shabby little nightclub with only her pianist to accompany her on a piano that sounded as if it had been left outside during a long winter; the next night it was all glitter and glory with Count Basie's Orchestra celebrating her presence among them.

Just as there are many contradictory accounts of Billie's state of mind and health and the quality of her singing, there are also different stories of where she went and what she did when she got there, and how long she stayed before she moved on. But because I am only working with the voices of people who are speaking about their memories of being with her, I do not need to cling to one version of the truth at the expense of all the others.★ So now I will follow

★ As Farah Jasmine Griffin has said, all biographies of Billie 'fight to situate a version of her life as *the* version. Even as these versions and counter-versions are launched, we are simultaneously both closer to and farther away from Holiday' (p. 64).

Memry Midgett's description of Billie's life for several months during 1954 – and never mind if it takes her to places that others say she never reached, or if she is made to sing a song that others say she never sang.

Memry Midgett came from Oakland, California. She said that she and Billie were 'physically about the same size, but Billie was a little darker than me'. Memry was something of an armchair psychologist, always very busy exploring and analysing Billie's personality, 'to part the curtain between what I had heard and what I was actually experiencing from her'. She was particularly fascinated by what she called Billie's 'malformed heterosexuality' and her 'need for self-punishment'. But at the same time Memry was impressed by what she called 'Billie's humility and her search for self and understanding'.

Memry said she first met Billie at the Downbeat Club in San Francisco, which could seat a big audience of some 300 people. Billie had arrived without any written music and without even the back-up of a pianist who knew how to accompany her. She was supposed to be singing with Vernon Alley's combo, but the musicians were not familiar with the arrangements and Billie was disgusted by what she felt was their lack of professionalism.

Memry was just twenty-three years old and she was playing piano during the intermission. Billie decided to hire her on the spot, even though she had no previous experience of such work. As Memry explained it, 'She would get on the bandstand and call me a tune I had never played before and I just had to do the best I could.'*

After performing in San Francisco, she and Billie had two weeks in Hollywood at the Crescendo, and then they set off

---

* The two-week engagement at the Downbeat Club went very well. According to the *San Francisco Chronicle* of 15 August, Billie 'flew into San Francisco last Monday morning . . . lined up three musicians, rehearsed for five hours on a coffee diet, went back to her hotel for an hour of sleep and then returned to put on four shows before a house that kept crying for more . . .' Helen Noga, who ran the Downbeat with her husband, spoke of 'all the warnings she received' about Billie and her dope addiction before she arrived, but she said, 'I'll take her any day' (Vail, p. 162).

for two weeks in the newly booming city of Anchorage in Alaska, a place where many East Coast Americans had recently come to find work because 'the money was flowing like wine'.

While they were on the plane flying to Alaska, Billie suddenly announced that she had given up heroin. She said she had done it often enough before and knew what the physical effects would be. She asked Memry to explain to the stewardess that all the shaking and shivering and coughing were due to the fact that she was recovering from a bad bout of influenza, nothing more.

When they arrived at their destination it was much colder than either of them had anticipated. Memry said she had never been so cold in her life, and Billie had nothing suitable to wear — only a little silver fur shoulder wrap and a few thin dresses. Her mink coat would have been ideal, but she had left it behind; or perhaps it was waiting for redemption in a pawn shop somewhere in New York.

So there she was, with nothing to protect her against the elements, coughing and shivering all through the day and standing with chattering teeth in front of the little heater in her dressing room, before taking the plunge and going on stage. Memry was convinced that, along with the symptoms of withdrawal from heroin, Billie was in very poor health and might even have contracted pneumonia. She also felt that, like anyone who was using a combination of drugs and liquor, Billie didn't eat much and as a result was suffering from malnutrition.*

For all her performances Billie stuck to the songs she knew well, the words and music intensely familiar, but grown slower and more surreal with the passing of time. She did 'Them There Eyes' and 'Easy Living' and made them sound like a lament, and she kept returning to 'Willow Weep for Me', but with such long pauses when she asked the tree for

---

* Memry blamed Louis McKay for Billie's state of health. She said he was 'the worst pimp ever' because he didn't look after her, and 'a good pimp will see that you get a milkshake, or vitamin pills, or some kind of sustenance to keep you going'.

some sympathy that it was as if she was really waiting for it to answer her in a gentle, willowy voice. Memry said Billie avoided 'My Man' and 'Fine and Mellow,' because they were too demanding, both emotionally and musically, but she could not avoid 'Strange Fruit', when each new audience insisted so vociferously that she sing it for them.

It was while they were in Alaska that Billie started calling Memry 'my little baby' and she would often talk to her as if she was talking to herself while thinking aloud. On one occasion Memry remembered that they were sitting side by side in the hotel living-room when a letter was delivered. It contained the details of Billie's royalties: the name of each record, the number of copies sold, the costs incurred by the company, the percentage taken by the agent and the monies that were due to be paid. The sales figures were very bad and made it apparent that Billie's public no longer cared whether she sang or not. Her star had risen, and now it was falling back into the darkness of obscurity. Billie handed the papers to Memry, so that she could share the realisation that 'her total life had just got to be nothing'.

Louis McKay had come with them to Alaska, but he kept disappearing for days on end. It was rumoured that he was buying great swathes of land in Alaska as property speculation, but no one was really sure. He had told Billie that, because of her police record, everything had to be done in his name even though her money was being used. Memry said he had been banned from 'any number of places' and that included the club in Anchorage where Billie was singing. This was because he had the habit of standing at the bar steaming with belligerence, waiting for the moment when he could engage a complete stranger in a violent argument.

Memry hated Louis McKay and believed that as she got closer to Billie, he began to see her as a 'formidable enemy'. She described him as 'one of the most ruthless men I have ever met', although her hatred must have been quite complicated, because she also said that he and Billie used to have a game about who was going to be 'the first to screw her . . . even though it was never more than a game'. She said

Louis McKay had a 'technique of trying to control Billie's mind. It was like hypnotism. He'd tell her, "You can't depend on anyone but me. You have no friends but me."'

Apparently Louis McKay sometimes arrived unexpectedly in Billie's hotel room, very early in the morning. Then he would pull down the blinds on the windows and tell her that she must stay quiet. He'd give her a tin of chitterlings to eat and a sterno can to heat them on, so that she had enough food for the day, and then he'd go out and lock the door behind him. In his presence Billie always became like a child, unable to break the habit of fear and obedience.

Billie was often alone all night and would phone through to Memry's room because she had woken from a nightmare and couldn't get back to sleep. 'I'm frightened and I'm all alone,' she said, choking on her tears.

Billie told Memry that she kept dreaming of her mother and, when she opened her eyes, the dream would not leave her; Sadie was in the room, staring at her. It seems that the longer Sadie was dead, the more vivid she became. Memry didn't think it was the bonds of love that gave Sadie's ghost the freedom to enter her daughter's room like that, but rather the accumulation of Billie's sense of guilt at having abandoned the woman who had so often abandoned her. She told Memry she should have done something when Sadie was dying in hospital; at the very least she could have sent some money, because she was making a lot at the time. Instead she did nothing and stayed away until after her mother was dead and cold and waiting to be buried.

Billie asked Memry if she thought God would judge her and condemn her to some sort of hell, because of all the things she had done – and failed to do – in her life. Maybe then she remembered the House of Good Shepherd for Colored Girls: the rosary beads she used to clutch to keep danger at bay, and the little golden cross she wore glinting around her neck in the days when she was still as sleek and round as a seal. Maybe she wished she had some of the holy water that she and her friends would collect in jamjars, because then she could sprinkle it into the corners of this cold hotel room and make it seem more like home.

Talking to Memry about her childhood, Billie kept mentioning her grandmother, and Memry felt 'there was something kind and warm and something positive about their relationship'. Billie seems not to have told the story about how her ancient grandmother died peacefully in her arms, a story she had invented for herself long ago, and which William Dufty used to great dramatic effect in *Lady Sings the Blues*. Instead, she just 'spoke fondly' about her grandmother and said something about how she learnt to scrub steps from her.★

Billie kept asking Memry what on earth it was that had made someone follow such a hard and painful road. She had known so many men, she said, men like Bobby Henderson and Freddie Green, who were good and kind and gentle. They were men who would have cared for her and protected her, and given her the children and the security she always longed for. But instead she had been drawn irresistibly to the hustlers and the pimps; she had chosen to be cheated and beaten and humiliated, and shared with other women and discarded when she was no longer useful.

Memry asked Billie about John Levy and whether he had been as bad as all the others, and suddenly that particularly unpleasant man was transformed in Billie's mind into a relatively good one. At least he had treated her like a lady, she said. He 'didn't permit her to wash dishes' and had sent her an orchid every day. He had made sure she was well dressed and always looking her best. He would never have let her come to Alaska without even a coat to keep her warm, and he never did anything so cruel as locking her in a dark room, leaving her alone with her fears.

★ Billie always adapted the story of her life to suit the person she was telling it to. William Dufty got everything he wanted about the horrors of drug addiction, while Memry, who was very interested in Billie's lesbian experiences, was told that 'At the time she was thirteen she had her own girls on the street. This was when she started in prostitution. I suppose she was a prostitute herself, but at the same time she was doing the bisexual part of a man.' If this were true, it seems odd that no one from Baltimore mentions that Billie was a female pimp.

Memry was determined to help Billie. She persuaded her to take the bold step of asking the club manager to pay her directly, instead of having the money passed on to Louis McKay. And then suddenly there was money to spend, and the two of them went shopping together and Billie bought herself a new coat and a dress, amazed by her own show of independence. 'This is the first time in many years that I've known what it's like to get up and be around in the daytime,' she said.

When it was time to return to New York, Louis McKay did not travel with them, although he gave them the surreal task of taking the frozen and butchered carcass of a whole deer back with them on the plane. It had begun to 'thaw and bleed' by the time they landed.

As soon as they arrived in New York, Billie wanted to get hold of some heroin and, when they got to the apartment in Flushing, the pianist Carl Drinkard turned up at the door, ready to return Billie to her old ways. The two of them began their preparations, but while Billie was tightening a tourniquet on her arm, Memry became hysterical and kept screaming, 'No! No! Don't! Don't!' She 'cried so hard' that Billie was woken out of her somnambulant state. 'Well, my little baby, if it's going to affect you like that,' she said, 'to hell with it!' And with that she ripped the tourniquet from her arm and told Carl Drinkard to 'get the hell out of here!'

Memry tried to persuade Billie that she must take control of her own life. She had to stay away from drugs. She must leave Louis McKay. She must get rid of Joe Glaser and find herself an agent who had *her* interests at heart, rather than his own. Memry kept telling Billie that within a few years she could save enough money to retire. She could buy a house with a garden, have babies, be happy. Billie listened and kept saying incredulously, 'Do you think I can? Do you think I can do it?'

One morning the two women set off by train from Flushing to Manhattan, to confront Joe Glaser in his office. Memry said they got as far as the subway station, but Billie couldn't summon the courage to step onto the escalator that would carry her out of the subterranean world and onto the streets of the city. She stood there, caught in a panic, staring at the flowing river of stairs that rolled on as inexorably as fate. She kept saying, 'I can't do it! I'm too weak! I can't! I can't!' The decisive moment was lost and Billie knew she had been defeated. Dejectedly they made their way back to the apartment.

Billie was booked to sing at Carnegie Hall on 25 September 1954, as one of the Birdland All Stars. Count Basie's Orchestra would be playing, along with Lester Young, Sarah Vaughan and Charlie Parker.★ The night before the performance, Louis McKay turned up unexpectedly and the next morning he accompanied Billie and Memry to the rehearsal room. He had his four-year-old son with him, and he suddenly got very impatient and said it was the boy's birthday and Billie must come with him at once to help buy a present. He also informed her that he had invited a crowd of friends over for a party later in the day. And so that was the end of the rehearsal.

Memry arrived at seven to take Billie to Carnegie Hall. She found that Billie had cooked a big meal, had served her guests and was now busy with the washing up. There were people all around and they were 'yelling and screaming and drinking and drunk, and pressing Billie with all kinds of foolishness and nonsense talk'. They all seemed to know Billie in one way or another, but they were not musicians and they were keen to prolong the party.

At eight-thirty Billie was trying to do her hair in front of a broken mirror and still hadn't decided what to wear. And then at last she was ready to be bundled into a limousine, along with a noisy crowd who all wanted to come too. Memry was squashed beside her and trying to explain what songs they would be doing for the show, how many bars this or that introduction would have, how long the sets would last. But the people in the car were talking too loud

---

★ Memry said that Louis Armstrong was on the bill as well, but no one else includes him.

and Billie 'didn't grasp the half of it'. Memry said that Billie was sober and not using heroin, but 'she was sick from lack of nutrition . . . and part of malnutrition is to be addle-brained'.

The crowd that had been in the limousine now followed Billie enthusiastically into her dressing room and Louis kept on asking more and more people to come in, until the room was filled to bursting.

Then it was the moment for Billie to be called to the stage. It was a long time since she had appeared in New York and people were eager to see her. The audience roared a welcome out of the darkness as she came on. She moved towards the microphone, but tripped over a wire and fell down on the floor. She clambered back to her feet, completed the short journey and stood there, waiting for the music to begin.

Count Basie's rhythm section opened with an eight-bar introduction to 'Blue Moon',★ but Memry said they were playing it double-time, so the eight bars sounded like four and Billie failed to recognise the tune. They repeated the introduction six times and still Billie showed no spark of recognition.

Basie signalled Memry to play the introduction on the piano without the orchestra, but by now Billie was far away.

'What tune is this, Memry? What am I supposed to be singing?' she asked, as if they were rehearsing quietly together in an empty room. Her words, spoken into the microphone, billowed across the wide space of the auditorium.

Memry replied, 'Blue Moon', but she had no microphone to amplify her voice and Billie couldn't hear her.

By now the musicians were whispering, 'Blue Moon, Blue Moon!' and the audience had taken up the refrain, 'Blue Moon, Blue Moon, Blue Moon!'

And then suddenly Billie knew it. 'Huh!' she said, very loud, 'Ah! Blue Moon!'

★ According to Ken Vail in *Lady Day's Diary*, Billie sang six songs, but 'Blue Moon' was not one of them. Stuart Nicholson has the same list, but he puts Carl Drinkard behind the piano, instead of Memry.

With that she began and when she had finished her set, 'She sang encore after encore, going from one song to the next without a pause for an hour and thirty minutes.' Memry said, 'The people laid their hearts out and showed their love for her', and everyone agreed it was a triumph, and never mind if Billie was drunk or high or what the problem had been at the beginning.*

When they left the hall, a fight broke out between Billie and Louis McKay. It was one of those messy, chaotic, drunken fights that can end in disaster. It started when Memry told Billie very pointedly that she had done well 'in the circumstances', and Louis McKay asked her what she meant by that? 'Of course she had done well! This woman's not just anybody! She is Billie Holiday!'

By now Louis McKay was so angrily indignant that Memry thought he was going to hit her. She picked up a bottle to defend herself with, and that was the cue for Billie to get involved. In the confusion that followed, Louis managed to knock Billie right across the street with a single blow of his fist.†

Memry was frightened by all this violence and decided to go and stay with her ex-mother-in-law for the night. But she managed to get lost on the subway and 'rode the train all night'. She finally turned up at Billie's apartment in Flushing at four in the morning.

She rang the bell and Billie answered the door and said, 'Is that you? What the hell are you doing here?' And when Memry came in, she found Billie in what she called 'a love tryst' with the man who had just assaulted her so savagely. For Memry this was 'typical of the kind of person that needs

---

* Hannah Altbush was less enthusiastic in a review of the concert for *Downbeat*, saying, 'For Miss Holiday too, it seemed to be somewhat of an off-night. Part of the Basie band and her own accompanist backed Billie in excellent arrangements of "Lover", "My Man", "Lover Man" and several other songs' (Vail, p. 163).

† Louis McKay also gets mixed reviews, depending on who you listen to. Stuart Nicholson is full of praise for him, saying, among other things, 'he had brought a degree of order to her life' (p. 191). Gary Giddins in the notes for the *Complete Columbia Recordings* (2001) says, 'Louis McKay was a low-level hustler whose one saving grace was that he lacked Levy's unreasoning violence.'

punishment, and after they've gotten the punishment they've been so completely gratified that they can enter into a sexual love tryst'.

Memry felt that she had been betrayed and this night marked an ending of the bond between the two women. She accompanied Billie at clubs in Boston and Philadelphia, but by now Louis McKay had become 'uncontrollable in his hostility' towards her. Memry became convinced that he would soon take his revenge by planting drugs on her and arranging to have her arrested. 'That was the way he did things,' she explained.

Memry arranged for her mother to send her a telegram saying that her father had fallen sick and asking her to come home at once, and with that excuse she left. She didn't meet Billie again until 1958 when she went to hear her sing at a club in San Francisco. After the show was over, Billie invited some friends to come to her hotel room for a meal and Memry was asked if she would come too.

Memry said that Billie had a room in 'the cheapest, the dingiest, the dirtiest hotel imaginable'. As soon as she arrived she wanted to escape, but Billie was very warm and welcoming, so she was persuaded to stay for a while. There was only one little hot plate to cook on, but Billie had managed to provide spaghetti and a pot of black-eyed beans and red beans. There was also pigs' feet and coleslaw and potato salad and fruit salad.

At one stage in the evening Billie came and sat down next to Memry. She said, 'Well, my little baby. Everything you told me would happen has come true. You know that day when we went to town in New York and I was going to try to do what you said about getting a new manager? Maybe if I had done that, it would have been a turning point. But I stuck with Louis and he robbed me of every dime. I have no money. I don't have any health. And now Louis's got a white girl he's gone off with. But you know, I've finally filed for a divorce. I've put him down at last!'*

---

* Billie and Louis McKay had married on 28 March 1957, basically as a legal manoeuvre because of an impending court case. Memry said, 'The irony was

Memry did go to hear Billie singing one more time, at a club somewhere, a few months later. All Billie could do by now was speak the words of the songs in time to the music, but even that worked its magic. As Memry put it, there was 'little of what you could call singing, but there was a communication of emotion that overrode the vocal limitations'.

(cont. from pg. 259) that before Billie signed those divorce papers in the hospital, she died and that left all her estate to Louis McKay.'

THIRTY-TWO

Lady Sings the Blues

———

On 13 August 1968, more than thirteen years after the publication of Billie's ghostwritten autobiography *Lady Sings the Blues*, William Dufty sent a letter to the lawyer Lester Shurr in which he explained, among other things, how he became involved in writing the story of Billie's life.

Dufty said that in the summer of 1955 Billie was working in Miami when 'her pimp, later her husband' Louis McKay, had the idea of trying to 'cash in on the confessional book vogue'. McKay contacted a journalist, who was sent out to meet Billie, but 'she got disgusted with him and the project and fled to New York'. She got in touch with her old friend Maely, who was now married to Dufty, and was invited to come and stay with the two of them for a few days. Billie and Dufty soon 'got talking', and that was when the first plans for *Lady Sings the Blues* took shape.

Dufty said that the entire book was done 'pronto'. Within the first twenty-four hours of hatching the idea, he was ready to take three chapters to the New York publishers Doubleday. Lee Barker, who was the editor there, told Linda Kuehl that he had been 'interested in Negro celebrity books for a long time' and he remembered being 'electrified by the first chapter

– as you know, the opening chapter is a hell of a chapter. I bought the book on the basis of that, plus a short outline. I thought Dufty's work on this was terrific, because he'd taken her down very simply in her own language and that's what made it a damn good book.'

An agreement was signed on 28 July 1955. The advance on signature was $3,000, of which 35 per cent went to William Dufty and the rest to Billie, although she then lost a further 10 per cent to Maely Dufty, who was acting as her literary agent.

After Billie had gone, Dufty 'took a month off in the summer to finish the book'. It was then edited and checked for possible libel. Lee Barker remembered that they had 'a lot of fun doing it' and the book was scheduled for publication in March 1956.

On 23 February 1956, while Billie was appearing at the Showboat in Philadelphia, she and Louis McKay were arrested at the Radnor Hotel where they were staying. The police had apparently been watching the hotel 'on a tip' and at 3 a.m. two detectives and a policewoman obtained a search and seizure warrant and a key from the desk clerk. They flung open the door and, as Detective Ferguson said, 'police found in Miss Holiday's possession an ounce and a half of heroin', as well as half an ounce of cocaine and some hypodermic needles.★ A .25-calibre automatic revolver was also discovered in the room.

Billie and McKay were taken to City Hall and were examined by Dr Arthur H. Thomas, a police surgeon, who said that both Miss Holiday and her husband were 'under the influence of narcotics'. At 5 a.m. they had a hearing before the magistrate William Cibott and were granted bail of $7,500 each, pending a possible Grand Jury trial. The magistrate did not have anything to say to McKay, but according to the Doubleday editor Lee Barker, he told Billie, 'It is a shame

---

★ Again there is no way of knowing if any drugs were really found. Billie said they were not, and Louis McKay told the *Pittsburgh Courier* that the police harassed them both and tried to plant the evidence. 'But they found us completely clear, after all sorts of searches' (Nicholson, p. 204).

that such a talented singer as you has become involved in a habit that can result only in heartbreak.' Billie had brought her Chihuahua Pepe with her and he accompanied her into the jail cell while waiting for the bail money to come through.

Billie finished her engagement in Philadelphia before going to a sanatorium to take a short cure, which had been demanded by the magistrate. She then went on to fulfil her other commitments in Kansas City, Chicago and Detroit. Once again it was her public notoriety that was used to draw in the huge and enthusiastic crowds, rather than her singing. 'Ho, Hum, Billie Holiday Jailed on Dope Charges' was the headline in the *Chicago Defender*, while the *Pittsburgh Courier* lamented that her comeback was 'marred by another arrest'. There was even an article in the *Journal American*, which suggested that Billie's arrest had a 'tragic footnote' because the New York Police Department had announced that in that same week they had 'relented . . . and moved to issue Billie a permit to work again in the local nightclubs'. There is no way of knowing if this was true, or simply a private joke on the part of the police force.

According to Dufty's account of what happened next, the publishers, 'instead of cashing in,★ panicked and, on the advice of lawyers, hacked the book to pieces, taking out anything which they felt might cause trouble'. But as well as making the cuts − as a result of which, so Lee Barker said, almost everyone of note disappeared without trace − it seems that Doubleday felt it would be good for sales if Dufty updated the book to include Billie's most recent brush with the law. And so he added a final chapter about narcotics, to round the whole thing off.

In spite of her known fear of jail and bad publicity, Billie was made to speak of her most recent arrest in an uncharacteristically cheery tone. 'Sure, I'd been busted again. And I was in jail . . . It might look like old times, but it wasn't. There was a big difference. I didn't feel lost. I didn't feel

---

★ As far as advance publicity was concerned, Billie's arrest could not have been better timed.

alone. And I wasn't alone. Louis was with me . . . God has blessed you when he lets you believe in somebody, and I believed in Louis.'

In Dufty's words, Billie went on to describe the circumstances of her arrest as if she had seen it all as a glorious publicity stunt. Louis was 'as cool and gentle as a lamb' in his dealings with the detectives and the police officers – there were now five of them instead of the original three – and he even had the foresight to tell her to put on 'something pretty' when they left the hotel, because the photographers were all waiting outside and eager to get a shot of her. Dufty also managed to make Billie sound very coy about whether there were any drugs to be found in the hotel room. At one moment she was protesting that their only fault was Louis' gun, which had no permit, but then in the next breath she was undermining her case by adding, 'I've had my troubles with the habit for fifteen years, on and off. I've been on and I've been off . . . I knew when I started to work on this book that I couldn't expect to tell the truth in it unless I was straight when it came out. I didn't try to hide anything. Doubleday carried an item in their winter catalogue that I was writing about my fight with dope and that I knew it wasn't over yet. There isn't a soul on this Earth who can say for sure that their fight with dope is over until they're dead.'*

When *Lady Sings the Blues* was finally published on 5 July 1956, Billie was working in Las Vegas. She apparently hadn't seen the finished result yet, because on 23 July she sent a postcard to the Duftys saying, 'Hey. How's the book going there? You can't get it out this way and it's sold out in Chicago. If you can, send me a copy as I haven't read it yet.'

Lee Barker remembered that at some point after the book's publication 'my wife, my daughter and I went up to the Apollo in Harlem where she was singing, and I went

* *Lady Sings the Blues*, pp. 186–92.

backstage. We all went down to a joint on 43rd Street and had drinks and so on. We had a great evening, just marvellous, and I think she's a very interesting woman . . . She was attractive, damned attractive . . . She had beautiful bones, from an Irish father, I guess, or grandfather . . . She had beautiful Irish cheekbones and a lovely colour too . . . Everyone was on heroin except me, and her Chihuahua was on gin. Her Chihuahua was a wonderful little dog . . . He drank gin out of a one-shot glass and got plastered.'

In spite of Lee Barker's enthusiasm, Dufty felt that *Lady Sings the Blues* was 'published as an abandoned book' and not given enough publicity. Nevertheless it 'was on the bestseller list in nothing flat . . . and went into some twenty foreign editions. I have been getting royalties on it ever since.'*

Dufty also managed to sell a series of articles, based on the most salacious aspects of the book, to the *Sunday People* in England. The series ran under the title 'Body and Soul', with such headings as 'I was a slave to white dope! . . . Dope smashed up her marriage, dope sent her to jail for a year . . . Billie Holiday knew the full horror of a lust she could not conquer — a lust she knew was evil. Now she tells this story to the world.'

In America the book was seen as a 'lucid and candid' autobiography, and quickly entered the bestseller list. In November 1956, Billie did a show at Carnegie Hall in which she 'told her life story in her inimitable style, in song, while Gilbert Millstein of the *New York Times* reviewed it in prose' by reading passages from *Lady Sings the Blues*. Dufty was hopeful that a movie deal could be signed quite soon. He wrote to Billie in December 1956, saying, 'I just wanted to say it will be the thrill of my life if this movie deal comes through.' In fact, after endless legal wrangles, the film was finally made in 1972.[†]

★　★　★

* Letter to Lester Shurr, 13 August 1968.
† Farah Jasmine Griffin says, 'While the film kept [Billie] a victim, it turned her last husband, Louis McKay, into the knight in shining armour who sought to rescue Holiday from herself. The film shot Diana Ross into superstardom, sparked interest in Holiday and raised the price of the Holiday commodity. It also spawned two decades' worth of articles, essays and books claiming to reveal the "real Holiday"' (p. 32).

Meanwhile Billie continued with her hectic schedule, zigzagging this way and that across the United States, from one engagement to the next. Because she still had no Cabaret Card, she was forced to continue with the endless round of 'second-rate theatres, tawdry dressing rooms and inferior nightclubs'.★

In July and August 1957 she was back in New York. She sang at two Jazz Under the Stars concerts in Central Park. As she said on 30 July, in an interview for the *World Telegraph*, 'I'm allowed to sing in a park, where children can hear me, but I'm banned from nightclubs. I think it's pretty silly . . . I think maybe the police department is going to let me have the permit this Fall. I sure hope so. I'm tired of travelling. It would be nice to settle down in New York for a while.'

★ A comment by the English jazz critic Leonard Feather, who always asserted that Billie was destroyed by the treatment she received in America and, if she had moved to England, she would have survived for many more years and her singing would have gone from strength to strength.

THIRTY-THREE

Irving Townsend and Ray Ellis

'She wanted that cushion under her voice.'

One of Billie's last records was *Lady in Satin*, on which she was accompanied by the Ray Ellis Orchestra and an unknown choir. Billie was keen to work with Ellis because she admired what he'd done with Frank Sinatra on *Only the Lonely*, and decided she wanted to offset her growling voice with the unlikely background of strings and angelic voices.

Irving Townsend, who was the producer for *Lady in Satin*, obviously liked Billie very much and said he 'got more personally involved with her than you do producing a record'.★ Initially he couldn't believe she was going to do the album. 'It would be like Ella Fitzgerald saying that she wanted to record with Ray Conniff. But she said she wanted a pretty album, something delicate. She said this over and over. She thought it would be beautiful. She wasn't interested in some wild swinging jam session . . . She wanted that cushion under her voice. She wanted to be flattered by that kind of sound.'

★ He kept in contact with her after the *Lady in Satin* recordings and in the summer of 1958 Billie came to stay at his home in Connecticut while she took part in a Seven Ages of Jazz concert. 'I shepherded her up and back between the station and my house,' he said. 'She was very nice and gentle, to the dogs, the kids. She was warm inside, no matter what bitterness.'

The recordings were made in New York City during three days of February 1958. By that time Billie had moved to a one-bedroom apartment near Central Park. Irving Townsend visited her there and described it as a 'dark, run-down, dingy place'. It would seem that – thanks to all the talk about heroin addiction in Lady Sings the Blues, and to her image of complex notoriety, which was maintained in pretty well everything that was written about her in the press – Billie found it necessary to live more or less incognito. She was calling herself Eleanor and using either her family name of Fagan or her married name of McKay, but in spite of that the landlord almost refused to sign the lease when he realised her true identity. Irving Townsend felt that she was 'bitter and worrying about what was going to happen to her and what people had done to her and the advantages they had taken of her'.

Billie was very short of money, and Townsend made her a 'series of little loans to pay bills', letting her have a total of maybe $100 or $150. The reason why she was getting so little work was partly because of her reputation for unreliability and because her critics said she could no longer sing, although as Townsend explained, 'People didn't give a damn what her voice was like because she was Billie Holiday, with a style and a sound like no other woman ever had anywhere, and what she once was would carry her through with any audience. But the problem was she was losing confidence in herself, and as a musician she knew her singing wasn't what it should be, and she was drinking to bolster her nerve and the more she drank, the worse it got.'*

Ray Ellis remembered that the idea of doing a record with Billie began in the spring of 1957 when someone told him that she had been asking about him. 'I couldn't believe it,' he said, 'because I had never met the woman . . . I didn't know she was aware of me.'

---

* As Stuart Nicholson says, 'By mid-1957 Billie's use of drugs had become incidental; instead, she relied on brandy [or other spirits] to subdue her hunger for narcotics' (p. 212).

About six months later he received a call from Irving Townsend at Columbia Records. 'He asked me what I was doing October 11th, 12th and 13th. I said I wasn't doing anything and he said, "Good! You're going to do an album with Billie Holiday! She's in the office right now and she wants to do an album!"' Ray Ellis was full of eager anticipation at the idea of working with Billie. It was 'one of the greatest things that ever happened to my ego'.

A meeting was arranged and the parties involved signed a contract. Columbia was providing an 'unlimited budget'. The musicians in the orchestra would be getting $50 or $60 a session, and Billie was to get an advance of around $100 or $150 a side, against a 5 per cent royalty. As Irving Townsend explained, 'It was a one-shot deal. It was pointless to sign her, because you didn't know if you'd get two sides out of her, let alone an album.'

Ray Ellis remembered being deeply disappointed by his first encounter with Billie. He said she failed to live up to his expectations: 'I had seen pictures of her ten years before and she was a beautiful woman. When I met her she was a repulsive woman . . . She looked a little shabby, a little dirty . . . I was taken aback because I had this mental thing, like she turns you on and you can go to bed with her. But I don't think I could have gone to bed with her at *that* stage for anything . . . There was something a little funky about her, a little too funky . . . She just looked like she smelled . . . Her whole life structure existed on her getting her next fix. You don't think like a woman any more.'★

Ray Ellis wanted to make it clear that he was 'very sensitive to women, especially to a woman with that much talent. Even if a woman is not very pretty, I would see something vital in her that turns me on. I wanted to be turned on by Billie Holiday, but I couldn't because she was so unappetising to look at . . . But still I flipped, with all the talent she had.'

Linda Kuehl asked him if he always had a woman in mind when he did his arrangements. He replied, 'Damn

★ When Ray Ellis said 'She just looked like she smelled', Linda Kuehl asked, 'Did she?' To which the reply was, 'No, she didn't.'

right! If I am writing for you, I am making love to you.'

'So how did you make love to Billie Holiday?'

'I never made love to her in bed. But if I'm writing a song . . . I would make myself a lover at the time I was writing that song. At the time of writing that song, I'm in love with her.'

'So when you arranged for Billie, you . . . ?'

'I was in love with Billie. Not necessarily Billie, but . . . I heard her voice, I dug it. It turned me on, and maybe I was in love with that voice and I was picturing a very evil, sensuous, sultry, very evil . . . probably one of the most evil voices I've heard in my life . . . Evil is earthy to me. When *you* say somebody is evil, it means very, very bad. I don't mean bad. Let me tell you something. Music relates to sex. It always did and it always will. Anything she sang that meant anything had to do with sex.'

So, despite his disappointment in how Billie looked and his lack of desire to go to bed with her, they agreed on a list of songs. 'We went through a whole pile of music and she read the titles and the lyrics. More than half she'd only heard once or twice or hadn't heard at all. She just liked the lyrics when she read them. I showed her the melodies on the piano and she'd say, "Yes, I want that!"'

But the elation was short-lived, because whenever they made an appointment, Billie failed to turn up. Ray Ellis tried to meet her on 'about twenty-five occasions' and by then he said, 'I was getting very evil at this point. I was very busy in those days and at that point in my career I was the King of Arrangers. Everything else I was doing, I couldn't have cared less about. I wanted to do *her* and I wanted to do everything right, and we could never get together.' Finally he decided simply to go ahead with his plans anyway. He organised a thirty-five piece orchestra and got copies of all of Billie's records that he could find, and slowly he 'pictured the way to conceive these things'.

Once Ray Ellis had the arrangements ready, he contacted Billie. He told her to arrive at the studio for the first recording at ten o'clock on the evening of 18 February 1958. 'The dates were set for eleven, so I told her ten, figuring she'd show up late. She showed up at twelve.'*

According to Irving Townsend, 'She came all dressed up to the session, looking great, as if she was going to perform in public. Most don't give a damn and turn up looking like bums! She was very nervous and as soon as she saw the violin section, she fortified herself with gin. She was drinking like mad, straight gin, and by the end of the evening she was slurring so badly you couldn't understand her any more. We must have had three sessions and she did better than I expected her to do, considering she was working with twelve, sixteen, twenty violins, that just read sheet music and don't give a damn . . . Fiddlers represent the educated musician as opposed to the jazz player, and she's got to stick with this bank of fiddlers and I was surprised by how well she did it.'

But Ray Ellis saw things very differently. He said she hadn't learnt any of the songs. 'She was standing there with a bottle of gin . . . I was so mad at her, I actually fought through the first session. I was saying, "You bitch! You sing so great and you don't know what you're doing! You're blowing the whole goddamn thing!" It was an ego thing with me, because I'd slaved over the arrangements, picturing the way she was going to sing it, and she wasn't singing it the way I'd thought and I hated her. I literally hated her. I think I treated her badly . . .

'Finally I realised that this bitch is standing there and she doesn't know any of the songs. So I said, "Look, baby, I'm going to give the band a fifteen-minute break while you learn that goddamn bridge!" I had to treat her like a schoolkid. She stood there and pouted.†

* Ray Ellis implied that this meant they only had an hour to do each session, but Irving Townsend said that 'as each three-hour session went along, we'd get to the end and we'd have to stop, because she'd got so drunk we couldn't understand the words no more.' The bassist Milt Hinton, who was at the sessions, explained that Ray Ellis, 'a dear friend of mine, I like him very much', wanted to fit it into a three-hour slot, 'or else it goes overtime'.

† In the notes to the 1996 reissue of *Lady in Satin*, Ray Ellis was much more gentle: 'I remember how intimidated Billie seemed when she arrived for the first session and saw the forty-piece [*sic*] orchestra waiting for her. I introduced her to the musicians and they gave her a polite round of applause. That seemed to calm her down.'

'So she went into a corner with Mal [Waldron] and she learnt the bridge. And I realised why she was stoned all the time was because she had absolutely no confidence in herself. She was completely unprepared, and she figured if she came stoned, she could cop out. But the musicians dug her. That first session we had Urbie Green, Well Walter, Osie Johnson, they were all on drugs.'*

They did two sessions and they were getting ready for the third, but they had one song missing. Ray Ellis remembered saying to Billie, '"Hey, baby, we're doing another session tomorrow and there's still one song I haven't written!"

'She said, "All right. Let's go to the Colony!"

'It was three o'clock in the morning and she had been drinking gin through the whole thing. Straight gin . . . So I get into a cab, and you know the black-white scene and so we get double-takes. It's three in the morning and I ask the driver to get us to the Colony Record Shop.

'She really looks like a disaster. I'm trying to get her out of the cab and I'm trying to pay the cab driver, and I'm holding her up and I'm thinking she's going to fall. So I lean her against the telephone pole, the lamp-post, and I say, "Hold it, baby!"

'I live in Larchmont, which is a very nice WASP community. I don't know what two of my neighbours are doing on 52nd Street at that hour, but they see me and they walk across the street because they don't want to embarrass me. Can you imagine this? They don't know *who* this woman is, but all they could figure is that I'm out with some hooker and what bad taste I have, because she looks like a disaster.'

Once they were in the Colony Record Shop, Billie started going through sheet music, 'And she was out of her head. She was cursing everybody in the joint, cursing her mother. Nobody even recognised her.' She picked a song called 'You've

---

* Harry 'Sweets' Edison said he took part in the album, but this is not true and he must have been thinking of Billie's last recordings with Ray Ellis, which were done in March 1959. He said, 'I made her last album, *Lady in Satin*. She was still drinking gin. I guess it was the only thing she could do to keep from hurting so much. She and I were drinking out of the same bottle. One swig and pass it on. We got high.'

Changed'. It became Ray Ellis' favourite on the whole album and the favourite for many other people as well.

Finally the album was finished. 'Three sessions of torture,' as far as Ray Ellis was concerned. He said that by now he was 'completely frustrated, disgusted. I didn't want to hear that thing again. I can't stand the sound of her voice. The producer Irving Townsend says he's going to mix it next week and I don't want to go to the mixing. I'm so bugged I wish I'd never got involved in the project. I'm up to here with Billie Holiday. I tell him, "Mix it! Forget it! I'll destroy it!"'

Irving Townsend contacted him about three weeks later. He said, 'Hey, baby, I made a test of this thing! I think you should hear it!'

So Ray Ellis took the record and drove back to his house in Larchmont. His family was away. He made himself something to eat and listened to *Lady in Satin* for the first time. 'And you know what I did? I got into the car and I drove to New York! I couldn't stay in the house by myself, that's how despondent it made me! I could have jumped out of the window. It was the saddest thing.

'But I was despondent because I loved it. It was so sad. It didn't matter whether she sang the right note or the wrong note, because she sang twenty thousand wrong notes on that thing. But she poured her heart out. What she ended up doing was a recitation to the music, although I hadn't realised it at the time.'* Ray Ellis also realised that on that record Billie made him 'look good . . . She gave me the opportunity to be heard. If you listen to the album, you hear the orchestra very plainly.'

By the following year Ray Ellis had moved from Columbia to MGM. One day in March he got a call from Billie. 'Hey, man,' she said, 'I think I'm going to come over and do something with you!'

---

* *Lady in Satin* was released in the autumn of 1958, to instant controversy, with some people hating it and others, including Jimmy Rowles and Miles Davis, loving it more than anything she had ever done. Billie herself was very proud of the recording. John Magnus, who ran the KGFJ radio station in Los Angeles, remembered her materialising in his studio sometime in 1959. 'I hadn't expected her. A couple of guys had sort of dumped her there and left her

Ray Ellis didn't mention this conversation to anybody in the office, because, as he explained it, he didn't want to say to the President of the company, ' "Hey, I want to get Billie Holiday on the label!" and then I don't hear from her again and I'd have looked like a real jerk.'

But then, without any prior warning, Billie turned up at the MGM building. The receptionist at the desk was 'a real dumb broad . . . who wouldn't know who Billie Holiday was, and wouldn't know anything about her and is very anti-black . . . And Billie by this time looks like a real, old, tired, black hooker – the type you really wouldn't want to go near. She looks terrible, a pathetic thing.'

Billie said she wanted to see Ray Ellis, and the receptionist was 'giving her the brush' when Ellis' secretary overheard the conversation and realised who this was and brought her through to the office.

Billie came in and sat down and talked. Ray Ellis said she looked so bad that 'had she been a plain white chick she would have gotten bad vibrations . . . She was so out of it at this point, it was hard to carry on a sensible conversation with her. She said she wanted to do an album . . . with a smaller band than last time.'

The recordings were done over a period of three days in March 1959 and they were not a success.* Ray Ellis said Billie 'sang her ass off for about two takes and then she went *kerplop!*' For the other takes she was singing far too softly

(cont. from pg. 273) alone in strange surroundings, and dumped a six-pack of beer with her . . . Out of respect I opened up the mike to her and we talked. We tried sitting on the same chair, but that was uncomfortable, so we cranked the microphone up and that was better . . . She talked about the *Lady in Satin* album. I felt frankly this was one of the greatest things she had ever done and she was happy to hear that. She said she loved working with a big orchestra. It was a good feeling for her to hear all the holes filled. It was carpeted. She wasn't used to that.'

* *Billie Holiday: Her Last Recording.* With the Ray Ellis Orchestra and Harry 'Sweets' Edison (tp), Gene Quill (as), Hank Jones (p), Milt Hinton (b), Barry Galbraith (g), Osie Johnson (d). A review by Sally-Ann Worsford in *Jazz Journal International* said, 'Obviously there is an abundance of much finer Holiday recordings, but as the final chapter of a largely tormented and tragic life this immensely moving album is far better than it has a right to be' (White, p. 135).

and he couldn't get her to stand still behind the mike. 'Between the booze and God knows what she had done before she came there, she was almost like a pendulum. It was one take and if you didn't get it, that was it, baby! You almost got the feeling: Holy Christ! We're recording her last album! I was the producer on this one and trying to keep everything going and hoping she will not pass out.'

Billie died just four months later. I don't know if Irving Townsend was there, but Ray Ellis went to the funeral and said he was 'honoured to be one of the pall bearers' although he had no idea who asked him to do it. He found it what he called 'a funny situation. She had a Requiem Mass, which was sort of unusual for the type of life she had led.'

THIRTY-FOUR

Louis McKay

———————

'This bitch turns skunky overnight.'

Louis McKay was born in 1909 and died in 1981. He became Billie's boyfriend/manager in 1951 and the couple were married in 1957, although by that time their relationship had pretty much fallen apart. There was talk of a divorce, but when Billie died intestate in July 1959, Louis McKay was still her legal husband and he became her sole inheritor. Her personal property was assessed as being worthless and her assets were valued at a total of $1,345.36. She had a further $500 'hidden on her person' in the hospital. However, by the end of that same year the royalties from record sales alone had already brought in more than $100,000.

Some people liked Louis McKay and felt that he helped Billie as well as he could. Others did not like him and blamed him for much of her unhappiness and her financial troubles during the last years of her life. He himself was never a great talker, but you can hear him speaking about Billie in the transcript of a telephone conversation between himself and William Dufty's wife Maely, which was secretly recorded in February 1958.

The telephone conversation is an eleven-page document that was bundled in among Linda Kuehl's other research papers. The note on the first page states that it took place 'at time of recording session, *Lady in Satin*'. There is also a little scribbled note in the margin, which reads '*obligato* to Yvonne Chavedd', which I suppose might refer to the person who arranged the technicalities of having the telephone bugged.

Below is a slightly shortened version of this conversation, leaving out the sections that are simply too muddled to follow:

MCKAY: Maely, just since the last time I been out there, and I only went away and stayed five weeks, who's she partying with? Who's she giving it to? Because she can get it kind of easy. I'm through with her. That bitch is going to see some bad days around here. I put the skids on her tonight . . .

MAELY: Well, how you gonna put the skids on her?

MCKAY: All the money I made and all the things I bought her . . . This girl ain't never had a dime to buy nothing, Maely. I couldn't even buy a car with this woman in the last eight years . . . You know that.

MAELY: Well, I'm just flabbergasted about this. But don't you go and do nothing like you talk, because that's going to be bad, baby!

MCKAY: I know it's going to be bad! I'm going to end it all! Ain't going to let nobody make a fool out of me, good as I've been to this woman . . . She took the money and used it up . . . She go around here and give away all her cunt and everything and don't get no money for it . . . I don't do those kind of things, Maely. I do sell what I got!

MAELY: Don't talk to newspapers and stuff. Five hundred dollars aren't worth anything to anybody.

MCKAY: Seven hundred dollars . . . On top of that, the principle is involved.

MAELY: What principle? She'll pay it off!

MCKAY: Maely, I'm a man. I can do things that this woman can't do. I ain't never had a woman like this.

Milira, Juanita, every woman I had was great personalities, they is great people. They didn't do no skunky
things. How come I gotta take this from this bitch
here? This low-class bitch! I ain't never see a bitch
with that much low class in my whole fucking life.
Going fuck around with everybody in town and . . .
fuck me and my money up, too.

MAELY: You know she don't fuck around. She just sits
at home all night and all day.

MCKAY: You know I got the wire. I know what this
woman done . . . Fuck the seven hundred dollars, I
ain't involved with the goddamn money. I want some
of her ass this morning for playing me cheap. If I
got a whore, I get some money from her or I don't
have nothing to do with the bitch. I don't want no
cunt. I'm too old for cunt. I'm forty-nine years old.
What I want with her cunt? If I wanted some cunt
I'd marry somebody your age and we'd get along. I
could make a hundred dollars and she could make
twenty-five dollars and I'd be happy. I can make myself
two or three grand a week. Tell you the truth, I'm
frantic, I'm crazy right now.

MAELY: Don't be crazy. You'd better cool down and you
better not do something to Holiday, because you
know where it's going to wind up.

MCKAY: Holiday's ass in the gutter in the East River
somewhere! I'll get someone else to do it! Cheap
bitch! She's been getting away with too much shit!
I just got the wire and I can't stand it . . . I'll catch
her somewhere and whip her all over the goddamn
street. Then go and beat the goddamn case* in
Philadelphia. I don't give a goddamn about that case
in Philadelphia. Shit! That case been beat a long time

---

* He is referring to his arrest with Billie in Philadelphia, on drugs and firearms
charges, in February 1956, a month before *Lady Sings the Blues* was due to be
published. The trial was finally held in March 1958. A lot of what Louis
McKay is saying seems to relate to its outcome. McKay had been previously
arrested in Philadelphia on a firearms charge.

ago! People worried about that case! I ain't worried about it. I ain't worried about that case at all, because the right people are behind that case!

MAELY: What do you mean?

MCKAY: Every motherfucker I know tried to get me to turn that bitch loose and let her go ahead and get some time, don't worry about it.

MAELY: You mean she's supposed to do time?

MCKAY: She ain't going to do no time. I mean that's what happened two years ago. They told me to split her out from the case and then cut loose. 'No,' I said, 'she can't make it!'

MAELY: You know I wouldn't believe things that people say to you that Holiday said, Lou.

MCKAY: This is action. I got some photographs of her. They just give me the negatives. And I wasn't asking to spy on this bitch. They gave me the negatives and I got them under the light here now. I don't like that kind of stuff . . .*

MAELY: Louis, what can she have done to get you going like that?

MCKAY: I got enough. This bitch. I got enough to finish her off and go downtown and take a chance on my liberty.

MAELY: You think of killing somebody for seven hundred dollars, somebody you lived with for eight years and married.†

MCKAY: I ain't talking about killing her. I'm going to do her up so goddamn bad she's going to remember as long as she lives.

MAELY: Well, for heaven's sake don't do her up, because if you're doing her up she can't earn a dime!

MCKAY: She ain't earning anyway. She ain't even making

---

* There is no way of knowing what kind of photographs he was referring to, or in what way they were compromising for Billie.

† The $700 keeps changing its function. At first it seems to be money that Billie owes to Louis, and then it is money he is going to use to pay someone to hurt her.

a living. She owe the government four and a half thousand dollars and I ain't going to pay a quarter . . . I'm going to let her go ahead and rock it out . . . I hate her. How can you just sit up and tell me a lie, and you know I know the difference the next day when the people get to me?

MAELY: Well, she's so mad with me because she says that you said we were sleeping together.★

MCKAY: How could I? . . . You ain't no chippie† and you got a family . . . That woman owe you a thousand dollars right now.

MAELY: That's right! She says she's mad with me. She won't talk to me because we sleep together.

MCKAY: I say, when she talk of me fucking her, I say, 'Why don't you stop using this white woman's money,' that's what I told her! I say, 'You ain't earnt fifteen cents. In the last six months you're about four or five thousand dollars behind with me now . . . You ain't ever paid my salary and you never did give Maely nothing for working for you . . .' She never gave me a quarter. I took care of her. I kept that woman alive. Kept her away from junkies in the street and on the corners. Fronting it myself for years. And here this bitch turns skunky overnight!‡

MAELY: Well, if I knew where she is, I'd tell her not to go home, because I don't think you two should meet tonight!

MCKAY: Shit! I'm going to tear this joint up with that whore's ass. Do you know Alice's mother's phone number?§

MAELY: Louis, get some sleep, huh?

MCKAY: I ain't even sleepy, so help me God. I need a

★ When William Dufty and Maely were getting divorced, he also accused Maely of sleeping with McKay.
† A prostitute.
‡ I think this means double-crossing; to 'skunk' someone means to cheat them out of something.
§ Alice Vrbsky, who worked as Billie's assistant and secretary for the last two years of her life.

dexie to keep me awake a little longer. This house
is so damn cold, Maely honey. I'm freezing to death,
so help me God . . . She don't mean a damn thing
to me. I said, 'Well, baby, you and I let's go ahead
and get a divorce and stop fighting.'

MAELY: Well, you know also that I love her and that's
it . . . She don't know how much I love her. Louis,
take care. Take it easy, darling. Let me hear from you,
huh?

MCKAY: When I start work on her she'll know. I work
on her when she get to the door . . .

MAELY: Take care, darling. Take it easy.

MCKAY: Like something from Mars or something . . .

MAELY: Well, take it easy, darling.

MCKAY: Make both them motherfuckers commit suicide
this morning . . .

MAELY: Don't do that! Not my friend!

MCKAY: And I'm doing all right now and if I'm going
to stop doing all right, I'm going to end it all. Crack
this bitch's head or something. OK, honey?

MAELY: OK.

MCKAY: How's Bill★ doing?

MAELY: What? Bill's OK. He's getting better. Everybody's
getting better. It's too cold for him to go outside, so
he's raising hell inside. Take care, darling, and we'll
talk. OK?

Now, if that is the voice of Louis McKay talking about his
wife in February 1958, it is also interesting to listen to him
giving his account of his relationship with Billie during that
same time, in an affidavit that was presented on his behalf
to the Surrogates Court, towards the end of 1959.

This was the first of a number of legal battles in which
Louis McKay was involved after he had inherited his wife's
estate. It seems that as soon as the lawyer Earle Zaidins had

★ William Dufty.

learnt of Billie's death, he rushed to the hospital to tell McKay that Billie owed him some $12,000 in legal fees. Zaidins said he was prepared to waive this debt in exchange for a 10 per cent share of her estate and he immediately wrote out a contract that McKay signed.★

McKay quickly realised his mistake and, with Billie's lawyer Florynce Kennedy acting on his behalf, took Zaidins to court. McKay did not appear in court in person but, with Florynce Kennedy's help, he produced an affidavit in which he explained everything he felt was relevant about his relationship with Billie Holiday and her relationship with Zaidins.†

The language used in the affidavit is very formal and controlled. McKay is made to sound like an elder statesman as he tells the story of his love for Billie and how he tried, but ultimately failed, to protect her from her own vices and weaknesses. He explains that the task has been hard, and 'those who would judge me must have lived through what I have gone through with Billie Holiday'.

According to the text of the affidavit, McKay moved to New York during the 1930s and there he met Billie and 'dated her' when she was just sixteen. He 'befriended her and her mother' and when Sadie was worried about her

---

★ 'I acknowledge that Earle Warren Zaidins . . . has not been paid for any of his services. That in consideration thereof I agree as the surviving spouse of the decedent and as a logical administrator of the decedent's estate, when appointed, to pay Mr Zaidins ten (10) per cent of all gross monies received.' Contract signed 17 July 1959. Unattached file, Surrogates Court, County of New York. It is always possible that McKay suggested drawing up this contract.

† I have only read the sections of the affidavit quoted by Stuart Nicholson in his biography, especially Chapters 12 and 13, pp. 211–15, 226–7. He uses the text as if it were an ordinary interview with Louis McKay. He also quotes the opinion of Florynce Kennedy that Earle Zaidins 'was slimy. He was typical of the kind of sleazy people [Billie] seemed to surround herself with.' In fact Zaidins later became one of America's top show-business lawyers and then a judge. He did not try to contest the case, but in an interview with the documentary filmmaker John Jeremy in 1984, he dismissed McKay as a 'pathological liar'. When I spoke to his widow, Alice Zaidins, she said that her husband was one of the most honest men in the United States. 'He let it [the case with McKay] go, because those weren't very nice people to be dealing with.'

wayward daughter, she 'would send me to bring Billie home, or to see about her'.[*]

He said they met again early in 1951, while Billie was appearing at the Club Juana in Detroit, and within two weeks McKay had taken on the role of manager. In McKay's written version of that meeting, he was working in a car plant and 'Billie Holiday came to me for help, threatening suicide if I didn't help her. I told her I wouldn't leave my job in Detroit and abandon my obligations there, until she was ready to kick her drug habit. I refused to go on the road with her until this was done.'

Whatever the truth might have been, it was clear that Billie was at first overjoyed to share her life with McKay and was quick to tell the world of her new-found love. As Nat Hentoff wrote in February 1952, 'A large part of Billie's new sense of security and consequent ease is due to her husband and advisor Louis McKay. In fact, Billie's personal life has become so ordered that she is thinking now of retiring in two or three years because she just wants "to be a housewife and take care of Mr McKay".'[†] The relationship was obviously good for her career as well, because people remarked that she was 'singing better than anyone had heard her in the last few years, demonstrating a new sense of responsibility and co-operativeness'.[‡]

However, the happiness did not last for long and within a couple of years the relationship between Billie and McKay had become increasingly complicated, difficult and violent. Some people, such as Jimmy Rowles, who saw the couple together from a distance, felt that McKay really was looking

---

[*] No one else speaking about that time remembers McKay being around Billie. John Chilton, in his book *Billie's Blues*, said that the two of them had a 'casual acquaintanceship' and probably met when Billie was singing at the Hot Cha.

[†] Marie Bryant said of Billie's relationships, 'I have the feeling that Billie couldn't tell the real from the put-on and there was always this *want* for her to have someone in her corner. If they could make it look like that, then she'd fall . . . Louis to me is a weak guy. I don't think he dug her.' John Levy the bass player said, 'McKay was an idiot and a poor kind of pimp . . . compared to the rest of them he was a sweet cat up to a point . . . He was hanging on for dear life because that was all he had to hang on to: he was Billie Holiday's husband.'

[‡] *Downbeat* magazine, October 1951.

after Billie, but those who were closer to the domestic realities were less hopeful. Carl Drinkard explained how McKay
organised Billie's heroin supply as a way of controlling her.
And Memry Midgett realized that McKay was using Billie's
money to buy land and property, all of which he purchased
in his own name. One of his first acquisitions was the
house in Queens. In 1956 McKay bought a share of the 204
Club in Chicago, and the bistro attached to the club was
called the Holiday Room. McKay told Billie he intended
her to play there for several months every year, but the
promise never took shape.★

It was clear that by the time of their arrest on a narcotics
charge in Philadelphia in March 1956, the relationship
between Billie and McKay was in serious difficulties. The
pianist Corky Hale, who played for Billie in Las Vegas in
the summer of 1956, said, 'I don't know what the hell Louis
was doing. He was out running with girls. He put her down
all the time . . . She wasn't on any kind of dope at all. She
was drinking I don't know how much gin . . . Louis was
terrible, horrible. He made fun of her, but I don't think she
was even aware of it because she was so out of it.'

However, according to the affidavit, in 1957 McKay and
Billie were living harmoniously together in New York when
they both met a young lawyer called Earle Zaidins. 'We didn't
take him very seriously,' said Louis in his written statement.
'He said he was a jazz fan and was always following us around
and offering to help us. At the beginning we thought he
was just clumsy, like an overgrown friendly puppy . . . He
hung around our place sometimes when he wasn't wanted.'

McKay went on to explain that after about nine months
Zaidins began to get familiar with Billie when her husband
was not around. 'Billie would laughingly report that Zaidins
was making passes at her. She would say, "Would you believe
that fat faggot Earle Zaidins tried to talk sex with me? What's
his story?"'

★ In the affidavit McKay said that Billie had so few assets when she died because
she had been forced to sell everything she owned and to spend all the money
she earnt to pay for her heroin addiction (Nicholson, p. 226).

At this point in his statement McKay felt it necessary to explain that 'she always told me about people like Earle Zaidins, unpleasant though it was. I didn't take it very seriously because many jazz fans confused their admiration of Billie Holiday with their own romantic desires or problems . . . I realised Zaidins was nervous. He bit his fingers deeply.'

McKay said that to protect Billie from becoming too nervous or jittery, he seldom left her alone for any great length of time and always arranged for someone to be with her when he needed to be absent for a while. Zaidins was sometimes given the task of keeping an eye on her. McKay went on to say that on the weekend of 2 and 3 June he returned home to discover 'A number of my papers were gone. Earle was gone, and Billie was obviously under the influence of drugs . . . I knew she didn't have any cash because with her consent I handled all the money. To her, money meant drugs. The doctor had told me the last time she had been through withdrawal from drugs that her health would not permit her to "kick the habit" again. Earle Zaidins knew very well that he should not give Billie Holiday sizeable sums of money. When he went behind my back he co-signed her death warrant.'★

McKay said he realised that Billie was hooked again. He was so angry he resorted to violence. 'The reason was that she confessed to me that this was not the first time she had been supplied with money for drugs by Zaidins . . . Moreover, she confessed that Zaidins had attempted to perform an act of sodomy upon her . . .

'I blew my top, I don't know which hurt most . . . I was almost crying. I grabbed the phone from her and threw it. I guess I didn't care whether it hit her or not . . . All that I could think of was that for weeks she had been using again,

---

★ According to Nicholson, Zaidins was aware that McKay would leave Billie if she went back on drugs and 'This was a source of great torment for her. She loved McKay, but she loved to hate him for it. Her yearning for a fix was so strong it created an ambivalence that exasperated her and baffled those who knew her' (p. 212). This, in spite of the fact that everyone (including Nicholson himself) agreed that Billie had replaced heroin with alcohol and was sometimes off drugs altogether or using them very sporadically.

and she was so hooked by now that I could never go through what was necessary to get her off alive . . .

'I confronted Zaidins and demanded to know why he had helped her back on drugs and why he had stolen my papers and why he had made sexual advances to a woman who could not resist because of her condition. He did not deny one thing.

'I started after him and he ran out of the house and I ran after him. It's a good thing I couldn't catch him. Later Billie told me Earle called the police and she told him she didn't want any police, that I was her husband and it was her fault.'*

A few days after this incident McKay got in his car and headed for the West Coast. On the way, and after driving for many hours, he fell ill. He was admitted to hospital in Chicago, where he nearly died from perforated ulcers. He remained in hospital for several weeks. When he was discharged he said that he remained determined not to go back to New York until Billie Holiday was off drugs and had finished with Earle Zaidins.

'I was without the physical strength to do· anything with her until she made her mind up to help. I could never keep the pushers away from her. This was the first time there was anything like this, and I knew I couldn't win . . . Except for a bitter telegram which I sent, we were never estranged. Nearly every day or so we spoke. She phoned me nearly every week and I phoned her usually twice or more a week. I was trying to get well . . . I can't be sure whether Billie was on or off drugs . . . She told me Zaidins was keeping her happy. I stayed in the West Coast. Zaidins was in charge.'†

McKay won his case in the Surrogates Court and the lawyer Florynce Kennedy continued to work on his behalf

---

* Quoted in Nicholson, p. 213. This is obviously the same incident with the telephone that is described by Earle Zaidins (see p. 306), but in a very different way.

† McKay did go and see Billie in hospital. She told William Dufty that when her husband walked into her room she half-closed her eyes so as not to be bothered by him. To her amazement Louis threw himself on his knees beside her bed and began to recite 'The Lord Is My Shepherd'. 'I've always been a religious bitch,' said Billie, 'but if that bastard is a believer, I'm thinking it over!'

for several years. When asked in 1994 for her assessment of the character of her client, she said, 'I guess Lou was a kind of hustler, a gambler, and a lot of people said he had a string of whores. But this was not unusual; people in the black community did not have much money; this sort of thing happened. He lived off her earnings, but he was kind of compassionate and caring towards her, a "take charge" type. I think he made her feel he cared for her. He was knowledgeable in many ways, streetwise and a pimp. But it was a struggle with Billie Holiday and I don't doubt he hit her, but she depended on him. When I dealt with her I found her a difficult person. I did not admire her.'[*]

When the film version of *Lady Sings the Blues* was finally made in 1972, McKay was employed as the technical advisor, for which he received a percentage of the takings. He said later that he very much approved of the story that was told and the way his relationship with Billie was portrayed. 'Billie and I were very much in love, although we had our problems . . . She was much, much more woman than most people realise who saw her only as a glamorous star, then as someone caught up in the narcotics thing.[†] She was a tender, loving woman, who liked nothing better than being at home with her man, cooking meals for me and doing little things around the house.'[‡]

There was one point on which McKay remained particularly firm. He said that in accordance with the law, as a narcotics user Billie was liable to a twenty- to thirty-year

---

[*] Quoted in Nicholson, p. 227.

[†] On a TV show in August 1980, the singer Carmen McRae alleged that McKay 'caused Billie to become involved in drugs'. He filed a $2.5 million lawsuit against her, but the action lapsed with his death in March 1981.

[‡] Farah Jasmine Griffin describes the film as a 'post-Black Power fantasy of a beautiful, talented, but weak and childish woman, who is rescued time and again by a strong, supportive, wealthy, handsome black man. When Diana Ross as Holiday is kicking her habit cold turkey in a padded cell, Billy Dee Williams' McKay comes in with a doctor who injects her with something to make the going a little easier, and then her black knight slips an engagement ring on her finger. This is just the incentive she needs to pull her out of the nightmare. He pays for her time at a sanitarium, he arranges for her debut at a downtown club, he keeps her supplied with gardenias and he rescues her time and again. None of this ever happened' (p. 60).

prison sentence and 'If people get the idea that the Feds harassed her, then that's wrong . . . They could have made things really tough for her, if they had wanted to.'

THIRTY-FIVE

Endgame

In November 1958, Billie set out on a disastrously misman-aged European tour, which was supposed to earn her $10,000. In Milan she was 'starring in a mixed company of pop singers, comedians, acrobats and impressionists and her uncommercial style failed to please an obviously commercial audience'.* In Paris, she was booked to sing at the Olympia, but again it was the wrong kind of atmosphere for her intimate style; she was obviously lacking in confidence and was booed off the stage.

The contract for the whole tour was abruptly cancelled, leaving her without even the money for the fare home. So she sang for her supper, as it were, taking a cut from the door fee at a little club called the Mars. There the atmosphere was right and the audience was enthusiastic and appreciative.†

Not long after Billie returned to the States on 2 December

---

* *Melody Maker*, quoted in Vail, p. 199.
† Stuart Nicholson (p. 219) says that 'the truth was that Billie had become a sad bar-fly', but the singer and actress Yolande Bavan, who met Billie in Paris at this time, gave a very different account. 'Billie was terribly lonely. Not too many people came around her, possibly because they idolised her . . . They also respected her. She could be terribly funny sometimes . . . Perhaps she saw

1958, she was accused of having contravened the 1956 Narcotics Control Act. This Act was Harry Anslinger's most recent achievement in his battle against drug addicts. It made provision under federal law for making arrests without a warrant, on the belief that a drug offence had been committed, even if there was no proof of purchase or possession. It also stated that any US citizen who had spent more than a year in prison on narcotics charges must report themselves to Customs as a 'violator' before leaving the country and again on their return. The passing of the new Act had not been publicised and even lawyers were unaware of its existence and its implications.

On 14 January 1959, an Inspector McVeigh contacted Billie and demanded that she appear at Customs House in Manhattan the following afternoon for questioning. She was warned that, according to the regulations of the Act, her failure to register herself as a 'violator' could lead to a fine or imprisonment.

When Billie arrived with her lawyer Florynce Kennedy,★ she was told that the evidence against her had already been prepared and the matter would be referred to the US Attorney for the Eastern District of New York. The minutes of this first meeting are interesting. You can hear Billie speaking in her own voice, and you can hear how she was spoken to by the authorities.

These excerpts are taken from the statement of Mrs Eleanor Gough McKay, also known as Billie Holiday, made in the office of the Supervising Customs Agent, on 15 January 1959 at 3.40 p.m.

After the usual preliminaries, Billie took the oath and was asked for her name and occupation:

(cont. from pg. 291) some of the things that were in her reflected in me, because I was pretty strict about myself and my own behaviour at that time and she had a certain discipline . . . She told me that the essential thing about singing was to be as true as you could to the lyrics emotionally.'

★ Florynce Kennedy had been recommended by William Dufty.

BILLIE: My name is Billie Holiday. I am forty-one [*sic*].
I am a singer, that's my occupation.

QUESTIONER: Is your true name Mrs Eleanor Gough
McKay?

BILLIE: Yes.

The questioner then checked on her date and place of
birth, both of which she had answered incorrectly and she
apologised for the muddle. When asked about her 1947 arrest,
for which she received a sentence of a year and a day,★ she
explained, 'No, I wasn't really arrested. They were sort of
like you people; they were very nice to me.' She then said
something more about her arrest, but whatever it was remains
a mystery since it was marked 'off the record' in the transcript of the interview.

When Billie was asked about her 'purpose' in leaving the
United States, she replied, 'I went there [to Europe] to sing,
to do concerts.'

QUESTIONER: You went for a professional engagement
abroad?

BILLIE: That's right. Just myself and my piano player.
And my agent gave me the tickets, he gets the tickets
and tells us where to go and who to meet, and he
never tells us about registering. I never saw any sign,
so I didn't know. I went to the doctors, I did everything else I should have done, so why shouldn't I
have done this? I did not know . . .

QUESTIONER: . . . Did you register when you left the
United States and when you returned, as a convicted
narcotics violator, with Customs?

BILLIE: No. Nobody asked me. I never did it before.
This must be something new, because wouldn't they
ask me?

QUESTIONER: No. It's not the Government's responsibility to ask every individual passenger or person

★ The extra day was important because the Act covered only those who had
been sentenced to 'more than a year' in prison.

leaving the United States if they have a narcotic record.

BILLIE: Or coming back?

QUESTIONER: No, because it would be insulting a lot of people . . . Did you leave the United States on a French airline?

BILLIE: All I know, it was Pan American. They took a lot of pictures of me. I was standing on the step with a Pan American bag, you know – the newspapers and things. So it was no secret that I was leaving, or anything. I really – I couldn't have been trying to sneak away. I just didn't know about this, that's all.

Billie was then asked about her arrest with Louis McKay in 1956. She replied rather enigmatically, 'There wasn't anything to it; it was all wrong.'

QUESTIONER: Was there a trial held at which you were found not guilty and acquitted?

BILLIE: Yes. Well, you know, they have to trade a while and pick on you a little bit.

At the end of this statement, Billie was asked if she has anything to add, 'any comments or statements' that she would like to 'insert in the record at this time'. Her reply was eloquent.

'Yes,' she said, 'there's a lot I would like to add, but it would take a book. I'd have to write a book . . .* It just seems that a little thing like this I didn't know about, and nobody cared enough about me – my agents, and I've got managers for this and that – to tell me about it. And I have been trying my best to be a good girl, and a little thing like this. I have to come down here and go through all this. That's all I can say. It's terrible, that's all. Once you get in trouble for narcotics, it's the end. I think it's the worst thing

* She seemed to imply that this time she would have to write the book *herself* and not leave it to someone else.

that could ever happen to anybody in the wide world. That's all I've got to add.'

Billie had to wait for six weeks before her case was heard and she was terrified at the prospect of another prison sentence. She stopped eating and lost so much weight that a doctor was called in to see her. She drank more heavily than ever and when William Dufty remonstrated with her, she replied, 'If you had the Government breathing on you, you'd be drinking too.'

The US Attorney was finally ready to see her on 12 February. She was represented by Florynce Kennedy's partner Donald Wilkes and after a lot of wrangling the case was dropped. William Dufty said that once the case was dropped, 'She came home like a different woman. That night, she told us, she slept like a baby.'

However, it was obvious to everyone who saw her that Billie's health was deteriorating. A doctor friend, Terkild Vinding, described going with his wife to visit her in the sparsely furnished basement apartment where she lived alone with only her white Chihuahua for company.★ This must have been in the middle of May. He said that when they arrived Billie was obviously glad to see them. She played the *Lady in Satin* album and gave them a copy, which she dedicated in her sprawling handwriting 'for my Doc and best friend from Billie Lady Day Holiday'. Vinding said she was in bad physical shape, her legs swollen from oedema 'due to liver cirrhosis to a degree I had never seen before'. He told her that she must go to hospital immediately and offered to drive her there himself, but she refused.

On 30 May, just a few days after this meeting, Billie collapsed while her friend Frankie Freedom was with her. He called a doctor and she was taken to the private Knickerbocker Hospital and registered under the name of Mrs Eleanora McKay. But when an orderly smelt her breath and saw the old needle scars on her arms, the hospital insisted she be moved to a public hospital. She was taken to the

★ In a letter to Linda Kuehl, 12 July 1971.

Metropolitan Hospital. At first she was in a public ward, but once her identity became known and journalists began to turn up seeking an interview or a photograph, she was moved to a private one. For ten days everything went well; Billie was putting on weight and was full of plans for the future. But then a certain nurse Figueroa – Billie was sure she was a policewoman in disguise – reported the discovery of some suspicious white powder and the Federal Bureau of Narcotics was informed.*

Two detectives arrived and questioned her in her bed. They told her that unless she admitted possession and disclosed her supplier, they would take her to the Women's House of Detention, regardless of what that might do to her state of health. They removed her record player, her records, the radio and her comic books. She was officially arrested and refused bail, and three policewomen kept a twenty-four hour guard at the door of her room. Visitors were not allowed in unless they had a written permit from the 23rd Precinct, allowing access to Arrest Number 1660.

William Dufty and others made complaints. But even after a writ of habeas corpus had been obtained and signed, which should have got rid of the police presence, the police guard stayed. Apparently the District Attorney had plans to transfer Billie to Bellevue Prison Ward and this was only deferred by a legal request that she appear first before a Grand Jury as soon as she was fit enough to do so.

The legal manoeuvrings were complicated. But again it seems important to include some of the statements that were made when Donald Wilkes fought the case in the Supreme Court of the State of New York, on behalf of Eleanor McKay, against the Police Commissioner of the City of New York, on 16 June 1959.

---

* There are several contradictory accounts of what was found, and who found it and where. It was perhaps heroin, or cocaine, in a box of Kleenex tissues, under Billie's pillow, or by her bed, or traces of powder seen on her nose. There was also talk of finding a syringe, with which Billie was supposed to have injected herself, but this seems the most unlikely of all the options.

Mr Lang, on behalf of the Police Commissioner, said that: 'Far from attempting to deprive petitioner of any constitutional or statutory rights, I think the police department has been extremely solicitous of the conditions of this petitioner . . . We would have had her arraigned this morning if not for the fact the hospital authorities thought it would be detrimental to her health. We do not feel in view of the defendant's critical condition, although she does have a prior criminal record, that she will flee the jurisdiction or run away from the charge.'

Wilkes, on behalf of his client, tried to suggest that her treatment had been a little severe in the circumstances: 'Your Honour, I must say that the interrogation of a witness, who is classified by the hospital as terminal, by three detectives, hardly appears to be an act of solicitude for her welfare.'

Mr Lang saw no reason to accept this criticism and insisted that Billie had been treated in the proper manner. 'If, your Honour, this drug which is slowly killing, I believe, this defendant, if the detectives had prevented her from jumping off a bridge, they would be considered great heroes. In effect, they're doing the same thing by taking this heroin away from her and why they should be vilified by doing their duty, I do not know, your Honour.'

As a result of this hearing Billie was granted 'an adjournment of writ for a period of time' and was placed 'in the custody of her counsel . . . with the assurance that she will not leave'.★

The medical authorities at the Metropolitan Hospital were directed to inform the District Attorney when the condition of the petitioner Eleanor McKay would 'permit of an arraignment at the hospital' and she was to be 'subject to an additional criminal charge if her parole is violated'. Before the case was concluded, Mr Lang wanted to be reassured that the criminal charges against the defendant were still pending.

★   ★   ★

★ At this point Wilkes said, 'She is not going to leave. Your Honour, she will never leave that bed.'

On 21 June two more detectives arrived at the hospital and Billie was given what Donald Wilkes described as 'a bit of a going over'. They took 'mugshots' of her and fingerprinted her. As Wilkes said later, 'This was done while she was still in her hospital bed and without permission, knowledge or consent . . . She was refused bail, denied a hearing and held incommunicado.'

The date for Billie's appearance before a Grand Jury had been set for 26 June, but it was delayed until she was considered well enough to appear. Donald Wilkes felt that the whole episode following Billie's arrest was 'rank and redolent . . . a very, very shabby performance on the part of the State of New York'.

On 11 July 1959, Billie's heart began to falter and in the early hours of 17 July she died. Everyone agreed that she had been getting better, but then something snapped in her. She made jokes about it being the 'same old Keystone Kops routine', but the threat of imprisonment then facing her must have contributed more to her sudden decline in hospital than the cirrhosis of the liver, kidney failure and other medical complications that appeared on her death certificate. William Dufty had written a couple of pieces about her while she was in hospital, using such headlines as 'How dope changed my life'. As soon as she was dead he was ready with five new articles for the *New York Post*, in which he made such statements as 'The collision between her and heroin was fore-ordained. It had to happen.' He also included some useful promotion for *Lady Sings the Blues*.

Several years later, Dufty claimed that 'Billie's death changed my life'. By this he seemed to mean he was genuinely sad to lose her, but it was also a tacit acknowledgement that by linking his name inextricably with hers, his financial future was transformed. *Lady Sings the Blues* has proved to be a classic in the confessional autobiography mode and it has never been out of print in all the years since its publication.

THIRTY-SIX

Earle Zaidins

'She was very sensitive to bad publicity.'

Earle Zaidins had just completed his training as a lawyer when he arrived in New York from Wisconsin in the summer of 1956. He had his boxer dog with him and he found a room for the two of them in a broken-down hotel not far from Times Square. It was called The Flanders and was one of the few hotels in the city that accepted pets. He fixed a little wooden sign on the wall outside the hotel, announcing his name and profession, in case anyone was interested.★

Zaidins was in the habit of taking his dog for a walk late at night and sometimes he encountered a woman dressed in a black diamond mink coat that was so long it almost touched the ground. She was accompanied by the ghostly apparition of a white Chihuahua, its eyes bulging and its naked-looking body trembling in spite of the little jacket it was wearing.

The relationship between these two solitary night-walkers started with a simple greeting of recognition, but after a

---

★ This chapter is based on the interviews with Linda Kuehl and with the film producer John Jeremy, who used parts of his conversation with Zaidins in his 1984 documentary film, *The Long Night of Lady Day*. Zaidins himself died in 2002, but I spoke at some length with his widow, Alice.

while they began to talk. The woman had a room in the same hotel. She said her name was Eleanor Fagan and her dog was called Pepe. She said she loved boxer dogs and used to have one called Mister; the best dog she'd ever known. Perhaps she muttered in her dark and rasping voice that Mister was more faithful than any of the goddamn men she had come across, lifting her eyes to meet the eyes of this tall, dark-haired, pale-skinned and rather cadaverous-looking stranger as she spoke.

At first Zaidins had no presentiment of the identity of the dog-walking woman. But then he must have asked her what were the songs she sang that Mister loved so much and where had she sung them, and did she still sing sometimes? He thought her face was familiar and she reminded him of someone, but he had never heard of Eleanor Fagan McKay.

Billie told him who she really was and explained that these days it was safer for her to remain anonymous. *Lady Sings the Blues* had recently been published and that was making everything worse. She wished her ghostwriter, William Dufty, had not put in all that stuff about drugs and her being a prostitute, but he had promised her it was the best way to sell the book and she could certainly do with the money.

Already during these early meetings Billie was eager to tell Zaidins that she didn't do drugs any more; she even rolled up her sleeves to show him there were no new needle scars among the old ones. Not that it made any difference to the cops and their interest in her. She was a mark at all times, she said, and whenever she was performing some-where she'd see two or three men walking together and she'd know they were cops or federal narcotics agents and she'd panic. She said, 'If I was arrested again and sent to prison, I would never live through it. I couldn't go through that experience again. I'd rather be dead.'

And so these two strangers talked in the night in the company of their incongruous dogs and a sort of friendship began to emerge. Zaidins told Billie that he was a lawyer. He said he planned to specialise in trade regulations, but he had done some work defending people on drugs charges and so he might be able to help her if she got into trouble again. And there were other things he could do for her as well, because how come she was living at this down-at-heel hotel? She should be rich from all the record sales. Who was her agent? Who was her manager? Who was looking after her, for Christ's sake?

Zaidins realised at once that Billie could be very useful to his career, and as a young man he was ambitious for success. He was determined to seize the opportunity and get what he could from her. As he said, 'Everybody wanted something out of her. She attracted this kind of thing. She made herself vulnerable. She invited people into her life and people figured it was easy to get into the life of Billie Holiday. I got into her life very easily . . . I used her too.'

Billie asked Zaidins some legal question about a contract and he looked into that for her, and after a while she took him on as her lawyer. He said she told him 'She was in and out in terms of her relationship with Louis McKay and she had various cases pending. She wanted me to be on hand in case a problem came up.'

Zaidins was surprised by how aware Billie was of the technicalities of her contracts and of her precarious legal position. She explained that when she was arrested in 1948, her lawyer had told her to play dumb and that had worked with the judge, so she had played dumb ever since. She said she hoped that if people saw how helpless she was, it might persuade them to have pity on her and leave her alone.

The first job that Zaidins took on for his new client was drawing up her will. He said, 'She had a thing about wills, but every time it came for her to sign it, she wouldn't discuss it.' He thought she was afraid that if she signed, it would be like signing her own death warrant. She confessed to him that she was very superstitious and said she had once 'put a whammy'* on John Levy. She had wished him dead and he died, just like that. She felt she was in some way to

* 'To wish someone ill fortune . . . especially by predicting failure' (*Dictionary of American Slang*).

blame for his death – it was as if she had killed him with her maledictions, even though everybody knew he had a weak heart.

As her lawyer, Zaidins advised Billie that he could manage her money more efficiently if she had a bank account. He opened one for her at the Chemical Bank, but that did not last because she quickly withdrew more money than she had put in. She was used to spending her earnings before she had received them and she was very generous. Zaidins said, 'She wanted to keep alive that she was Lady Day. So when she had a little bit of money, or when she had borrowed a bit, she would give it to people, to show she had it . . . She used to tell me, "Don't ask for the advance. I don't want them to know I need it! I'm Lady Day!"'

Zaidins questioned Billie about her relationship with her agent, Joe Glaser. She said he had often promised to get her Cabaret Card back, but had achieved nothing. 'She was griping that he wasn't booking her enough, for enough money, and she could never get an exact count of the guy. She always felt she wasn't getting the proper accounting.'*

Worse than that, Joe Glaser never got the right sort of bookings for her. She was forced to do the same music over and over again and 'all those small jazz groups gave her a headache'. What she wanted was to 'sing her heart out with strings', like Frank Sinatra. Her best audiences had always been white and she wanted to play 'big white rooms' like the Plaza, the Waldorf, the Empire Room, the Bandbox. As Zaidins saw it, 'She wanted to be a big act. She wanted to be booked regularly. She wasn't that well recognised by everybody and she wanted that recognition and she wanted to pay the bills.'

But still Billie felt obliged to Joe Glaser. After all, he had stood by her and was always there when she got in a jam.

---

* Zaidins said, 'There were people who agitated her and convinced her she was being stolen from. She probably earnt a gross of thirty to fifty thousand dollars in her last years, which isn't a hell of a lot considering expenses: musicians, commissions, her piano player, to whom she had to pay a regular salary whether she worked or not . . .'

'Whether for good or bad, and even though she was unhappy with Glaser, she felt she had security with him. Glaser was to many people a father image. When you were broke you went to him and got some money, for a new coat, a car, or just to get home.'

Zaidins became convinced that he could pull the right strings to get Billie her Cabaret Card, but she refused to cooperate. She was afraid it would only lead to more publicity about her police record, her drug addiction, her unreliability. She said, 'I don't want the goddamn thing! I don't want that mess! I can live without it!' In spite of her protests he continued privately with the application, but it was again turned down.

However, sometime in 1957, Zaidins did manage to find Billie a little apartment on 87th Street, not far from where he had moved to. Even that was not easy. She signed the lease under the name of Eleanor Fagan McKay, but the land-lord wanted to cancel the whole thing when he discovered his new tenant's real identity. It was only by 'making a big stink' that Zaidins managed to push the contract through, because, as he said, 'It meant so very, very much to her.'

Zaidins obviously enjoyed Billie's company, although he was insistent that he did not have a sexual relationship with her. They used to listen to records together in his apartment and he found her to be a 'brilliant conversationalist who could hold a conversation about everything: clothing, babies, musicians, furnishings, her house . . . everything'. She'd tell endless stories about her life, whether it was events from years ago or from the day before, but Zaidins realised that 'There were some things she might not have wanted to remember and she did have a fantastic imagination. Not that she'd make up stories, but to repeat what happened yesterday, she'd completely fantasise.'

Zaidins said that after a while 'I had a feeling that Billie was dependent upon me. She was honest with me. She was a good friend.' In return she helped him with his career. 'She took me by the hand and took me to different jazz places and other clubs at night. She introduced me to the giants of the jazz world. She kept introducing me as her lawyer and saying how wonderful I was, and really I was nowhere near it then, I was just a kid. But as a direct result a lot of artists thought: if he can represent Billie Holiday, he sure can represent me. And I received a lot of clients that way.'

But Zaidins realised there was a certain one-sidedness to this friendship and an innate loneliness in Billie that could not be bridged. 'She had no real friends, no close friends.' He said that people who had known her in the past would drop by to pay a hurried visit to the apartment and then vanish again, while 'Total strangers would arrive out of nowhere and you had the feeling they had never been there before.'

Apart from Zaidins, William Dufty and his wife Maely 'passed in and out'. Then there was a 'tall, black, slender, nice-looking boy' called Frankie Freedom, who did her hair and made meals for her,* and her 'quiet and loyal' secretary Alice Vrbsky, who walked the dog and dealt with letters and other practicalities, such as filling out Billie's monthly probation reports, which explained where she was going to be playing and affirmed that she was 'being good'. None of these helpers was ever paid much for their services, simply because there was so little money around. Zaidins said he often lent Billie money when she needed it. On one occasion she pawned her black diamond mink so that she could stock up on food and drink.

Zaidins got married in 1958 and Billie quickly adopted his young son as one of her numerous godchildren. She sang him lullabies and had infinite patience with him, as she did with all the children to whom she became close. She often told Zaidins 'It was her dream to retire somewhere and get a big spread of land where she could have a home for orphan children.' On a more realistic note, she asked him if he could

---

* It was Frankie Freedom who took Billie to hospital at the end and was said to have been responsible for giving her the 'white powder' that led to her final arrest. But that part of the story is very hard to verify and Frankie Freedom himself disappeared without trace.

help her to adopt just the one. She told him she had only agreed to marry Louis McKay because, as a single woman in show business and with her police record, she knew she didn't stand a chance. But she felt it might be possible now and was sure she would make a good mother. She said she had recently heard of a child available for adoption in Boston. She was finding out about that. The house in the country would be surrounded by flowers and trees.

It is difficult to know if Zaidins really believed that Billie's dream of motherhood could come true, but he did set about collecting affidavits from all sorts of people who were willing to swear that she would be a reliable parent. He added his own affidavit as well, for good measure. This was Billie's second adoption application and it was turned down just as swiftly as the first and 'she cried for days, for days' when she was told the news.

But at least Zaidins was proud that he managed to fulfil another of Billie's dreams. He helped her to get in touch with Ray Ellis, who did the musical arrangements for the *Lady in Satin* record in February 1958. He said she did her first rehearsal for *Lady in Satin* in his living-room, going through the lyrics with her pianist Mal Waldron,★ and after that she was ready for the real thing. The recording sessions were held in a church on Lexington Avenue that had 'this magnificent, resonant sound' and Zaidins as well as Alice Vrbsky made sure Billie was there on time and stayed to listen to the recordings.†

Zaidins remembered how one night Billie turned up at his apartment, complaining that a tap was dripping and keeping her awake. 'You've gotta help me!' she said. 'That goddamn thing goes drip, drip, drip, drip, drip! It wouldn't

---

★ 'Mal Waldron was a very quiet guy and he didn't play funky, soulful music. She'd criticise him saying, "How come you're a black man and you can't play funky music?"'

† Ray Ellis remembered Earle Zaidins coming to the sessions. 'He was like her manager, almost a manager-lawyer. He was very dedicated to her. He really dug her. He would just flip out when he listened to her sing – have an orgasm is the only way I can explain it. He is the last guy in the world you'd imagine to flip out over Billie Holiday!'

be so bad, but it don't swing! It don't swing!' She was laughing and serious and angry and desperate all at the same time. Earle Zaidins told her to put a towel under the tap to silence it.

Another night she arrived at the door with blood dripping from a cut to her head. Louis McKay had turned up unannounced at her apartment. They had a fight and he hit her over the head with the telephone while she was trying to make a call. Earle Zaidins said, 'I locked her in the bathroom and Louis came knocking at my door. I locked my wife and kids in another part of the apartment and Louis came in.

'He said, "I got a gun! A pistol!" and he pulled it. I went for it and threw him out.

'I was going to call the police, but Lady prevailed upon me not to. She didn't want to press charges. At first I thought it was because she didn't want the police involved – and she didn't. But she was also afraid of the publicity. She was very sensitive to bad publicity.'

Zaidins was not contacted when Billie was first taken to the private Knickerbocker Hospital on 30 May 1959, but he went to see her after she had been moved to Harlem's Metropolitan Hospital. She had been registered as Mrs Eleanora McKay, but once her identity had been revealed, she had been placed in a private room because so many reporters began to hound the hospital. Zaidins had difficulty in persuading the orderly in charge that he had a right to see her and was told that, in her state, they doubted if she could recognise anybody. But finally they agreed to take him up to her room, where she was lying in some sort of plastic tent. He said, 'She looked like half of herself. She had wasted tremendously. The orderly pointed to me and asked Lady if she recognised me. She said, "What the fuck do you mean? That's Earle, my lawyer!" She smiled and the man went away.'

When Billie was first in hospital she had friends visiting her and well-wishers sending her messages. She had a radio and comic books, and Zaidins even brought in a gramophone so that they could listen to the recordings she had just made with Ray Ellis for MGM. One nurse allowed her to drink a bottle of beer. William Dufty provided her with cigarettes and also arranged to earn her some money by producing an article for *The Inquirer*, entitled 'How drugs saved my life', for which she received $500.

There was obviously a rather mad party atmosphere in Billie's room. Zaidins wanted to arrange a new recording deal with MGM and when Billie doubted if she would ever be able to sing again, he reassured her, saying, 'Look, Lady, these people at MGM are business people. They check into things. They've already talked to the doctors. Would they pick up your option if they thought you were going to die?' Billie warmed to the idea and said they could bring the recording equipment into the hospital and call the new record *Lady at the Met.*

But then, on 11 June, Billie was arrested in her hospital bed on the charge of possessing narcotics and everything became much more serious. According to Zaidins, 'She was free from drugs when she went into that hospital and I believe the tests proved she was free of drugs . . . She had no need for drugs, mentally or physically. So her involvement with the drugs found under or by her pillow had to be phoney.'★

Everybody who was involved had a different account of what drugs were found and where, and they all disagreed as to whether Billie was 'clean' or not. For his part, Zaidins was convinced that Billie's worst fears had come true and somebody had planted the drugs in her room. In the interview he said, 'I can only speculate as to why, and I don't want to do that here.'

Whatever the truth was, it does seem that Billie's arrest and the very real threat of imprisonment then facing her contributed more to her sudden decline in hospital than the medical complications that appeared on her death certificate. Everyone agreed that she had been getting better, but

★ According to Alice Zaidins, her husband was certain that Billie was completely free of drugs, but later he was persuaded by Alice Vrbsky that she must still have been an occasional user.

she told Zaidins 'She didn't think she was going to make it. She said she was tired. She was unhappy.'★

When Billie Holiday died on 17 July, there was an immediate flurry of activity as the people who had been involved in her life got ready for the financial, legal and emotional battles that were bound to follow. Zaidins, who had fallen out with Joe Glaser after a recent quarrel, suddenly found himself 'buddy-buddy' with Billie's agent. At the funeral he even travelled with Joe Glaser and Louis McKay in the first limousine behind the casket, and the three of them were among the pall-bearers.

Zaidins said he couldn't remember much about this final stage in his relationship with Billie. 'I was in a state of grief,' he said. 'I actually cried for a couple of weeks after this woman died. I don't know what it was, don't ask me how or what. It was as if she was somebody in my own family. I was very emotional about it.'

Thinking about it all those years later, Zaidins wondered if Billie might not still have been alive 'had this country treated her the way she should have been treated, given her the respect to which she was vastly entitled . . . In America we somehow or other do not place our jazz personalities on the same level as classical musicians and singers. We seem to look down on them as fair game, when we ought to elevate them to the status to which they are so richly deserving.'

And if she had lived, he thought she would probably have changed her style. 'She loved recording with violins and flutes and I think she would have gone in that direction.'

★ Like many others, Zaidins saw Billie as a masochist. 'She was only happy being miserable . . . Why else would she have gotten involved in that marital life?' But later in the interview with John Jeremy he added, 'To be a girl singer, you've got to be a masochist. You're going from town to town in hotel rooms and you're alone.'

THIRTY-SEVEN

Alice Vrbsky

'A woman of her word.'

A lice Vrbsky speaks very slowly and clearly and when
she needs to think about a question before answering
it, she doesn't seem to mind that the tape recorder is listening
to her silence. I have here combined two interviews with
her. The first was made by Linda Kuehl in 1971, when Alice
was in her late thirties, and the second was made by the jazz
collector Norman Saks in 1985. On both occasions Alice
gives pretty much the same account of her friendship with
Billie, although in the later interview she is far more
outspoken in her opinion of Louis McKay and in her talk
about drugs. She giggles quite often, making a shy, rumbling
sound when she explains how young she once was and how
little she understood about the world. As she draws closer
to the end of her story, her voice gets even slower and you
have the sense that she is not simply remembering the past
– she is also walking back into it, until she can see that
woman called Billie Holiday, as she knew her during the
final two years of her life. Here is Alice Vrbsky talking.

I'd only heard her on records, but then in the summer
of 1957 I got to see her in Central Park. I enjoyed the

performance so much that I went up to thank her afterwards. She'd signed the programme and I was trying to tell her how much I admired her. I said I'd got the album *Lady Sings the Blues*, but I hadn't got it with me, and I asked would she mind if I brought it down for her to sign and, she said, 'Fine, bring it down!'

So the next day I showed up with the record and the first thing she said was, 'Ah! A woman of her word!' – just like that. And on the album she wrote, 'Thank you for loving me.' You see we hit it off. I can't explain it, but we hit it off.

Her husband, Louis McKay, asked if I would be her secretary. I was really surprised, I was just a novice. But he made it sound wonderful and I thought this was great, I'd get to see some of the country and I'd get to hear her sing. For the first two weeks he paid me cash – sixty-five dollars I think it was – but that was the one and only time I was paid by him because then he sort of disappeared. She paid me after that. She'd pay for all the travelling and everything, although I didn't really earn anything. I was twenty-four years old and living at home. I didn't need the money.

When I started with her we went to Los Angeles. Her husband made arrangements to get us an apartment, but then he faded out quite promptly. The apartment was in a pretty lousy condition; the floors and walls were grimy and we were both scrubbing and wiping and mopping, but she did the major part of it, it was I who was helping *her*. She was a hard worker. It wasn't as if she just laid around and didn't do anything.

We had that apartment for four weeks and then we went on to San Francisco. This was around September 1957. I remember we'd been gone for six weeks and she had this Carnegie Hall concert booked, and so we had to finish the last show in California and pack and get right into the show in New York. Thirty-six hours without sleep. She did wonderfully.

She always fixed her own hair and make-up. She used

an ordinary eyebrow pencil – in fact, I have a small stub of it at home: Maybelline, orangey-red on the outside. At home she just put on lipstick and eyebrows with an ordinary eyebrow pencil. For stage she wore stage jewellery that was not in the best condition and she used a pancake make-up with a little powder over it. She put the pancake on her body. All I had to do was to take care of her dresses and make sure they were clean and zip her up, and lots of times I would zip her skin up.

She wore a light girdle, just to hold her stockings, white or pink; an ordinary bra, white usually; white panties, not lacy or anything. She wasn't a frivolous woman; the things she wore every day were not very outlandish and not very expensive. She liked slacks. She had very good wool slacks. When she had money before I knew her, she knew what to buy and bought quality things, but she didn't buy too much when I was with her. She was hard up, in the sense of money. And she wouldn't sit around undressed between shows in her dressing room; she just stayed the way she was dressed. Maybe that was different when she was young.

In New York when I first worked for her, she was living at the Wilson Hotel. She was a Chinese food addict and she often asked me to bring back some Chinese food from the restaurant next door. She'd put it on regular plates or eat it out of the box. She wasn't the kind of person that needed to be waited on. Steamed porgy with rice was what we got most of the time. She liked plain white rice. I never saw her use chopsticks.

My parents liked her. She came to dinner once and she kept them up until three in the morning, and my folks weren't used to that. But fortunately it was the weekend and they didn't mind. Her hours were always irregular. She was a night person and she'd never go to bed before 5 a.m. She usually got up around noon and often slept through appointments, if she had any.

Sometimes she'd drag me down to Broadway and

we'd go to these all-night shows on 42nd Street. We were like two old moles. I remember once she took me to 7th Avenue and 125th Street and we went into this bar, and she ordered me a club soda because I still wasn't drinking in those days and she showed me the atmosphere – what it was like in a Harlem bar. We usually took a cab. That was the way we got around.

She said she'd tried every drug in the book, and she was on drugs all the time I knew her. Someone would bring her drugs, maybe a couple of times a week. She said Louis McKay had not helped her at all and had put her back on drugs; I presumed he was supplying her. I'd seen her melting the stuff down on a spoon and using an ancient needle to put it in her veins. It was a very primitive kind of arrangement and not very sanitary and must have been painful. I'm a diabetic and the only thing I did was to give her a syringe because I couldn't stand to see the way she was injecting herself. Today you can walk into any place and get a dispos-able needle, but in those days it was different. I never got involved in her drugs in any way, but a guy once offered me some marijuana and I said, 'No, thanks. I get drunk on the music!' And later Lady would often say, 'She gets drunk on the music!' She liked that.

She said it was all wrong the way they treated drug addicts as criminals and made criminals out of them.★ And one time she said to me, 'If I ask you to help me, you can help me, but if I don't ask you, there's nothing you can do.' And I think she was really admit-ting it was up to the drug addict to give up the habit. She had a couple who were friends and she felt bad because they took stuff, and their children would play games of taking the stuff because their parents were hooked and Billie said those children didn't have a chance.

★ When Alice Vrbsky asked Billie whether she was 'set up' for the arrest and jail sentence in 1947, 'She said she was on drugs when she went to jail, but she was set up in the sense that she wasn't the problem, she wasn't a pusher, and the people who were with her got off.'

She told me when she first got married she wanted children very badly and she would sometimes lie in bed with her feet up after intercourse, because she thought that might help. But by the time I knew her she realised it would have been too late. Still, I think she would have been a good mother. I saw her with the two boys Louis had with a woman in California. She often took care of them and they liked her. She swore they weren't really Louis', and said his woman told her they were trick babies.

She wasn't always the easiest person to get along with, because of the things she was under the influence of. One time I walked out because nothing I did was right and I was trying the best I could, so I said to hell with it. Two days later she called me and said, 'I can't find so-and-so and would you come over?' and so I went. I remember she said to me, 'If you want to hang around show people, you can't be sensitive. You've got to get over that.'

I enjoyed being with her. Of course I enjoyed her as an artist, but I also enjoyed just talking to her. She'd talk a lot about her mother. I got the feeling there was a lot of friction between her and her mother, because Sadie didn't approve of the things she was doing, but they were very close. She said, 'I haven't spoken to anybody the way I speak to you since my mother died. I almost feel as if she has come back to me in some way.' I had the feeling she needed to have somebody who loved her enough to understand her.

She was a very intelligent woman who knew about many things I knew nothing about, and who knew about sizing things up. She always said what she meant, and I learnt a great deal about real feelings rather than phoney feelings from her, just by watching her and seeing how she treated people and how she talked to them. She'd be friendly with someone if she liked them, no matter who they were, and she wouldn't be friendly with someone just because he was a bigshot. She'd say,

'People don't think I like laughing. They don't think I lead any kind of normal life.' I think it bothered her that people thought she was something peculiar, in the sense of being totally depressed and out of everything. She didn't live such an unusual life, but she was bitter against society and the phoneyness.

I never felt she used people and that might have been part of the problem, because people were using her all the time, but she never learnt to use them. In her heyday, when she had scads of money coming in, she told me how people asked for money and she gave it to them and nobody ever gave it back to her. They weren't people I knew, so the names didn't mean anything. But they weren't around when she needed them later.★

She wasn't the kind of person who pitied herself, or if she did, it was only when she was alone. She wasn't the kind of person who complained. But she used to say, 'I can sing in Carnegie Hall and in a place where they sell ice cream to kids, but I can't sing where people drink.' I think she missed being in the clubs in New York. I remember she was in the Apollo Theater to see Al Hibbler, and they called her up to the stage and she sang with him and the response from the audience was fantastic.

One of my main jobs was making out her parole reports, because she'd been arrested a year or so before. All that was required was information about where she was performing and where they could find her, if they wanted to find her. So I'd give them the itinerary for a month and we'd say, 'Oh, I'm doing fine. Everything's going well.' It didn't really mean anything at all, but she hoped they wouldn't bother her so long as she sent them in. It was a scary time for her because she was always expecting them to walk in and arrest her again.

★ Apparently Billie's mother was also very generous and used to say, 'If we give it out now, we'll get it back later.' But 'It didn't work out quite that way,' said Alice with a soft giggle.

She wasn't working regularly, she was working when she could. You can't live if you don't work, and this was her problem in the last two years I knew her – just finding enough work to keep ahead of things. I don't know if the clubs felt she wasn't reliable, or that she was past it, or what. I usually went to every engagement and I don't recall her missing a set. The owner of Birdland said he could arrange a deal with her and he would buy a licence★ for her, if she would sing in his club for six months of every year, but Billie said, 'I'm not going to sell half of myself, contract-wise, to anybody.' But she was bitter about the fact that it could have been done.

She told me her father died in a similar way to Bessie Smith; he was shunted around from place to place and she felt his death was very close to a lynching, although the exact facts were never known. She said she could have gone to the South and made a lot of money when she became a soloist without the big bands, but she just felt she couldn't bring herself to go down there. Even in 1958 there was as much segregation in Las Vegas as in Baltimore. She played Baltimore twice while I was working with her and we stayed in a Negro hotel because it couldn't be otherwise. But even when she played places like Detroit, she wasn't allowed to stay in a white hotel.

The club owners and the guys who ran the hotels assumed that, because I was travelling with her, I must have been a black woman who was trying to pass for white.† She said as soon as people saw her together

★ By a licence she means a Cabaret Card. When Alice asked Billie how it was that after-hours clubs were permitted to stay open, even though it was against the law, she said, 'The police know where they are and they don't worry them if they pay. I'm sure it's the same with drugs, prostitution and everything else.'
† Looking at a photograph of Alice Vrbsky, it would seem impossible to think she was 'passing for white', but as the writer Langston Hughes explained in his autobiography *The Big Sea*, 'Here in the United States of America, the word Negro is used to mean anyone who has *any* Negro blood in his veins.'
My own father, Thomas Blackburn, had a grandmother who was born on the island of Mauritius and was a 'woman of colour' as it was called there,

with a white woman, they assumed it was a sort of relationship. And she said that the white men she may have
had affairs with didn't want it to be known that they
knew her when they met her in public, and they'd just
cut her off. It was the basic dishonesty of society at that
time.

I remember in Detroit she was sitting in a bar with
two musicians who were white, and one of the club
owners came to her later to say she wasn't supposed to
have drinks with customers at the bar. She said, 'My
God, I've gone through this so many times before!' In
Los Angeles she stayed at the Sahara Hotel, but that
was only because they made special arrangements
because she was playing there, and her musicians had
to stay somewhere else. She asked one of her black
friends, 'Why don't you come and see me at the Sahara?',
but no black person was allowed to come to the show.
She said, 'They wouldn't even hire me to be a maid
here, or to wait at the tables, and they would never let
me in.' In Detroit when she was with Artie Shaw's band,
she had to put on white make-up.

She wanted to take me to Europe with her, but she
couldn't afford to. She went to Europe with the idea
that people were more liberal there, not as prejudiced
against everything. She was really looking forward to
it, but she was really glad to be home when she came
back. She said she missed New York. She was a little
disappointed by not being able to understand the
language and she had some trouble with management,
from what I gathered. She didn't come back with any
overwhelmingly happy memories. She bought me a

(cont. from pg. 315) and a descendant of slaves. That would make me a Negro
in many of the southern states, where 'any ascertainable trace' of Negro blood
defines one as being black. There are endless stories in which a person who
looks white, but who is officially black, is denied the job they are qualified
for, thrown out of the hospital they are lying in, or ostracised by those who
were their friends, once the 'secret' is out. All this might have an *Alice in
Wonderland* humour to it, were it not so serious and had the consequences
not been so disastrous for so many people, black and white.

kerchief from Milan and that was about all. I don't know
what she did about drugs and that might have been
part of it too, but I'm only guessing.

For the last year and a half she lived in an apartment
in New York. There were no religious objects around.
She didn't really have any possessions because she'd
been living in hotels and so she wasn't somebody who
could accumulate things. She had a radio and she'd
carry it with her from room to room. She had her
phonograph and maybe twenty-five records. She didn't
turn it on that often and when she did, she'd play more
instrumental music, not for background but as something she'd really listen to. I remember one time she
said about Miles Davis, 'You know it bothers me. It
sounds as if he's playing off-key on some of the notes.'

I used to mix her drinks. She smoked heavily and
she had a cigarette and a glass in her hand more often
than not. When I was there I tried to make her eat
something for breakfast, but this was in the early days;
in the end she wouldn't even eat. By June 1959 she
was mainly drinking Gordon's gin and Seven-Up, and
that was what she was living on and that was why she
started losing so much weight. She stayed at home and
watched TV mostly at the end. Her only bad habit was
that she would often fall asleep while she was smoking
a cigarette and she'd burn holes in her nightgown or
bathrobe. She'd make jokes about it and say, 'I'm real
holy!'

She seemed to go suddenly, like my father, who looked
well six months ago and then suddenly he had cancer
and he was dying. Two months before she went to
hospital she looked very haggard and her cheeks were
sunk in and she wasn't eating much. She got yellower
as she got sicker. A young Negro boy called Frankie
Freedom was staying there for the last weeks and helping
her. I don't know where he came from. He was tall
and thin and young, about seventeen or eighteen. He
had ambitions to be in the theatre and I don't know

how Lady got to know him that well, but maybe she needed somebody around in the daytime, especially since I had to get a job, so I couldn't be there all day and all night. I just came in the evenings, or she'd call and ask me to take care of her clothes. I took her clothes to the cleaners, took the dog out. She'd see her lawyer and Bill and Maely Dufty, but there weren't other regular visitors.

She told me the book she wrote with Bill Dufty, *Lady Sings the Blues*, was devoid of the truth, it was utter baloney. It was Louis McKay who put pressure on her and Dufty to say certain things, and Louis insisted that she clean up the story of her childhood. But the worst thing in the book is that Louis became the great hero at the end of it. Now, in many ways Billie was a dreamer, and she always wished that some man would come along and be the man she really needed, but Louis McKay was not that man.

The Duftys were negotiating movie rights and record contracts. I think she got on better with Bill than with Maely. Bill was very quiet, very mild, but I think Maely was the driving force, and she felt she had a corner on Billie and she didn't want anyone getting in. I remember I was playing opera records and Billie was talking about how much she loved them, and Maely was surprised and said, 'Oh, I didn't know *you* like opera!' And Billie was indignant and said, 'Well, I like good music, so why can't I like opera?' And once Maely said to me about Billie, 'She's not stupid!' or something like that. This whole attitude struck me as strange.

Still, I didn't realise that she was as ill as she was and I was kind of surprised when she was taken to hospital. I didn't see the doctors too much in the hospital, but the nurses were there. In a city hospital I guess you don't expect more than them just doing their job. I don't think she got any special service, because that's something you have to pay for. When I first visited her in hospital she was sitting up in bed. She was wearing a bed jacket, a pink one that was kind of tufted, and she had her hair pulled back and clipped with an ordinary clip because she didn't have anything valuable that I knew of.

I hoped she might get better, but as I kept going I realised she was getting worse and worse and she knew by then herself, I'm sure. She was too honest and she wouldn't have reacted that way if she didn't know. She was having trouble breathing, but she could talk. The timbre of her voice had gotten harsher and slower, but her reactions were still sharp. She didn't complain. She wasn't the kind of person who said, 'I don't feel good.' She never did. Maybe that was why I was so shocked. Whatever happened inside her body was probably building and building until it reached a certain point. But she was declining in the last month. Her spirit was willing, but the flesh had had too much of everything.

I don't think she went into hospital thinking she wouldn't come out. She was very practical in the sense – not that she knew she was going to die, because no one knows★ – but in the sense that she was very composed and ready for it. She wasn't a desperate dying woman by any means. Whatever she was thinking at the end, it was as though she wasn't in trouble in not wanting to die, maybe she was even looking forward to it. But she never talked much about her own death, or what she wanted done, and she never spoke of a will.

I guess that boy Frankie Freedom came at the time when all the trouble started. She told me that Frankie brought some powder to her and that's what they found. She wasn't angry with him; she had asked him for it. And that was when the nurse must have noticed it. She wasn't withdrawing, because the one time that I saw her when she was having trouble, she was sweating and shaking, but she wasn't like that in hospital, so they

---

★ Alice said that 'If she had known she was dying, she might have signed the will that her lawyer Earle Zaidins had got ready for her.'

must have been giving her something – morphine or something. She didn't talk about the nurse who reported seeing traces of white powder round her nose, but of course she wasn't happy about being arrested again.★ From that point it was as if the heart went out of her. She just wasn't herself.

When she was arrested they only allowed so many people to go up and see her, and it was more difficult. Then there was the police guard, and you had to give your name and you had to show your card to the policeman outside the door. At that time she was too ill to have gotten up and walked out, so I don't know what they were protecting her from or for. She was bitter about the arrest, in the sense that it was the last thing she wanted at that point. They took everything away in the hospital, even the hope she had.

She did get flowers, especially when the publicity about her arrest got out, but it is an exaggeration to say she always had a room full of them. People who didn't necessarily know her, but who appreciated her music, sent her cards. Mostly these cards were from ordinary people and that is why she didn't get flowers from them, because ordinary people can't afford that much, especially black people. I think then, when she saw all the cards and letters, that really made her feel much better, because she probably didn't realise how many ordinary people cared for her and how many people she touched. She read them all. I helped her open them, but she read them. One day I took home two bags of cards and I answered them, with her permission.

She was still not in terrible spirits, even after she got arrested. She sort of reacted like: 'What do you expect? This is the way things have been going! I've been busted before.' Even the day before she died I didn't see her in an oxygen tent. But I saw the same thing in my

---

★ Alice was very confused on one point. 'She said she asked Frankie to bring cocaine, but it said in the paper it was heroin . . . Why didn't she tell me if she asked for heroin, too? And how could she have taken a fix? It's a mystery.'

father's face, the day before he died. She died the following night, but I didn't go to see her that day. I felt almost that she didn't want me to come. By then she must have known. I saw death in her face.

I think her husband Louis McKay may have been out of town when she went into the Metropolitan Hospital. I don't know how soon he got back, but I know he called me when she was laid out in the funeral home. He wanted me to act as receptionist there, but I said, 'No,' I said, 'I can't do it!' He said, 'Oh, but I'll give you some of Lady's coats!' I felt this wasn't going to take her place, but he didn't understand.

I knew her. I felt I knew what she would have wanted. She wouldn't have wanted any phoney fuss being made over her, which was what Louis was doing. He was playing the dutiful husband who had lost his loving wife, but from what she told me there had long since been no love between them any more. I went to the church and when they took the coffin out I cried. I couldn't listen to her records for a year.

THIRTY-EIGHT

Laughin' to Keep from Cryin'

———

I have been looking at a video recording of Billie singing 'Fine and Mellow'. It is taken from the television film *The Sound of Jazz*, which was made on 8 December 1957. The entire sequence lasts for about three and a half minutes. I reach the end and spin the flickering images back to the beginning. I press Stop, Rewind and Play, over and over again. I am watching faces. I am trying to read the story that is being told here. I am watching how people look at each other, how they stand, how they move. Some appear to be very strong, while others look frail. There are those who close their eyes with concentration and those who keep their eyes open all the time.

Billie is here with a gathering of old friends.* Many of them used to play together in the 1930s and '40s, but then things changed, their paths rarely crossed and they hardly ever had the opportunity to perform on the same stage. The reason for this was very simple: they were all recognised individually as stars in their own right and they were making good

---

* Billie's All Stars included Roy Eldridge, Doc Cheatham (tps), Vic Dickenson (tb), Lester Young, Ben Webster, Coleman Hawkins (ts), Gerry Mulligan (bs), Mal Waldron (p), Danny Barker (g), Milt Hinton (b), Osie Johnson (d).

money, their names emblazoned in big letters in front of one club or another. But few club owners were prepared to pay for more than one star at a time, and so they tended to appear on their own, which meant that the excitement of working together and sharing skills and experience was lost.

Some, like Lester Young, couldn't bear the isolation and the lack of compatibility he felt with young and unskilled players. Perhaps that was one of the reasons why he increasingly withdrew into a cocoon of drink and marijuana and pills and sadness, unable to play with anything like his old fluency, until the moment when he was back among friends and could become himself again. Others were stronger, but still they were unhappy with the situation. The bassist Milt Hinton explained how Billie's old friend Ben Webster was 'going crazy . . . because he gets five hundred dollars a week in Rochester, but with three high-school kids to accompany him, and every afternoon he needs to sit down with them to teach them the chords. They'll forget by the time they get on the bandstand, and God forbid if one of them takes an extra break!'

Milt Hinton said that Billie was in the same situation. 'She's going to some club . . . and they're giving her a fairly high price, but in order to do that they can't support her with the kind of musicians she should be supported with, like the ones who made her records. So they're taking this little stinking joint and they pay her whatever her price is and they get some local musicians, which is just ridiculous, for the simple reason that they haven't the experience. They'll probably be great later, but they're just terrible now and they're only getting fifty or sixty dollars a week. And she has to scuffle through a performance with this kind of a background.'

And so it was an important event when two music journalists and a television film producer* put forward the idea of bringing a number of top jazz musicians together in

---

* Nat Hentoff, Whitney Balliett and producer Robert Herridge. Nat Hentoff was 'a champion of Billie's cause, who made a point of emphasising his devotion to her singing from all eras' (Chilton, p. 230).

Studio 58 on 10th Avenue and letting them play like they used to play in the old days. Here were the Count Basie All Stars, the Henry 'Red' Allen All Stars, the Thelonious Monk Trio, the Jimmy Giuffre Trio and the Billie Holiday and Mal Waldron All Stars. Everybody had just one day to rehearse, to listen to each other and to talk. The programme was then ready to be broadcast live the following evening.

During those two days in December the streets of New York were engulfed by a heavy snowstorm and some of the players were not at all well. Nevertheless everything was forgotten with the sheer joy of walking into that studio and seeing the old familiar faces again. Milt Hinton remembered 'the ecstasy, just to be flitting around' and how they kept saying, 'Here we are, playing together. We know who we are, the people know who we are. We never get to play with the good guys any more, but now here we are together.'★

During the rehearsal all the musicians were milling around together. Count Basie and Thelonious Monk were seen talking, while Billie stood smiling beside them.† Milt Hinton remarked on the 'princely demeanour and majestic presence' of Jo Jones the drummer, and Vic Dickenson was overheard saying 'Jazz am a bitch' and making people laugh with his gentle humour. And there was Roy Eldridge, whom Billie still called Little Brother, and Gerry Mulligan 'the Sax King', who was the only white man in her group and the baby of them all.

Even Lester Young had made it, although he was sitting by himself on a bench and was wearing carpet slippers because his feet hurt, and he was looking much older than his forty-eight years. Milt Hinton said everyone was aware that Pres 'wasn't so well', but he didn't remember anyone saying they

---

★ There was a similar joyful gathering in 1958 when *Esquire* magazine organised the photograph by Art Kane of jazz musicians gathered on the front steps of a house in Harlem. A crowd of top musicians turned up, even though the shoot was set for ten o'clock in the morning and several people said that until then they hadn't known there were two ten o'clocks in a single day.

† Milt Hinton was also a keen amateur photographer and had his camera with him for this event. He took a picture of Billie 'through the piano with her long pigtail, standing next to Basie'.

thought he was going. 'We had no thought like that and certainly we had none of Billie then.'

Billie was in fine spirits and exuberant, although Roy Eldridge said he was shocked by how much she had changed since the last time he saw her. 'She was just a little bitty woman. She had gotten so small. I'd never known her so small, and I knew her when she was fourteen or fifteen.'

When that day's rehearsal was over, Doc Cheatham said that 'Everybody was kidding and laughing and talking a mile a minute . . . and Billie invited us to have greens and ribs and stuff at her place after the session, and a lot of 'em went.' Only Lester Young declined. 'He just kept to himself, sat apart. He was very quiet and sad that day. He didn't have much to say to anybody.'

The following day, the bassist Walter Page collapsed on his way to the studio and was taken to hospital, where he died a couple of weeks later. But everyone else stumbled through the snow and arrived when they were supposed to. The cameras were rolling. Roy Eldridge remembered how gracious the producer was. 'He let people mingle and he didn't disturb them and he had a feeling for jazz . . . "Let the boys play," he said,' and the cameras continued to roll.

Billie was the only woman among them, but there was nothing new in that. In the film sequence that I have been watching, you see her and her eleven All Stars taking up their positions. The dark air is pierced by the beams of television lights and is full of the swirling smoke trails of cigarettes.

Billie goes to sit on a high wooden stool in the centre of the stage and the musicians gather round her in a semi-circle. She is wearing a pale woollen dress with a round neck and a hemline that just covers her knees. She is wearing flat shoes and a wristwatch, and her hair is pulled back into a pony tail. She settles herself very quietly with her hands in her lap and looks for all the world like a schoolteacher who is preparing to read a story to a class of young pupils. The only hint of glamour is in her shining earrings, which sparkle like stars when she moves her head.

There are two main camera angles that are used throughout. From one of them, Billie is bathed in a soft light and the paleness of her dress is answered by the luminosity of her pale skin. She looks younger than she is, almost like the young girl she once was. She looks soft and innocent and possessed by an almost ethereal beauty, especially when she smiles.

The other camera seems to be focusing on a completely different woman, who is illuminated by dark and dramatic shadows. This woman is gaunt and tired and her eyes are glittering black pools that keep filling with tears. From this angle you don't see the prim dress or the wristwatch – just the floating apparition of a face and the shifting emotions it contains.

Billie gazes at the men who surround her. With several of them she has been engaged in what Roy Eldridge called 'a little light housekeeping' at one time or another, but she is just as close to the ones she has never slept with. As Harry 'Sweets' Edison once explained it, 'She romanced everybody in the band, so far as friendship was concerned. Because she was *your friend*.'*

Now you see her busy with all of them, going from one to the next, smiling at them, getting them ready to do their best for her. As Doc Cheatham said, 'You had to be exceptional to play for her. She wanted everything to be just right. One wrong note, no matter how quiet or short, and she noticed it. She could let you know something with her eyes, like if the trumpet was too loud. She'd be polite, but tough.'

The music begins and she is singing 'My man don't love me, treats me oh so mean. My man, he don't love me, treats me awful mean. He's the lowest man, that I've ever seen.'

Ben Webster is her first soloist. As he rises to his feet you can see the solid power of his body and how dangerous he

---

* Billie called him Sweetie-Pie. 'We'd kiss and she'd say, "Sweet, Sweet, you still carrying on that same old shit? Sweet, Sweet, Sweetie-Pie!" Only she could say that in her way. And when her life went on, her voice got lower and lower. Nobody's like her, there'll only be one Billie Holiday!'

might be if he became drunk or angry. He and Billie did a little light housekeeping in the late 1930s and he used to beat her up, and on at least one occasion gave her a black eye. Now she looks at him with extreme tenderness, because everything is starting just right and he is doing well.★

The camera moves to Gerry Mulligan, who has his eyes tight shut and his head dipped forward, so that he seems to be lost in a deep sleep. And then we see Lester Young rising to his feet and shuffling forward to stand beside his old friend, his Lady Day. The camera moves onto his face, exposing how ill he looks and how tired. His last recording, made earlier that year, was called *Laughin' to Keep from Cryin'* and Lester looks as though he has been crying for weeks, his eyes are so swollen and puffy. He raises the saxophone slowly towards his lips and his mouth opens in thirsty anticipation of receiving it. The music he makes is slow and measured and heartbreaking. As the *New York Times* journalist Nat Hentoff described it later, 'He blew the sparest, purest blues I had ever heard.'†

The camera leaves Lester Young's face and examines his hands and the fingers that hardly seem to be moving at all. Then it turns to Billie, watching her as she watches the man who was once the closest of her close friends. Her eyes are fixed on him. It is as if she is giving him strength and keeping him safe from harm with the concentration of her gaze. She nods her head in agreement to what he is saying in the

---

★ Ben Webster remembered the occasion and how Billie's mother got very angry and refused to let him enter the apartment again. When Billie went to join Webster in a waiting car, Sadie rushed down and attacked him with an umbrella, telling him he'd 'get worse' if he ever hurt her daughter again. Webster said, 'Naturally I could see that Billie's ma was real mad, but what made it worse was that Billie was just bursting with laughter at the sight of me being whupped. That made *me* mad, but we all ended up friends' (Chilton, p. 23).

† Nat Hentoff felt that Billie was more close, more intense with Lester Young than with the other musicians. In this interpretation of the session, when Billie was looking at her old friend, 'she was looking back with the gentlest of regrets at their past. Prez was remembering too. Whatever had blighted their relationship was forgotten in the communion of music. Sitting in the control room I felt tears and saw tears in the eyes of most of the others there. The rest of the program was alright, but this had been its climax – the empirical sound of jazz' (Robert O'Meally, *The Many Faces of Billie Holiday*, 1991, p. 163).

language of his music, and she bites her lip because she can feel the effort he is making, the thin edge he is balancing on.

The words of the song continue: 'He wears high-draped pants, stripes are really yellow. He wears high-draped pants, stripes are really yellow. But when he starts in to love me, he's so fine and mellow!' And now Vic Dickenson is on the trombone. In the film, the skin of his face is very pale and from his features he could be mistaken for a white southern farmer. You can see the gentleness of his character as he plays. Billie smiles him through his solo.

In comes Gerry Mulligan. He is wearing a flashy, dog-toothed sports jacket that tightens over his back as he bends forward to blow on his instrument. He is very blond and Nordic and tense with concentration.★ Billie gives him a broad, welcoming smile as she watches his anxious face, as she listens to the heavy footstep tread of the baritone saxophone.

The words return: 'Love will make you drink and gamble, make you stay out all night long. Love will make you drink and gamble, make you stay out all night long. Love will make you do things, that you know is wrong.' Billie no longer seems to be aware of her musicians – she is staring inwards, lost in some private world of thought and memory. It is as if she is not singing about a particular man she has loved, but about love itself and her own driving need to love and be loved, no matter what the consequences might be.

Now it's Coleman Hawkins and the heavy-toned, gruff voice of his saxophone. Coleman Hawkins, his head full of literature and politics, his apartment full of classical records, his belly full of brown lentils and brandy. Gerry Mulligan has opened his eyes and is standing very close behind him, swaying like a thin tree in the wind.

★ Gerry Mulligan was born in New York in 1927 and died in 1996. Like 'many of the most gifted musicians in jazz [he was] lost for a time to narcotics . . . Heroin stretched out the natural high that playing produced . . . It served to soften the edges of the gritty world in which musicians were forced to earn their living' (Ward and Burns, p. 358).

Roy Eldridge is next. He wears a striped shirt and a broad-brimmed hat. He pushes the trumpet notes higher and higher, and it is as if he might burst from the effort. Billie is there as a gentle, smiling presence and at one point he catches her eye for approval, just before he takes the notes to their final, squealing heights. 'Stand up, Little Brother!' she used to say to him. 'Stand up! You're small enough as it is!'

And then the song is ready for its promise: 'But if you treat me right, baby, I'll stay home every day. If you treat me right, baby, I'll stay home every day. But you're so mean to me, baby, I know you're gonna drive me away.' And with that Billie emerges from whatever place her private thoughts took her to, and she lifts her head and fixes her dark eyes on the camera.

She leans forward in a confidential manner and again she is a schoolmistress instructing her class. She shakes her head with solemn authority as she explains that 'Love is just like a faucet, it turns off and on' and then she faces the camera a second time. She stares straight into the lens and with a wistful smile and a little shrug of her shoulders she explains, 'Sometimes when you think it's on, baby, it has turned off and gone.' With that the story is told in its entirety.

BIBLIOGRAPHY

Anslinger, Harold, *The Traffic in Narcotics*, New York, Funk & Wagnalls, 1953

Baldwin, James, *Notes of a Native Son*, Boston, Beacon Press, 1955

Berry, Mary Frances and Blassingame, John W., *Long Memory: The Black Experience in America*, Oxford and New York, Oxford University Press, 1982

Brandt, Nat, *Harlem at War: The Black Experience in World War II*, Syracuse, N.Y., Syracuse University Press, 1996

Büchmann-Møller, Frank, *You Just Fight for Your Life: The Story of Lester Young*, New York, Praeger, 1990

Carr, Ian, Fairweather, Digby and Priestley, Brian, *Jazz: The Rough Guide*, London, Penguin, 2000

Cash, W. J., *The Mind of the South*, New York, Knopf, 1941

Chilton, John, *Billie's Blues*, New York, Stein & Day, 1975

Clarke, Donald, *Wishing on the Moon: The Life and Times of Billie Holiday*, London, Viking, 1994

Davenport-Hines, Richard, *The Pursuit of Oblivion: A Global History of Narcotics*, London, Weidenfeld & Nicolson, 2001

Dyer, Geoff, *But Beautiful*, London, Jonathan Cape, 1991

Ellison, Ralph, *Invisible Man*, New York, Random House, 1952

Gottlieb, Robert, *Reading Jazz*, New York, Pantheon, 1996

Gourse, Lesley, *A Billie Holiday Companion*, New York, Schirmer, 1997

Griffin, Farah Jasmine, *If You Can't Be Free, Be a Mystery*, New York, Free Press, 2001

Hammond, John, *John Hammond On Record: An Autobiography*, New York, Summit, 1977

Hardwick, Elizabeth, *Sleepless Nights*, New York, Random House, 1979

Holiday, Billie (with William Dufty), *Lady Sings the Blues*, New York, Doubleday, 1956

Hughes, Langston, *Selected Poems*, London, Pluto Press, 1986

Israel, Lee, *Miss Tallulah Bankhead*, New York, Putnam, 1972

Jones, Max, *Talking Jazz*, London, Macmillan, 1987

Lees, Gene, *Meet Me at Jim and Andy's*, New York, Oxford University Press, 1988

Lewis, David Levering, *When Harlem Was in Vogue*, New York, Knopf, 1981

Litwack, Leon F., *Trouble in Mind: Black Southerners in the Age of Jim Crow*, New York, Knopf, 1988

Margolick, David, *Strange Fruit: The Biography of a Song*, New York, Ecco Press, 2001

Myrdal, Gunnar, *An American Dilemma: The Negro Problem and Modern Democracy*, 2 vols, New York, Harper & Bros, 1944

Nicholson, Stuart, *Billie Holiday*, London, Gollancz, 1995

O'Meally, Robert, *The Many Faces of Billie Holiday*, New York, Arcade, 1991

Porter, Lewis (ed.), *A Lester Young Reader*, Washington, DC, Smithsonian Institute Press, 1991

Shapiro, Nat and Hentoff, Nat, *Hear Me Talkin' to Ya: The Story of Jazz by the Men Who Made It*, New York, Rhinehart, 1955

Sinclair, Andrew, *Prohibition: The Era of Excess*, London, Faber & Faber, 1962

Vail, Ken, *Lady Day's Diary: The Life of Billie Holiday*, New York, Castle Communications, 1996

Ward, Geoffrey C. and Burns, Ken, *Jazz: A History of America's Music*, New York, Knopf, 2000

White, John, *Billie Holiday: Her Life and Times*, New York, Universe Books, 1987

Wright, Richard, *Black Boy*, New York, Harper & Bros, 1945

——*Native Son*, New York, Harper & Bros, 1940

ACKNOWLEDGEMENTS

Above all I am indebted to Linda Kuehl for the perseverance she showed in making contact with so many men and women who had known Billie Holiday and for listening carefully to what they had to say.

While I was in America I had the pleasure of meeting Billie's pianist, Bobby Tucker, whose vivid memories of Billie were filled with humour and wisdom.

I became friends with the distinguished singer and actress, Yolande Bavan, who got to know Billie when they met in Paris in the late 1950s. Yolande had many insights on Billie's character and especially her professionalism.

Robert O'Meally, Professor of English at Columbia University and author of the book *The Many Faces of Lady Day* and the screenplay for the documentary film version, shared his understanding of Billie's music and the world she lived in.

Farah Jasmine Griffin, visiting professor at Columbia University and author of *If You Can't Be Free, Be a Mystery* also gave me many valuable insights into Billie's life.

Dan Morgenstern, the Director of the Rutgers Institute of Jazz Studies in New Jersey, helped me to find my way around the Archive and told me of his own fascinating memories of meeting Billie in the 1950s.

The collector of Charlie Parker memorabilia, Norman R. Saks, kindly sent me a tape recording of a long interview he had made with Billie's secretary, Alice Vrbsky.

On my second visit to New York, my husband and I stayed at Lenny and Elka's New York Guest House in Harlem and they were charming and friendly hosts.

In England I am indebted to David Nathan at the Loughton Jazz Archive, and to Stuart Nicholson who made several suggestions for initial lines of research and whose Billie Holiday biography helped to steer me through some of the complexities of Billie's life, especially during her final years.

Dr Ditti Smitt van Damme of the HKPD gave me valuable information on the nature of addiction.

The documentary film maker John Jeremy, who made the wonderful *Long Night of Lady Day*, gave me access to transcript interviews from his film and his private jazz archive. He also lent me a number of very useful and hard-to-find books.

My English editor, Dan Franklin, did a Mohammed-to-the-mountain journey when I could not get to London for the editing and he, along with my American editor Dan Frank, made it possible to carry this book through its final stages.

My agent and dear friend, Toby Eady, has followed *With Billie* right from the beginning.

My husband and first reader, Herman Makkink, has kept close to this book, throughout the stages of its development.

PERMISSIONS

INDEX